D1436325

WORLD SPORTS CAR
CHAMPIONSHIP

CYRIL POSTHUMUS

WORLD SPORTS CAR
CHAMPIONSHIP

LONDON

MACGIBBON & KEE

1961

FIRST PUBLISHED 1961 BY MACGIBBON AND KEE LTD
© CYRIL POSTHUMUS 1961
PRINTED IN GREAT BRITAIN BY
COX AND WYMAN LTD.
LONDON, READING AND FAKENHAM

CONTENTS

1	Seven Races, Seven Countries	*page* 11
2	That Horse Again	40
3	Enter the Silver Arrows	66
4	A Prod from the Trident	88
5	Three-pronged Attack	105
6	Feltham Forces the Pace	128
7	Ferraris Meet their Match	144
8	Towards Gran Turismo	161
9	1961—The Last Championship	185

ILLUSTRATIONS

List of the illustrations to be found between pp. 96–7

The American 5.4-litre Cunningham which won the 1953 Sebring, Florida. *Associated Press*

Stirling Moss with his disabled Jaguar. *The Autocar*

After the Jaguar victory, Le Mans 1953. *Associated Press*

Piero Taruffi pushed his Lancia two miles to the pits. *Associated Press*

Reg Parnell surveys the wreck of his Aston Martin. *Klemantaski Studio*

Duncan Hamilton in the first D-type Jaguar, Le Mans 1954. *The Motor*

Ascari, Lancia's No. 1 driver, heads the field. *The Autocar*

Umberto Magliolo in his big Ferrari. *Associated Press*

Le Mans 1955. *The Motor*

Moss, the winner, follows Musso during 1955 T.T.

Winning the 1955 Targa Florio. *Bernard Cahier*

Castellotti in his Ferrari. *Associated Press*

Maserati drivers Jean Behra, Stirling Moss, Piero Taruffi and Harry Schell.

Moss's Maserati, Hawthorn's Jaguar and an Aston Martin are first off.

Akton Miller's American 'Caballo II'. *Autosport*

Winner of the 1957 Nurburgring. *Autosport*

Stirling Moss's ultra-low Maserati coupé at Le Mans 1957. *The Motor*

ILLUSTRATIONS

Ivor Bueb at full chat. *The Autocar*

Partners in victory at Le Mans 1957. *The Autocar*

Rear wheels spinning, Mike Hawthorn motors his Ferrari through a field. *Bernard Cahier*

Shock is recorded on Harry Schell's smoke-blackened face. *Associated Press*

Blazing fiercely, Schell's 4½-litre v8 Maserati. *Associated Press*

Aerial view of the 1957 Swedish G.P. *Bernard Cahier*

Peter Collins and Olivier Gendebien. *Car and Driver*

The start at the 1958 Goodwood T.T. *Motor Sport*

A burst tyre on his Ferrari brings Mike Hawthorn's No. 4 to the pits. *Motor Sport*

Out goes Fairman, in goes Moss, 1959.

Ambition achieved—an Aston Martin wins at Le Mans. *The Autocar*

The Aston Martin team at Goodwood. *Maxwell Boyd*

Roy Salvadori's Aston Martin on fire. *The Autocar*

Dan Gurney's 'Birdcage' Maserati No. 5. *Bernard Cahier*

The Camoradi car at Le Mans, 1960. *The Motor*

Briggs Cunningham's prototype E Jaguar. *The Autocar*

The same race a few hours later. *The Autocar*

The ugly but effective 'Birdcage' Maserati Type 61. *Motor Sport*

Following G.P. trends, Ferrari put their 2.5-litre v6 engine behind the driver. *Motor Sport*

WORLD SPORTS CAR CHAMPIONSHIP

CHAPTER 1

SEVEN RACES, SEVEN COUNTRIES

ODDLY enough, the World Sports Car Championship seemed to come into existence almost as an afterthought. The first and most famous motor racing championship is, of course, the World Drivers' Championship, inaugurated in 1950, and no contest of similar type was mooted until October 1952. It was then that the International Sporting Commission (C.S.I.) of the Federation International de l'Automobile (F.I.A.)—the International body which controls all motor racing—announced during their Autumn Congress in Paris that a European Touring Championship for rallies was to be inaugurated in 1953.

This set various minds thinking, and in subsequent weeks the question formed itself: 'Why not a sports car racing championship as well? It can't be for drivers—the Drivers' Championship looks after that—but why not for makes of car, Ferrari versus Jaguar versus Lancia, and so on?'

Like most things, championships have their good and bad points. In motor racing, they can impart much extra interest to the scene, and ensure a consistently good field of starters throughout the season—a major point for organizers as well as the public—*providing* the contest remains close between rivals.

Again, their publicity value is considerable, ensuring strong trade support. To win one race on somebody's petrol and somebody else's tyres is good advertisement for these commodities and for the car, for a limited time, but to win a championship on them is a far greater advertisement. A single race victory loses topicality with the public after a fortnight in these days of crowded sporting calendars, whereas a championship victory lasts for twelve months.

The C.S.I. took their decision at the Monte Carlo winter Congress in February 1953, quietly announcing the instigation of a World Sports Car Championship—just five weeks before the first qualifying round! Technically the contest was termed the Manufacturers' Championship, and the principal awards were a diploma and the C.S.I. Cup, which would be awarded on a points basis. In general, however, it came to be referred to as the World Sports Car Championship, a title well merited, since the seven qualifying events in the first year took place in countries widely apart—U.S.A., Italy, France, Belgium, Germany, Northern Ireland and Mexico—and embraced the world's major sports car races.

The list of qualifying events for 1953, as issued by the F.I.A., was as follows:

> Sebring 12-hour race, Florida, U.S.A., March 8th.
> Mille Miglia, Italy, April 26th.
> Le Mans 24-hour race, France, June 13th–14th.
> Belgian 24-hour race, July 25th–26th.
> Nurburgring 1000-kilometres race, Germany, August 30th.
> Tourist Trophy Race, Northern Ireland, September 5th.
> Pan-American Road Race, Mexico, November 19th–23rd.

Each race had to be over a minimum distance of 1000 kms. (621.4 miles), and competing cars had to comply with Appendix C of the International Sporting Code drawn up by the F.I.A. This lengthy Appendix lays down a series of structural dimensions, equipment details and other requirements for all sports cars competing in International events. Thus, all cars had to have proper wings of adequate dimensions, two seats, self-starters, rear mirror, efficient silencers, full lighting equipment and horn, spare wheel, etc., and although such impedimenta were often an irritant to enterprising constructors bent on keeping weight to the minimum, a set of rules was obviously necessary to keep sports car racing under reasonable international control. As will be seen, however, that control was inadequate.

The championship was to be decided on a points system of scoring, eight points being awarded for first place, six for second, four for third, three for fourth, two for fifth and one for sixth. The make of car amassing most points on its four best performances

out of the seven qualifying events would be proclaimed World
Sports Car Champion and winner of the Manufacturers' Cup.

Only the highest-placed car of each make could earn points, a
proviso which meant that team reliability would go unrewarded.
A make which gained first, second and third places in a race
would gain no more points than if it won first place only, with
two retirements, a point which aroused some criticism; however,
all competing makes were equally affected, and at least it would
assure fast racing rather than comparative soft pedalling to ensure
a full team finish.

Apart from that one quibble, the new championship sounded
fine, particularly as the scoring was on straight placings without
irritating complications over class-capacity successes. A potential
battle, in fact, between the world's fastest sports cars—Britain's
Jaguars and Aston Martins, Italy's Ferraris, Alfa Romeos and
Lancias, and America's big Cunninghams, with the smaller
German Porsches and Borgwards and Italian Maseratis joining
the hunt amongst the larger cars.

Yet reaction to the championship was lukewarm at first.
Notice of the contest was too short, and the first round, the
Sebring 12-hour in Florida, too quickly upon them for potential
Sports Car Champions to argue 'we must be there or we may
miss vital points'. The expense of the transatlantic crossing with
a team of cars and personnel was also a deterrent, and as no starting
or prize money was available at Sebring in those days, the general
tendency on the European side was to sit back and 'see how
things shaped'.

And as things worked out, they 'shaped' most interestingly.

FLORIDA: FIRST ACT

'*Altogether this was a very interesting race indeed, and a good start
to the* 1953 *season*'—THE AUTOCAR, March 20th, 1953.

The sole European marque officially represented in America's
Sebring 12-hour, was Aston Martin of Britain, whose patron,
that enthusiastic industrialist David Brown, decided to send two
2.9-litre DB3 cars of 1952 pattern, to be driven by Reg Parnell/

George Abecassis and Peter Collins/Geoff Duke, the latter trying car racing for the first time that year.

Enzo Ferrari decided to rely on American talent with privately owned cars to uphold the 'prancing horse', while Jaguar did likewise, with the comforting thought that several well-prepared XK120CS were down to run. In all, the organizers under the indefatigable drive and enthusiasm of Alec E. Ulmann, raked in sixty entries for their race, mostly of amateur status, apart from Briggs S. Cunningham's single 5.4-litre Chrysler-engined Cunningham and the two dark green Aston Martins. A 2.3-litre Gordini from France was a lamented non-starter, leaving the blue to be borne by two tiny 750cc D.B.-Panhards, constituting a potent threat to the Index of Performance category, but hardly to World Sports Car Championship contenders.

As the scene of America's most important motor race apart from the Indianapolis 500-mile track classic, Sebring is a surprisingly remote and dreary place. Formed from a vast airfield known as Hendrycks, where once Boeing 'Fortresses' disported themselves during the war years, its concrete runways and 'blacktop' link roads provide a tough 5.2-mile circuit which is flat, featureless and notoriously hard on brakes owing to numerous corners ranging from 120mph to a 35mph hairpin.

But with rare exceptions there is warm Florida sunshine to grace the scene, and in 1953 it was fine and hot when fifty-seven starters lined up for the Le Mans getaway at midday. A diverse collection they were, ranging from 5½-litre Cadillac and Chrysler-engined Allards, the lone Cunningham, Ferraris, Jaguars, Aston Martins, down through 2-litre Frazer-Nashes, Ferraris and a Maserati, to smaller Porsches and Oscas and tiny 750cc Siatas, American Crosleys and D.B.S.

Practice had indicated that the main struggle would be between the blue and white Cunningham C4R, a beautifully prepared machine with Le Mans experience behind it, and the two Aston Martins with only 2.9 litres under their bonnets as against 5.4 in the American car. The Feltham team under John Wyer realized that much would depend on a really rapid getaway. Acknowledged a master at the Le Mans start in those days despite his bulk was Reg Parnell; during practice Peter Collins, then twenty-one years old and on his way up the racing ladder, asked his older team mate: 'How d'you manage to move so fast without hurrying, Reg ?'

The famous Parnell grin appeared. 'I hurry all right, Peter, don't you worry.' Then he explained his technique—eyes never off the starter's flag, the sprint across the track, into the car without panic, switch on and away. . . . 'As if you were in your private car, Peter, but a bit pushed for time. And don't panic. Time you're away, some of 'em are just getting their trouser legs off the gear lever!'

When Captain George Eyston, famous pre-war recordman, swept the flag down, both master and mentor made splendid starts, but by the irony of fate, Reg Parnell's car, first of the fifty-seven to move, stalled its engine. By the time he'd got it going again, aided by a good English cuss-word or two, the field was well away, with Peter Collins's Aston and Phil Walters's Cunningham at grips for the lead, a length or two apart.

Parnell moved up like a bullet on that first lap, but the entire lack of flag marshals on the course, and a curious rule permitting passing on either side which made drivers of slower cars somewhat carefree in their cornering, nearly caused his undoing. He was about to burst past a little French DB when it moved out to take a corner; the Aston was forced farther outwards to miss it, and struck one of the very substantial 50-gallon oil drums serving as course markers. The nearside headlamp was smashed, the wing crumpled on to the wheel, and the body door damaged.

Three minutes were lost at the pits, pulling the wing clear, then Reg grimly resumed the race. Two hours later he had caught the entire pack save for the battling Collins and Walters, and was in third place.

At quarter-distance, however, when Collins had pulled out a half-minute lead, the race pattern took a dramatic change as cars rushed pitwards to refuel, and co-drivers took over. John Fitch took Phil Walters's place in the Cunningham, and Geoff Duke, two-wheeled racing star, relieved Collins. Aided by Aston's excellent pitwork, Duke set off with a minute's lead, but four laps later he was caught out by the same hazard which almost eliminated Parnell, coming up to pass an M.G. just before a right-angle corner as it began to move outwards.

Duke had little option but to accelerate hard to miss the M.G.; as a result he arrived at the corner too fast. Even then he might have scrabbled through sideways had not an XK120 Jaguar occupied the space he needed. The two cars collided, the DB3's rear suspension was damaged, and although the unhappy Duke drove it back to the pits, team manager John Wyer decided it was unsafe to risk continuing, and the race-leader was withdrawn.

Now the Cunningham led comfortably from George Abecassis in the Parnell Aston, with Bill Spear's 4.1-litre Ferrari moving into third. Not for long, however, as Spear's co-pilot, a talented Californian named Phil Hill, crashed the car at the chicane. Meantime the Parnell/Abecassis Aston Martin was out to catch the Cunningham, and despite such unusual hazards as ice-cream salesmen cheerfully using the edge of the track to get to various enclosures, officials buzzing from corner to corner on motor scooters, and aircraft taxi-ing across the course with only a white flag as forewarning, the pair managed to get within forty seconds of Fitch and Walters after eight hours.

Nightfall brought a setback, however, for the Aston's broken nearside headlight meant Cyclopean motoring on the long, dark circuit for Reg and George, no easy task with numerous slower cars around, and the Cunningham, most expertly driven and pit-controlled, could not be caught. With two hours to midnight and the finish, the British pit decided to ease the pressure and ensure second spot, Abecassis finally crossing the line three and a half minutes behind the blue and white Cunningham.

It was a popular win for Briggs Cunningham, who had tried so hard, and dipped so deep into his pocket, to field a worthy American competition sports car; and an equally popular second for the Aston Martin, which also won the 3-litre class. As Chief Steward Alec Ulmann later told David Brown and John Wyer, the British DB3 'made the race'.

American-driven C type Jaguars were third, fourth and seventh, Ferraris sixth and eighth, and other Jaguars tenth, twelfth and seventeenth. That an American car had taken the lead in the first World Sports Car Championship (the score was Cunningham eight points, Aston Martin six, Jaguar four) was frankly unexpected, but Enzo Ferrari, with but one point to his marque's credit for sixth place, shrugged it off.

'Let us await the result of the Mille Miglia' was all he said.

937 MILES IN 10 HOURS, 37 MINUTES

'We climbed the Futa well and were making the descent of the Raticosa when the car suddenly slowed and Reg shouted "Throttle gone". . . . Terribly disappointed, I expected we would lose ten minutes rigging up some makeshift control, but quickly "my man" said "Open the throttles wide and tie them up". I thought the humour misplaced; but he meant it !'—Louis Klemantaski, passenger to Reg Parnell, THE MOTOR, May 27th, 1953.

What a contrast the second round of that first Championship was to Sebring! Italy's unique 1000-mile race from Brescia, down the Adriatic side of 'the leg', across mountains to Rome, then back north via Florence, across the Apennines to Bologna, Modena, Parma and back to Brescia. 937.5 miles actually, in 1953 form, every one of them over public roads heavily lined with wildly enthusiastic, not to say suicidal spectators, who formed human 'funnels' in every town through which competitors drove at 100mph.

The race which began in 1927 and has brought a total of over fifty deaths during its thirty years' existence is now no longer run, but memories of it will never die. Dangerous it was, but intensely dramatic and exciting, a revival of the town-to-town races of pioneer racing days, and a prodigious test of driving skill, courage and human and mechanical stamina.

Before the race, all Italy caught 'Mille Miglia' fever, banners were plastered everywhere proclaiming the famous drivers in the contest—Villoresi, Fangio, Farina, Bonetto, Ascari and so on, not forgetting Britain's Moss, Parnell and Collins. The race had extensive television coverage, while many towns en route installed public address equipment to keep their citizens up to the minute on race progress. As for Brescia, start and finish point of the great race, it was like a disturbed antheap, with people rushing hither and thither in a turmoil of excitement and little apparent object other than at the hub of it all, the Piazza Vittoria.

There the competing cars gathered for scrutineering and assembled for the start, not in their thirties, forties or fifties of the other major road races, but in *hundreds*. The entry list for the 1953 Mille Miglia totalled over 500 cars, contesting eight classes for sports and touring cars, and there were 488 actual starters.

Moving to the Via Rebuffoni, they set off at one-minute intervals, mounting a huge ramp, receiving a control card, then being flagged away on their long journey. On the suggestion made several years before by that great Italian driver, the late Achille Varzi, the cars' competition numbers also denoted their starting time; thus the first car away was not No. 1, but No. 90, leaving at 9.0pm; the second No. 91, leaving at 9.1pm. By the time the last car, Tony Rolt's XK120C Jaguar, had been dispatched, dawn had broken and it was almost 6am.

Amongst that endless stream of cars careering round the giant figure-of-eight course on April 25th-26th, 1953, were some of great mechanical interest and significance. Not surprisingly, Italian red was preponderant, and amongst its most illustrious wearers were four works 12-cylinder Ferraris in the capable hands of Villoresi, Farina, Ascari and Britain's Mike Hawthorn, and three exciting new six-cylinder 3.6-litre Alfa Romeo coupés, driven by the great Fangio, the German Karl Kling (second in 1952 with a Mercedes-Benz 300SL) and the Italian, Sanesi.

Then there were five completely new and startling 2.9-litre Lancia coupés, with vee-six twin o.h. camshaft engines, all-round independent springing, tubular space frames and inboard brakes front and rear. Such technical enterprise, allied with the driving talents of men such as Clemente Biondetti, four times a Mille Miglia winner, Taruffi, Maglioli and Bonetto, meant a serious challenge to Ferrari domination of the race.

For Britain, three of the 'portcullis'-fronted DB3 Aston Martins ran in the care of Sebring heroes Parnell, Abecassis and Collins, while Jaguars had two XK120Cs, both with a daring innovation, disc brakes, and with Stirling Moss and Tony Rolt driving them. A third Jaguar C was Leslie Johnson's own car, works-chaperoned. Others amongst the 'Championship class' included a blue and white Nash-Healey driven by Sebring co-victor John Fitch, and a string of private Ferraris in the hands of such men as Bracco,

1952 winner, Scotti, Castellotti, Cabianca, etc. Also running, but
unlikely to disturb the masters as much as the public, were Prince
Aly Khan's Alfa Romeo and Roberto Rossellini in a Ferrari.

With each car starting separately, the Mille Miglia is no neck-
and-neck, wheel-to-wheel race, although it often develops that
way in the later stages. But the 'tigers' in the fastest Ferraris,
Alfas and Lancias were at grips metaphorically from the very
moment they shot down the ramp at Brescia, even though their
'closest' opponents might be many minutes away.

Along the fast straight roads southward from Brescia, the big
cars rocketed through villages at over 140mph despite inter-
mittent showers of rain, their horns blaring and headlights
flashing a warning to the carefree populace. At Verona, 80 miles
from the start, Sanesi led for Alfa Romeo at an average of over
113mph, from Taruffi's Lancia and Farina's 4½-litre Grand Prix-
engined Ferrari.

A hundred miles farther on, at Ravenna, however, Taruffi had
dropped out, Farina was now second, and Kling's Alfa was close
behind, followed by Bordoni's fast Gordini and Fangio. Alfas
first, third and fifth! Alas for Britain, Moss's Jaguar, lying
twelfth at Rovigo, went out early, giving no chance for a demonstration of its disc brakes; Johnson's c type also retired, and
Descollonges' privately owned 'c' plunged down an embankment, killing the co-driver Ugnon. Rolt's disc-braked Jaguar also
retired, while the 3-litre Aston Martins, losing on maximum
speed on the long straights, lay some way behind the leaders.

The harsh pace took its toll. Out went Villoresi's Ferrari,
Bordoni's Gordini, Fitch's Nash-Healey and Mike Hawthorn's
Ferrari, but still Consalvo Sanesi, the Alfa Romeo mechanic-
turned-driver, led at fantastic speed, dashing into Pescara ahead
of Farina, Kling and Fangio. Then steering trouble struck, and
poor Sanesi's race was run. Into the lead, then, went Farina, but
briefly, for the forceful Dottore went off the road near Aquila
and had to retire.

Now Karl Kling of Mercedes-Benz, on loan to Alfa Romeo
for the 1953 season, found himself leading at Rome, with his
team mate Fangio behind, followed by the Ferrari of Giannino
Marzotto, one of four brothers of a wealthy textile concern who

raced as amateurs. As for Rossellini, his wife Ingrid Bergman forced him to give up at Rome, after a stormy scene which gave the gossip columnists much joy!

'He who leads at Rome never wins' is an old Mille Miglia adage; one which was true in Kling's case, for he crashed on the Radicofani Pass, slamming through the guard rails and severely damaging his neat red Alfa coupé. So it was Fangio who led through Florence, with Marzotto closing on him, while third came another Marzotto, Giannino's brother Paolo, chased by the Lancias of Bonetto and Maglioli, with Reg Parnell now sixth in a DB3 Aston Martin, passengered by the valiant Louis Klemantaski.

Between Florence and Bologna come the Futa and Raticosa passes, and it was on the Futa that the track-rod mounting of Fangio's Alfa came adrift, so that his steering wheel controlled the nearside wheel only! *El Chueco* pressed on regardless, but his pace inevitably dropped, and when Bologna was reached Marzotto had seized the lead. Parnell had trouble on the passes, too, his Aston's throttle control breaking. He and photographer 'Klem' wired the throttle fully open, after which Reg controlled his speed with the ignition switch!

Ovet the final flat-out stretches to Brescia, Fangio's crippled Alfa could not keep the 4.1-Ferrari in sight, and it was Giannino Marzotto who rocketed into Brescia to win the twentieth Mille Miglia at 88.39mph. Behind him there was further drama, his brother Paolo's Ferrari catching fire less than fifty miles from the finish, being burnt right out.

Bracco's Ferrari had retired, Musso's 2-litre Maserati crashed, and Abecassis's Aston Martin was another retirement. Felice Bonetto's Lancia took over Paolo Marzotto's third place behind Fangio's crippled Alfa, while that great Anglo-American enthusiast, Tom Cole, was fourth with a Ferrari; Reg Parnell's Aston Martin was a splendid fifth on three litres and full throttle, and Giletti's 2-litre Maserati came sixth, just nosing into the Championship scorings.

Gallant indeed was Clemente Biondetti's effort; the four-time winner was stranded about two and a half miles from the finish when his v6 Lancia engine failed. He and his mechanic began to push in, but the latter collapsed and had to rest in the car while

Biondetti pushed alone, finally taking a hard-earned eighth place.

And as tough 'Biondo' followed the trail of other drivers weary in every bone after over twelve hours of the most gruelling motor racing, and thankfully retired to his hotel to rest, the delirium amongst the Brescia crowds went on, and would continue through the night. Italy's *Corsa dei giganti*—the race of the giants—came but once a year, and they made the most of it!

SON ET LUMIERE

'*The Jaguar team humbly present their loyal duty to Her Majesty and advise her that in her Coronation year they have won for Britain the world's greatest international car race at Le Mans, France, yesterday.*' Telegram from Jaguar Cars Ltd. to the Secretary to H.M. The Queen, June 15th, 1953.

Marzotto's Mille Miglia victory for Ferrari, following the retirement of the entire official team, earned the warm approval of Enzo Ferrari, and eight Championship points for his factory. These, added to the single point gained at Sebring, placed Ferrari ahead in the contest by one point with Cunningham and Aston Martin lying equal, second.

Round three was Le Mans, the world-famous French 24-hour classic on the very fast, triangular Sarthe circuit—again a contrast to barren Sebring and the over-populated Mille Miglia course. As a spectacle, Le Mans can attain the zenith of drama and the depths of boredom, but as a test of stamina for motors and men it stands unequalled. The romance and glamour of Le Mans have been heartily overdone by ultra-keen penmen through the years, but there is no denying that indefinable Continental *ambiance*, with the bustling crowds, the exciting atmosphere, the funfair, the cafés and bistros, the gay lights, and the savage, intoxicating speed of the race itself, with cars of all sizes and many nationalities slashing past on *la ronde impitoyable*.

For the drivers it is different. Le Mans is a gruelling race, not because the circuit is hard, but because of its length, and the hazards of mixing cars of all sizes, driven by men of widely varying ability. Grand Prix professionals in 160mph 'prototype' sports-racing cars bred by the regulations, have to share the course with amateurs in cars incapable of exceeding 100mph, not in daylight alone, when at least they can be seen, but at night, with only headlights to pick them out at high speed on the long, dark circuit, often enough in pouring rain or mist.

Few drivers profess a genuine liking for the famous *Vingt-Quatre Heures* on the Sarthe, but it is a race which the big sports car manufacturers cannot afford to miss, being of immeasurable importance as a world shop window for their products.

Le Mans, 1953, drew a magnificent entry, the sixty acceptances including teams from Alfa Romeo, Ferrari, Lancia, Jaguar, Aston Martin, Talbot, Gordini, Cunningham, Nash-Healey and Allard—all cars of Championship status, plus numerous smaller-capacity entries down to 610cc. Amongst the great 'names' competing were Fangio, Ascari, Villoresi, Gonzalez, Moss, Hawthorn, Chiron, Rolt, Farina, Rosier, Kling, Parnell, and many, many more. Thus the weekend of June 13th–14th, 1953, brought an unequalled gathering of human and mechanical talent to Le Mans, and a vast throng of spectators, estimated at over 240,000, to watch the great battle.

Up to 1960, there have been twenty-eight Le Mans 24-hour races, but few can have been as 'wide open' on paper, or as interesting from every aspect, as the 1953 event—nor as satisfying from the British point of view, since it resulted in a brilliant Jaguar victory. The works 3½-litre six-cylinder disc-braked XK120C cars, much improved on the earlier edition which won at Le Mans in 1951, finished first, second and fourth, avenging their 1952 debacle, when the hasty fitting of ultra-streamlined bodywork caused the entire team to boil itself out of the contest within the first two hours. The winning pair of drivers, Tony Rolt and Duncan Hamilton, averaged 105.85mph, covering 2,534.6 miles in the twenty-four hours, an increase of 9mph on the 1952 winning average by Mercedes-Benz.

It was a race won by shrewd team control, splendid driving, superb mechanical reliability—and disc brakes. These components gained the Jaguars vital yards on each corner, and continued to do so while rivals wore out their own drum brakes, clutches and transmissions, striving to hold the British cars.

Deeply worrying to team managers is the annual 'Grand Prix' waged amongst the fastest cars during the first three hours or so. Twenty-four hours is eight times longer, and it behoves teams to 'hold their horses' and conserve the machinery. On the other hand, the fastest rivals must not be allowed to get too far ahead, lest they remain there, declining to blow up—the usual fate of the Le Mans 'hotheads'.

Jaguar tackled this annual problem in 1953 by instructing Stirling Moss, their fastest driver, to 'travel as fast as he thought comfortable' without overstressing the car, while his team mates Rolt/Hamilton and Peter Whitehead/Ian Stewart lay further back, waiting.

Manifestly travelling very comfortably indeed, Moss joined the opening 'Grand Prix' with a will, snatching the lead from the formidable Villoresi/Ascari 4½-litre Ferrari coupé on lap four, and drew the race on to record-breaking pace until, half an hour later, fuel starvation afflicted the Jaguar, leaving Moss and Peter Walker the rest of the race to work back from twenty-third to second place.

Out, then, went signals from the Jaguar pit, and Tony Rolt put on speed, passed Villoresi and led the race, while in response to other pit signals, the very fast 3.6-litre Alfa Romeo coupés began moving up. The three Italian cars—one Ferrari and two Alfas—dogged the Jaguar mercilessly until, during the night, the Alfa challenge suddenly collapsed through transmission troubles. But the big Ferrari remained a constant menace until the nineteenth hour, when its long-suffering clutch, hard used in efforts to save the brakes, failed at last to function, and Villoresi and Ascari were out of the race.

Thereafter, only a magnificent drive into third position by the Americans John Fitch and Phil Walters in the newest Chrysler-engined Cunningham, the C5R, split a British 1-2-3-victory formation. Trouble stalked the rest of the field. Fangio's Alfa broke a piston early on; Reg Parnell most uncharacteristically crashed his Aston Martin in the Esses during the first hour; the other two Astons—all were new, much improved DB3S models—retired; only one Ferrari (fifth), one Gordini (sixth) and one Talbot (eighth) survived; poor Tom Cole was killed when his

4.1-litre Ferrari crashed at White House on the Sunday morning; all three 3-litre Lancias, fitted for this race with superchargers to augment the power from their v6, four-cam engines, were forced out; poor Sidney Allard led the entire race on lap one in his Cadillac-Allard, and retired on lap two with brake trouble.

In all twenty-six cars finished, of which the four Jaguars which started occupied first, second, fourth and ninth positions, the latter taken by a Belgian privately entered xk120c. No wonder Mr (later Sir William) Lyons smiled—it was the most magnificent demonstration of British supremacy at Le Mans since the Bentley days of old—greater, in fact, since the opposition was much stronger.

As a result, Jaguars found themselves sharing a joint lead with Cunningham in the World Sports Car Championship, both makes having twelve points, with Ferraris the runners-up, one point behind, followed by Aston Martin (eight) and Alfa Romeo (six).

ECURIE ECOSSE MUSCLES IN

'. . . I tucked in behind Villoresi . . . and drove on sidelights only. As the 4½-litre was touching nearly 170mph at some places, this was not particularly pleasant. . . .' The late Mike Hawthorn, THE MOTOR, March 3rd, 1954.

Seven weeks later, the fourth round of the Championship took place in Belgium, where another famous sports car classic, the Belgian 24-hour race, was staged at Spa-Francorchamps, a splendid wooded road circuit, first used for sports car racing back in 1922.

It proved an absorbing race, disappointing only in the lack of interest shown by several Championship contestants. Jaguar, vastly content with their Le Mans triumph, withdrew their team entry, being represented instead by three private, drum-braked xk120cs, one from the Scottish Ecurie Ecosse stable, one from the Belgian Ecurie Francorchamps, and one from the Dutchman, Herman Roosdorp.

Cunningham had an entry for Spa, but the car had crashed

during the Rheims 12-hour race and could not start, while Aston
Martin, Lancia and Gordini did not go to Belgium at all. But
Ferrari sent a strong team of three $4\frac{1}{2}$-litre 12-cylinder coupés,
and Alfa Romeo sent one of their 3.6-litre coupés. One reason
for the feeble entry at Spa was the lack of starting money. Money
brings performers, and on the same weekend, July 25th–26th,
the non-Championship but better paying Portuguese Grand Prix
for sports cars took place at Lisbon, where the complete Lancia
team were to be found, and Stirling Moss and Peter Whitehead
with Jaguars.

In all, ten Championship-sized cars turned out amidst the
thirty-six car field at Spa for the 4pm Le Mans-style start. The
large, genial and apparently leisurely Sir James Scott-Douglas
made a magnificent sprint at flag-fall, and took his blue Ecurie
Ecosse Jaguar out ahead, leading the long string of cars over the
Eau Rouge bridge and round the sweeping right-hand climbing
curve before being overwhelmed by the Ferrari trio and Fangio's
Alfa.

Lap one, a rising whine, and Farina hurtled past the pits, his
team-mates, Ascari and Maglioli, in close pursuit, followed by
Fangio, Scott-Douglas, Laurent and Roosdorp (Jaguars) and
Tom Meyer's private DB3 Aston Martin coupé. Then the meteoric
Ascari put on speed, took the lead, and with his co-driver 'Gigi'
Villoresi skilfully put two whole laps before midnight between
their 4.5-Ferrari and that of Farina/Hawthorn, while the three
private Jaguars, unable to match Maranello's $4\frac{1}{2}$ litres and 12
cylinders, boomed along behind, awaiting developments.

Consalvo Sanesi spun off during a rain shower when essaying
to pass a slower car on a fast bend, damaging the lone Alfa and
saving Fangio, sleeping calmly in his car behind the pits, the
trouble of waking up. The Laurent/Swaters Jaguar also retired,
as did Meyer's Aston Martin and Maglioli's Ferrari, with a broken
final drive.

By midnight, the remaining two Ferraris had things apparently
in the bag, with the Scottish and Dutch Jaguars next astern. But
the Farina/Hawthorn Ferrari was suffering dynamo trouble, and
Mike Hawthorn dared not use the headlights during his night
spell for fear of draining the battery. He therefore tucked in

behind Villoresi's car, having a hair-raising drive on sidelights with both Ferraris lapping at around 105mph on that very fast, very difficult Spa circuit, only switching his headlights on as he passed the pits each lap, to comply with regulations!

Still Ascari and Villoresi flogged round until by 8am, two-thirds distance, they were four rounds ahead of their team mates, and no less than nineteen ahead of 'Jimmy' Scott-Douglas's third-place Jaguar, co-driven by Guy Gale, who had taken Ninian Sanderson's place at short notice. Then, as at Le Mans, the leaders retired after nineteen hours, this time with a broken differential, letting the Farina/Hawthorn Ferrari into the lead.

It promptly made for its pit, much to the excitement of the Jaguar contingent, but it was simply a precautionary stop to check the rear-axle oil level. Nasty noises indicated that all was not well with the back end of this Ferrari either, and the last hours were extremely tense for the Italians, fervently hoping the car would last, and for the Ecurie Ecosse, hoping with equal fervour that it wouldn't!

The twenty-fourth hour ran out painfully, and at last the Ferrari clanked over the line to score a lucky yet nonetheless convincing victory, eighteen laps ahead of the blue Ecosse Jaguar and the orange one of Roosdorp/Ulmen. The victors' average was 94.91mph, whereas Hawthorn's record lap was at 111.22mph, indicative of their much retarded pace later on.

Spa meant that Italy moved into a narrow lead in the Championship. Thanks to David Murray's Scottish Ecurie, Jaguar now had eighteen points, but Ferrari had moved ahead by one point, having a score of nineteen—a close issue which, it was hoped, would be resolved by the respective works teams in round five, the Nurburgring 1000-kilometre race on August 30th.

FORTY-FOUR TIMES ROUND THE RING

'To speak frankly, we would have liked to have seen the official Jaguar team enter this race after their success at Le Mans. It is quite possible that they would have had a possibility for victory, which would have proved to the Italians the superiority of the Jaguar'. Corrado Millanta, ROAD AND TRACK, January 1954.

Although world-renowned as the scene of the German Grand Prix, the ever-winding, climbing, plunging fourteen-and-a-quarter-mile Nurburgring circuit, set in the heart of the Eifel mountains in Germany's Rhineland, was used for sports car racing in its earliest days, during the late 'Twenties. The A.D.A.C. —*Allgemeiner Deutsche Automobil Club*—had twice already tried without success to promote a major long-distance sports car event at Nurburg since the Hitler War. Now, in 1953, their ambitions were at last realized, and a big race became possible, with added status as a qualifying round in the *Weltmeisterschaft für Sportwagen*.

A month before, prospects looked very bright, with team entries secured from Alfa Romeo, Ferrari, Lancia, Maserati and other makes of smaller engine size, with further hopes of works Jaguar and perhaps Aston Martin representation. Then the German member of the Alfa Romeo team, Karl Kling, crashed during training, seriously damaging both himself and his car, and eventually the entire team was withdrawn. Next it became known that Jaguar and Aston Martin would not come, but the Ecurie Ecosse entered three xk120c Jaguars instead.

Juan Fangio, released by Alfa Romeo, then joined the Lancia team, which had been practising assiduously during the previous month with new 3.3-litre, de Dion-axled cars. Meantime there came a major upset in the Ferrari camp; Italian newspapers announced that Enzo Ferrari was to reduce his motor racing activities that season, withdrawing completely after the Italian Grand Prix in September. This news did not improve the morale of his team at Nurburg, already harassed by the bursting of one engine during practice. In the end the coupé's engine was transferred to the Farina/Ascari open car, and the other two Ferraris were withdrawn.

Next Jimmy Scott-Douglas, grappling with Nurburg's sinuous curves, overturned his c-type Jaguar during practice, fortunately being thrown clear. Hastily 'Wilkie' Wilkinson, the team's chief mechanic, got to work on Scott-Douglas's private xk120 as a substitute, giving it a hurried valve grind and tappet check the evening before the race.

The organizers must have been relieved when race day dawned

without further mishaps or withdrawals. Fifty-three cars started at the uncharitable hour of 7.30am, on a cold but dry morning, and Ascari quickly warmed himself and his Ferrari by beating the Lancia trio into the lead. One Jaguar, the c-type of Roosdorp/ Ulmen, was out after a mere lap, going hedging and ditching in a big way. The former Mercedes star Hermann Lang also retired, having seemingly lost his famous mechanical 'sensitivity' for his 2-litre Maserati was well over-revved. But all eyes were on the new open Lancias of Taruffi and young Eugenio Castellotti, both going very quickly, overhauling Ascari and pulling away.

Fangio in the third Lancia had disappeared, however, stopping somewhere with fuel pump trouble, while it was apparent that all was not well with the lone Ferrari's rear suspension. On swept the leading Lancias, holding a commanding lead during the first 300 kilometres, when both came into the pits to refuel and change drivers. The pitwork was executed swiftly, and Manzon climbed into Taruffi's car, Bracco into Castellotti's.

Then came bitter anti-climax. Both cars declined to start, their batteries being utterly unable to turn the engines over. The incessant buffeting of the *Ring* was believed to be the cause, the Lancia's batteries being carried near the rear axles; but whatever the reason, the effect was demoralizing for Gianni Lancia and his drivers. Attempts were made to pushstart the cars, but officials declared that this contravened the regulations, and Italy's latest sports-racers had to retire when looking all set to win.

Ascari/Farina in the big Ferrari were very fortunate to inherit Lancia's lead, especially as their rear suspension deteriorated further. But the two masters nursed the car round for the next five-and-a-half hours at sufficient speed to stave off the private Jaguars, winning the first Nurburgring 1000-kilometre race at the modest average of 74.7mph, after a trying and boring drive lasting 8 hours, 20mins. and 44secs.

Second until the very last lap was the 2-litre Maserati driven by Giletti and Onofre Marimon, a protegé of Fangio. Through bad luck, however, their engine blew up two-and-a-half miles from the finishing line, letting the Ecurie Ecosse xk120c driven by Ian Stewart and Roy Salvadori into a lucky second place. Third came a 1½-litre Borgward, while John Lawrence/Jimmy

Stewart in another Scottish c-type were sixth in spite of broken front suspension. As for the dauntless Scott-Douglas, he and Ninian Sanderson brought their substitute xk120 home tenth, running on wheels borrowed from David Murray's Mk. VII saloon when their own broke up. The result was a 100 per cent team finish and a special prize for the Ecurie Ecosse—and a Mk. VII Jaguar standing on four jacks!

Now Ferrari had a Championship lead of three points over Jaguar, the score before round six standing thus: Ferrari twenty-seven points, Jaguar twenty-four, Cunningham twelve, Aston Martin eight, Alfa Romeo six. The next round took place in Great Britain.

TO THE BANKS OF DUNDROD

'It is to be hoped that this new Championship, with its importance to manufacturers, will put an end to most of the frustrations which have prevented the T.T. from being an annual affair, and that at Dundrod it will settle down to a long period of prosperity. . . .'
W. A. McMaster, 1953 T.T. race programme.

Seen from the Sports Car Championship aspect, the 1953 R.A.C. Tourist Trophy race at Dundrod, outside Belfast, was handicapped from the start. It took place on September 5th, just six days after the Nurburgring 1000-kilometre, allowing very little time for even the keenest contestants to prepare cars, and get them to Northern Ireland.

Unfortunately, none of the Continentals seemed keen at all. Ferrari had promised to send two cars for Farina/Hawthorn and Villoresi/Maglioli, but what with the Commendatore's much publicized avowals to withdraw from racing after Italy's G.P. on September 12th, and his excessive financial demands on the keen but hard-pressed Ulster A.C., upon whom the R.A.C. had delegated organization of the T.T., no Ferraris landed on Irish shores that year.

Nor did any of the hoped-for Lancias or Alfa Romeos enter Britain's Championship qualifier, leaving the works Jaguar and Aston Martin teams to fight it out between them, with only the

French Gordinis to join in amongst the faster stuff. Then even Gordini failed them, two 2.3-litre cars non-starting. The Ecurie Ecosse caused further depression by withdrawing their three XK120C Jaguars on the just grounds that they had insufficient time to prepare after the German race the previous weekend, while Porsche and Stanguellini were other defaulters.

As at Spa and Nurburg, one answer to the entry problem was insufficient starting money. Although a grant of £5000, made by the Northern Ireland Government, greatly assisted in financing the race, the promotion of a major motoring event is notoriously costly, and the hapless Ulster A.C. found themselves running a classic event with insufficient cash in the kitty.

Fifty-four starters was the maximum permitted; forty-five the number of entries received, and twenty-seven the actual number of starters in Britain's finest race, on Britain's only real road circuit. Dundrod was a splendid course, 7.4 miles round, winding and twisting uphill and down, left and right, and offering a tremendous test of speed, braking, acceleration and roadholding. But apart from its comparative inaccessibility for Continentals, Dundrod had two other handicaps—much of its lap was narrow and bordered with banks; while every yard lay within a water catchment area west of Belfast, so that 'Dundrod weather' could be very wet and unpleasant indeed.

That year, however, Dundrod brought a third handicap, and a major headache for the organizers and the competing teams. The entire circuit had been resurfaced with a non-skid dressing of rather large stone chippings which, in practice, proved extremely abrasive to tyres, completely sabotaging calculations as to the number of changes necessary during a race lasting an estimated nine hours and covering 108 laps for the largest-engined cars, a total of 800 miles.

It looked at one stage of the crisis as if even the big teams might withdraw because of this tyre problem, but they decided against this, while the Dunlop and Avon concerns rallied to the cause, flying over huge loads of extra covers as reserves, and the Ulster Club breathed again.

But their troubles were not yet over! Race day dawned without the dreaded Dundrod downpour, but instead the elements conjured up a heavy mist which blanketed much of the course at starting time, 9am. The race had to be postponed, first for half an hour, then for a further hour, so that it was 10.30am before the flag fell on the Le Mans start, and restive drivers sprang at last into action.

Stirling Moss made a brilliant getaway, being in his Jaguar and on the move before other engines could be heard. His team-mate Tony Rolt was next off, with Collins's Aston and White-head's Jaguar at his heels, fleeing from the main pack, a storming, snarling mass of cars which vanished towards Leathemstown, leaving a strong concentration of exhaust gases and an uncanny vacuum of silence. Little more than five minutes later, it was riven by the three green Jaguars of Moss, Rolt and Whitehead, slamming past in a howl of sound, hotly pursued by the DB3 Aston Martins of Collins, Parnell and Salvadori.

The roads remained moist during the opening stages, which minimized the much-dreaded tyre wear, but also caught out the unwary. The Kenya driver C. J. Manussis crashed his C-type Jaguar, two Kiefts, a Frazer-Nash and a Lester-M.G. had lurid moments, and many a tyre flirted with Dundrod's unsympathetic banks in scrabbling past.

Trouble struck at Jaguar on lap five, Rolt's car going out with serious gearbox faults, but Moss evaded the Aston Martin pur-suit in spite of needing tyres about every sixteen laps to the Astons' twenty-two. Mist still lay at high points during the morning, but after midday the sun strengthened, dispersing it and drying the roads. Speeds increased—and so did tyre wear. Whitehead's XK120C threw a tread and lost much time crawling in, and later Ian Stewart in the same car burst a tyre near Quarry, changing it on the spot.

Peter Walker took over from Moss, lost some time with a loose bonnet, then set the fastest lap of the day in 5mins. 1sec.—88.70 mph, but paid for it by skidding badly on worn tyres, hitting the bank at Cochranstown and damaging a rear wing. Then Aston Martin lost a car, Dennis Poore crashing when striving to pass Ken Wharton's very fast 2-litre Frazer-Nash at Tornagrough and suffering severe cuts and bruises.

The confusing handicap system beloved for so long by Ulster

T.T. organizers left the public hazy of actual race positions until after half-distance, when the warring Jaguars and Aston Martins had shaken clear of smaller cars granted many 'credit laps'. But Jaguar suffered a second blow when the Whitehead/Stewart car developed gearbox trouble identical to that on Rolt's car, and soon the hard-noted Astons, deftly controlled by John Wyer, began to press their attack home.

By 4pm the Moss/Walker XK120C's lead over the Parnell/Thompson DB3S was uncomfortably narrow, while the Collins/Pat Griffith DB3S, though troubled by water losses, was moving up fast. By 4.30pm Reg Parnell was in front, Collins was harrying Walker, and Wharton's astonishing Frazer-Nash was fourth.

Now Collins was seen at his brilliant best. Going like the wind, he pulled out a lap one second slower than Walker's lap record on an extra half litre, and took the lead from team-mate Parnell, while the Jaguar began to drop back. By 6.45pm, when Moss relieved Walker, the car was almost a lap behind and obviously not at its best. On the 99th lap, with seven to go, Collins lapped Moss and roared on to clearcut victory, while the final drama centred on the hapless Jaguar.

Just as Moss was negotiating the hairpin, between Wheeler's and Quarry Corners, his gearbox failed as had the other Jaguars'. He managed to crest the rise to Quarry, then coasted down towards the pits, halting just short of the finishing line to await the winner. Then, as the Aston crackled past to take the chequered flag, Moss started his engine, revved it up, and managed to judder his crippled car over the line, to take fourth place behind Collins, Parnell and Wharton. Feltham's triumph was rubbed in by two private entries, those of Graham Whitehead/Tony Gaze and Tom Dickson/Desmond Titterington, finishing fifth and sixth.

But that fourth place meant three Championship points, so that Moss's shrewdness had brought the Coventry marque on a par with Ferrari again, both now having twenty-seven points, with but one round of the contest to go. On the face of it, this was an intoxicating situation, but there was a 'catch' to it, namely the C.S.I. Championship regulations. These stipulated that out of a total of seven events, only the four best performances by a marque would count for the contest. As the 1953 score chart shows, this put Ferrari two points ahead of Jaguar, with twenty-six points to twenty-four—still close enough to be exciting.

MARATHON IN MEXICO

'*We must say that, merely reading all the names of villages, cities and towns steeped in Mexican history of revolutions, passionate rebels and fiestas in warm, penetrating sunshine, makes us want to pack our smog mask and be off on the next boat*', 'Grande Vitesse', THE MOTOR, November 18th, 1953.

To the great regret of countless British race followers, the Jaguar Company declined to exploit the opportunity of winning the Championship, so hard-earned for them by Stirling Moss and Peter Walker in the T.T., and did not send cars to Mexico for the *Carrera Panamericana*, decisive round in the contest. With but two points between them and Ferrari, and Ferrari not sending any works cars to Mexico, Jaguar's chances were high. They had the cars, they had the men, they had the money too.

The Autocar's sports editor, the late John A. Cooper, made an impassioned plea in his columns after the T.T., saying:

'It is to be hoped, for the prestige of this country, that the Coventry firm will be able to see its way clear to entering a works team in this event, especially as it carries great weight in publicity over the whole American continent, probably only exceeded by the incomparable Le Mans classic. In fact, I think it would pay dividends for them to enter two teams, of three XK120C and three Mark VII models, for the production car class is also of great prestige value and the relative increase in expense would not be proportionately great. They have enough drivers, for only one is required per car, a mechanic occupying the passenger's seat. What about it, Mr Lyons ?'

Alas, the company decided against it, their policy being never to participate in a race unless they had the whole operation planned properly beforehand. The fact that they were so close to victory in the World Sports Car Championship left them unmoved, it being their opinion that a major success such as Le Mans brought adequate publicity. With an eye to the future,

B

however, they decided to send Stirling Moss and team manager Raymond ('Lofty') England out to reconnoitre the course—a regrettable waste of talent.

The Panamerican road race was verily a marathon affair, more closely a revival of the pioneer town-to-town races even than the Mille Miglia, since it was run in stages with rest periods in between. It was inaugurated in 1950 to celebrate the opening of Mexico's portion of the great Panamerican highway, planned some day to link North and South America end to end. That first race ran from the Texan frontier at Ciudad Juarez on the Rio Grande, down to El Ocotal in the humid green south near the Guatemalan border, but from 1951 onwards, they reversed the direction south to north, and cut out the El Ocotal leg, starting at Tuxtla Gutierrez.

The distance was 1908 miles, split up in 1953 into five daily stages from November 19th to 23rd, the cars being impounded in a *parc fermée* each night, after an invaluable but all-too-short three-hour period for servicing and repairs. The long, long route included gruelling mountain sections comparable in all but temperature with the Alps, serpentine high-altitude stretches which affected carburation, and tremendously long straight stretches under the torrid sun, where the fastest cars could top 170mph for mile after mile, if their engines could sustain the pace.

In the towns and villages, Mexican and Indian crowds massed in true Mille Miglia style, right on the road verges, forming a wall of humanity which made the sighting of corners tricky, and intimidated all but the most callous of drivers. In contrast there were great desert stretches occupied solely by huge cacti, windswept plains where the dust whirled in thick clouds, and pastureland where wandering cattle, sheep, goats and burros would be encountered. It was a unique, dangerous, but immensely fascinating race.

There were two main categories, sports cars and catalogue touring cars, both with first prizes of around £5750, and cash awards up to tenth place; as a result, entries were numerous. Although Enzo Ferrari stuck to his vow and sent no works team, the 'Prancing Horse' was nonetheless well represented by the Scuderia Guastalla, which fielded five Ferraris, with Maglioli,

Chinetti, Stagnoli, Mancini and Ricci to drive them. The Mexican Echeverria and the Californian Phil Hill also drove privately entered Ferraris.

But the most powerful contenders of all were Lancia of Turin, who staggered the Mexicans by the lavishness of their equipment and the superb preparation of their cars. They brought no less than five V6 *Competizione* models, with the great Fangio, an old hand at long-distance town-to-town racing in South America, and the veterans Taruffi, Bonetto and Bracco, each driving a 3.3-litre car, and the up-and-coming Castellotti with a 3-litre.

France was well represented by two Gordinis, ultra-fast but fragile, for Behra and Lucas, and a 4½-litre Talbot, rapid and rugged, for that shrewd 'stonewaller' Louis Rosier. Welcome American rivalry to the Europeans in the big sports class came from Akton Miller's genuine 'hot rod' special, with a much-souped up Oldsmobile V8 engine in an old Ford chassis, plus a *soupçon* of Cadillac and Nash in the transmission department; and also from two Kurtis sports cars, one with a Cadillac engine for Jack Ensley, the other Chrysler-powered, to be driven by Duane Carter. There were also two Jaguars, an XK120C being entered with Mexican state backing for Paco Ibarra to drive, while Guillermo Giron of Guatemala ran an XK120 coupé.

The great race began at 6am, November 19th, when 177 cars were dispatched singly at one-minute intervals, on the first stage of their long journey. Their destination was Oaxaca (which sounds something like 'Oh-hwaca' the way the natives say it), 329.34 miles distant. Lead-footed Jean Behra in his Gordini caught Rosier's Talbot and Hill's Ferrari to lead the cavalcade into the town, but on time all were overwhelmed by four of the Lancias, which simply outpaced everyone, including Maglioli's ex-works 4½-litre Ferrari coupé which won the Belgian 24-hour race.

Alas, the first retirement was a Jaguar, Ibarra's XK120C breaking its timing chain two hundred miles from the start, while Ensley's Kurtis-Cadillac ran out of fuel. Stage one winner was that ebullient fifty-year-old Italian, Felice Bonetto, who led his great rival, Piero Taruffi, home by two minutes, followed by Fangio and Castellotti, Maglioli, Behra, Bracco and Lucas, while next

came two Porsches driven by Hans Herrmann and the 1952
'Pan-Am' winner, Karl Kling, and a Borgward, all contesting
the 1500cc sports class.

It was on this opening stage that grim tragedy struck. Travelling a straight, two-lane section, almost one hundred miles in
length, the 4.5 Ferrari coupé of Antonio Stagnoli burst a tyre
when motoring flat-out, rolled over and over, and caught fire.
The two unfortunate occupants hadn't a chance, passenger
Scotuzzi being killed instantly, while Stagnoli died a few hours
later in hospital.

Then Micky Thompson, today a World Land Speed record
aspirant, heroically steered his Ford saloon over an embankment
approaching the Tehuantepec River bridge to avoid a woman
and child running across the road, only to dive on to a concealed
crowd gathered around Bob Christie's Lincoln, which had
plunged down into the muddy river verge earlier. Six people died
and several others were injured in this tragic accident.

Stage two led from Oaxaca to Puebla, a severe section travers-
ing mountains, plateaux and valleys, and skirting Popacatapetl,
Mexico's famous volcano. Here Taruffi got the better of Bonetto,
while Fangio contented himself again with third position.
Maglioli, Bracco, Castellotti and Mancini followed in, while
Chinetti's Ferrari retired with a 'blown gasket'.

Run that same day after a half-hour break was Stage three,
shortest of all, from Puebla to Mexico City; 81 miles of dangerous
mountain pass traversing a pass nearly 11,000 feet above sea level.
Taruffi knew this stretch well from his 1951 and 1952 drives in
the Carrera, and won from Bonetto, Maglioli and Fangio. Phil
Hill's 4.1-Ferrari fell one hundred feet down a precipice, Hill
and Richie Ginther emerging unhurt, to discover that a sign
warning drivers of a turn had been removed by local Mexicans
'to add to the fun'! Less spectacular was Duane Carter's retirement in the Kurtis-Chrysler with simple overheating.

The third day also comprised two stages: Mexico City to
Leon, 267 miles away, then Leon to Durango, a further 333
miles. It was another day of tragedy, for the fiery Bonetto, duelling for the lead with Taruffi, lost control when braking fiercely
from high speed on a bend in the village of Silao. The Lancia

slewed round, bounced off a wall, and struck a lamp post with cruel force. 'The old Pirate' as his many admirers called the hapless Bonetto, died from a broken neck.

It was the first stage not won by a Lancia. Taruffi, close behind Bonetto, stopped to aid his team mate, and eventually came into Leon with damaged front suspension, lying tenth, while Umberto Maglioli put on a sensational spurt to win from Fangio. Mancini, Castellotti and the two Gordinis followed in.

Making up time, Taruffi won stage five, Leon to Durango (where the finish-line was marked by two vast twenty-foot Pepsi-Cola 'bottles!) from Fangio, although the latter now led the race on overall time. The biggest threat to Lancia was Maglioli's Ferrari, but the car lost a wheel during this stage at about 130mph, the driver luckily escaping unhurt, and promptly taking over Mario Ricci's Ferrari instead. The blue Gordinis had both retired with trouble, but Rosier's Talbot moved into fifth place behind Mancini.

After a rest day in hot, dry Durango, stage six was a largely straight and simple 251-mile drive to Parral. Maglioli fairly flogged Ricci's 4.5-Ferrari along, beating Taruffi and Fangio, though the latter's overall lead was not imperilled. From Parral to Chihuahua (they call it 'Chee-wa-wa'—where the miniature dogs come from!), a very fast 186 miles, it was Maglioli first again, at a 127.46mph average, moreover. And in the eighth and final 223-miles of flat-out motoring, the last few miles in a 30mph dust-storm, to Ciudad Juarez (sounding something like 'Thewdad Hwaareth'!) it was Maglioli yet again—at the staggering average of 139·3mph.

Yet this grand effort secured him only sixth place in overall race order, since the car, in Ricci's hands, had been far behind in the early stages. The outright victor of the fourth *Carrera Panamericana Mexico* was Fangio the old fox, the shrewd tactician, who never won a single stage yet whose overall racing time of 18hours 11mins was 7mins. 51secs. less than second man Taruffi. Castellotti in the 3-litre car was third, completing a brilliant 1-2-3 Lancia triumph, and fourth came Guido Mancini in his Scuderia Guastalla 4.5-Ferrari.

With that fourth place, secured by an Italian amateur, the

1953 World Sports Car Championship, and the Coupe de la Commission Sportive were won by Ferrari and lost to Jaguar, by three points.

In ninth place overall, last of the unlimited sports car class, came the XK120 hardtop of Guillermo Giron, behind the three triumphant Lancias, Mancini's Ferrari, Rosier's Talbot, Maglioli's and Echeverria's Ferraris, and 'Ak' Miller's remarkably fast and tough 'Hot Rod'. A works XK120C Jaguar could have been placed much higher; third place and the four points gained, would have made Jaguar the first World Sports Car Champions. . . .

But hypothesis works both ways, and cannot alter hard fact. Automobili Ferrari were able to proclaim themselves 'Campeoni del Mondo, Vetture Sport', and on aggregate, of course, well merited the title. Of the seven qualifying events, they had won three, whereas Jaguar, Aston Martin, Lancia, and Cunningham, had won one each.

So it was 'Hail, Ferrari, the first World Sports Car Champion'.

CHAMPIONSHIP SCORE-SHEET 1953

Make of Car	Sebring 12-hour, U.S.A.	Mille Miglia, Italy	Le Mans 24-hour, France	Belgian 24-hour	Nurburgring 1000-km, Germany	Tourist Trophy, Gt. Britain	Carrera Panamericana, Mexico	Total Score	Best Four Performances
Ferrari ..	1 (6th)	8 (1st)	2 (5th)	8(1st)	8 (1st)	—	3 (4th)	30	27
Jaguar ..	4 (3rd)	—	8 (1st)	6 (2nd)	6 (2nd)	3 (4th)	—	27	24
Aston Martin ..	6 (2nd)	2 (5th)	—	—	—	8 (1st)	—	16	16
Lancia ..	—	4 (3rd)	—	—	—	—	8 (1st)	12	12
Cunningham ..	8 (1st)	—	4 (3rd)	—	—	—	—	12	12
Alfa Romeo ..	—	6 (2nd)	—	—	—	—	—	6	6
Borgward ..	—	—	—	—	4 (3rd)	—	—	4	4
Frazer-Nash ..	—	—	—	—	—	4 (3rd)	—	4	4
D-B ..	—	—	—	3 (4th)	—	—	—	3	3
Porsche..	—	—	—	—	3 (4th)	—	—	3	3
Talbot ..	—	—	—	—	—	—	2 (5th)	2	2
Veritas ..	—	—	—	—	2 (5th)	—	—	2	2
Maserati ..	—	1 (6th)	—	—	—	—	—	1	1
Gordini..	—	—	1 (6th)	—	—	—	—	1	1
Panhard..	—	—	—	1 (6th)	—	—	—	1	1

SCORING: First 8 points; second 6pts.; third 4pts.; fourth 3pts.; fifth 2pts.; sixth 1pt.

CHAPTER 2

THAT HORSE AGAIN

ONE OF Ferrari's pleasant traditions is the annual end-of-season dinner given at Modena, to honour those who have driven under the escutcheon of the famous 'Prancing Horse'. At the 1953 function on December 12th, Commendatore Enzo Ferrari announced that he had changed his mind about withdrawing from racing; his teams would again be seen in Grand Prix and sports car events, he said, but only in the most important races.

This was taken to indicate that Signor Enzo had encountered little difficulty in securing that extra financial backing he sought. Some said it came directly from the Italian Government, who had already assisted the far larger Alfa Romeo concern; others said the wealthy Marzotto family were backing him. But whatever the source, Ferraris were 'back' without ever having gone away, the news being hailed with pleasure and relief within Italy, if not in some quarters outside that country.

DOWN ARGENTINE WAY

'Ferrari clearly established its supremacy, for the moment at least. This author shudders at the thought of a faster car than the big 4.5-litre job, with Farina scowling over the hood. . . .' Bob Said; MOTORSPORT (U.S.A.), May 1954

Round one of the second contest for the Constructors' Cup and the World Sports Car Championship took place early in the year, on January 24th. It was a new event, the Buenos Aires 1000-kilometre race, sponsored by the Municipal Government of the famous 'beef city', and organized by the Automobile Club of Argentina, in conjunction with other races at other weekends, the meetings being collectively known as the *Temporada*.

The confines of the city's very modern permanent 'Ottubre 17' Autodrome were not considered suitable for a long-distance sports car race, so the A.C.A., with Municipal assent, simply went outside the Autodrome's front gates and incorporated part of the fast motorway, the *Avenida General Paz* (where the Nazi Adolf Eichmann was 'kidnapped' in 1960), linking it with the outer track of the Autodrome, where ultra-modern pits were installed.

Cars travelled up one side of the four-lane road, took a complex series of left and right hand sweeps, crossed the *Avenida* via a bridge, slammed down a one-and-a-half mile straight to a round-about, which took them back down the return side of the motor-way, re-entering the Autodrome by a short straight. The resultant 5.88-mile circuit was interesting, but potentially very dangerous where the cars travelled at high speed in opposite directions down the *Avenida*, separated solely by a central strip of grass and kerbs.

It was touch-and-go whether the Ferraris—two 4.5-litre VI2s and an interesting new 3-litre four-cylinder model—would get to Argentina at all, since the lorries carrying them from the Modena works to the boat at Genoa became snowed up en route. In the end they had to be flown across the South Atlantic to find, on reaching 'B.A.', that Britain had sent unexpectedly strong opposi-tion, in the shape of an Ecurie Ecosse team of three XKI2OC Jaguars—the ex-works disc-braked cars—and three works DB3S Aston Martins.

Also competing, on an 'all expenses paid' invitation from the organizers, was a team from the Sports Car Club of America, comprising a 4.1-Ferrari, an XKI2OC Jaguar, a J2X Cadillac-Allard, and an Osca, the drivers including Carroll Shelby, Phil Hill and Masten Gregory, three men destined for international fame. There was a miscellany of other Ferraris amongst the thirty-six starters, including a 3-litre VI2 driven jointly by the Spaniard, Marquis Alfonso de Portago, a seemingly languid new-comer to racing, and the tempestuous Harry Schell; and a potent 4½-litre car in French blue, actually Rosier's old Formula 1 G.P. car, still with central seat but converted to sports bodywork— one of the broader conceptions of the 'prototypes' permitted by Appendix C!

Rosier's co-driver was dapper Maurice Trintignant, who

performed a splendid getaway at the Le Mans start, to lead the pack on lap one from Scotsman Ian Stewart's Jaguar, Bonomi's fast Ferrari 3-litre 'four', Schell in Portago's V12, Parnell's Aston Martin and Ninian Sanderson's Jaguar—a cosmopolitan 'gaggle' emphasizing the international nature of the field.

Giuseppe Farina, seemingly under the impression that others should make way for his Ferrari at the start, got going rather tardily, then, using all the colossal power from his 4.5, he carved his way through the massed opposition, steering with one hand and waving his fist with the other. But it took him eight laps to catch the flying Trintignant, after which the works' Ferrari was never headed, Farina and Maglioli winning the 106-lap, 624-mile race, comfortably at 93.43mph.

But behind the contemptuous wake of the leading *Ferraristi* there were ample incidents—all too many, in fact. Sanderson went straight on over the roundabout, doing his Jaguar's handling qualities no good at all for the rest of the race; Phil Hill's 4.1-Ferrari spoilt its transmission and his day; while Bob Said's Osca also ran out of final drive. Said pulled up in an escape road near a group of policemen, who suddenly broke up and fled in all directions as a Ferrari charged in amongst them, very much out of brakes. It glanced off an ambulance, then bowled over several of the police, badly damaging its light-gauge alloy front against them, much to the rage of Pedro Llano the driver, who rightly argued that the escape road was for his use, not theirs!

Frenchman Elie Bayol in his 2.5-Gordini dodged the usual Argentinian spectator crossing the course, but lost control and smote a haystack; a wheel flew off the car, striking a policeman, while the Gordini hit a spectator and killed him. Then Ian Stewart's Ecosse Jaguar lost its line on a curve while passing two Porsches on the outside, hit the kerb, and smashed into a very solid retaining wall. Worse came when Eric Forrest-Greene, a Briton residing in the Argentine, struck a kerb with his private DB3 Aston Martin, which bounced across the road, overturned and caught fire. The unfortunate driver struggled out, his overalls ablaze, and began to run; severely burned, he died in hospital.

Then Rosier's Ferrari lost time at the pits, yielding second position to the newer Ferrari 4.5 of the Argentinians Ibanez and

Janices. But the latter had scarcely taken over when a brake
locked as he rushed up to the roundabout. The big Ferrari
slewed, hit the inevitable kerb and turned over, careering on its
back straight over the central dividing strip and into the stream
of oncoming cars on the return leg. The Masten Gregory/Dale
Duncan Jaguar narrowly missed the Ferrari, which skated on to
end up a total wreck—out of which Janices emerged, unhurt.

The third cars of the Aston Martin and Ecurie Ecosse teams
were handled by Argentine crews, but both were forced out with
transmission troubles. The other Astons of Parnell/Salvadori and
Collins/Griffith moved up steadily, however, until electrical
bothers spoilt Parnell's run, and let Harry Schell into a hard-won
second place.

Schell was the hero of the day, driving with fire and fury until,
exhausted, he pulled in and handed over to Portago. But when
the inexperienced Marquis dropped two places in two laps, that
was too much for Harry, who flagged him in again and drove the
rest of the long hot race himself. He fought a great duel with
Bonomi's 4-cylinder Ferrari until the latter ruined his transmission in the heat of battle, about ten laps from the finish.
Schell went on to second place, heading the Collins/Griffith
Aston Martin, the limping Jaguar of Sanderson/Scott-Douglas,
another Ferrari and the Musso/Giletti 2-litre Maserati.

Thus the world's 1953 Champion sports car marque took an
early lead in the 1954 contest, the score sheet after 'B.A.' reading:
Ferrari eight points, Aston Martin four, Jaguar three, Maserati
one. It was as well that only the highest placed car of a make was
eligible for points, otherwise Ferrari would have kicked off their
season with sixteen!

SEBRING—THE GIANTS FALL

*'Rarely in the history of sports car racing in America has pre-race
speculation run so high, and prognostications been so wrong. . . .'* Bill
Callahan; MOTORSPORT (U.S.A.), May 1954

If ever there was a 'turn up for the book' in motor racing, the
1954 Sebring 12-hour was it. Of the fifty-eight starters, about a
dozen were Championship-sized, driven by the élite of racing

men. Yet appalling luck, and the determination and skill of one British driver in a little Italian car half their size, robbed 'the giants' of victory in the second qualifying round of the 1954 Championship.

Most powerful entrant of all was Lancia, who that year had signed up Alberto Ascari and Luigi Villoresi, both formerly of the Ferrari team. In all, the Turin marque fielded four cars, pairing Fangio/Castellotti, Ascari/Villoresi, Taruffi/Manzon and Valenzano/Rubirosa, the latter a versatile Dominican more widely known to the press as a 'diplomat playboy' whatever that may be, than as a racing driver.

For the second year, Ferrari declined to send an official team; there was still no prize money or starting fees at Sebring; not a dollar! Prestige and Championship points were the sole rewards of victory, and Ferrari deemed these insufficient to warrant the long trip from Italy to Florida. But the Champion marque was still well represented, by Harry Schell/de Portago in a 3-litre, Phil Walters/John Fitch in a Cunningham-entered 4.5, and Bill Spear/Phil Hill in another 4.5. Briggs Cunningham had also entered a 1½-litre Osca, to be driven by Bill Lloyd and Stirling Moss, who had wanted, but couldn't get, a works' Jaguar for the race. Aston Martin made the journey, however, with three DB3S for Collins/Griffith, Parnell/Salvadori and two Americans, Carroll Shelby/Charles Wallace. A 5.4-litre C4R Cunningham was down for Sherwood Johnston/Briggs Cunningham, and Lance Macklin/George Huntoon had a 2.6-litre disc-braked Austin Healey.

Although Florida conjures up thoughts of sunshine and orange groves, the vast Hendrycks airfield was bleak, windy and uncharitable on race day, March 7th. The Lancia team had flown from Italy, via Prestwick aerodrome in Scotland, where, well-wrapped against the biting cold in overcoats and rugs, they had been interviewed by the Scottish monthly magazine *Top Gear*. Asked what difference there was between driving a sports car and a Grand Prix car, Ascari observed that a sports car was a little warmer owing to the all-enveloping bodywork—'But,' he added, pulling a rug closer about him, 'you wouldn't have to worry about that in your country, signor!'

Now Ascari and Co. were in 'sunny' Florida, feeling almost as cold in the cold, gusty north wind, and glad for the 10am starting bomb and the warmth of their cockpits after the rush across the broad track at the Le Mans release. Johnston's big, growling Cunningham and Goldschmidt's Cadillac-Allard were first away, but lap one gave the chilled American crowd of about 12,000 an impressive idea of the Italian way of motor racing. Four Lancias crashed past in close order: Ascari, Fangio, Rubirosa, Taruffi, with bulky Bill Spear's howling 4.5-Ferrari in chase and Macklin's astonishing Austin Healey next.

The three Lancia stars sported with each other, chopping and changing their positions and keeping the lap-scorers busy, but Rubirosa in the fourth Lancia—the actual Panamerican winner of 1953—lost much ground, and also first and second gears during the first hour! Walters' Ferrari had plug trouble, but Spear clung hard to the flying Lancias, which *somehow* seemed to use up all the road when he was close, though he managed to displace Taruffi awhile from third place.

Britain's Aston Martins were right off form. Collins's car went out with dire braking trouble when seventh, while Reg Parnell's run ended in a cloud of black smoke and a one-mile push, in vain, to the pits. The American-driven DB3s lasted longer, but the 5.2-mile circuit, notoriously hard on brakes and transmissions, eventually took its toll and forced Shelby/Wallace out with brake failure.

When Johnston brought the big blue and white Cunningham in for a refuel, a stream of 'Amoco' fuel slopped from the funnel on to the hot exhaust pipe, sending a pillar of flame high above the pits. But Briggs Cunningham was right 'on the ball', snatching a fire extinguisher and quickly quelling the blaze; he then set off in the now sooty and blistered car. Next burly Bill Spear came in, and Phil Hill, the very antithesis in physique, took over, just as the Lancia pit called their cars in, one by one, letting the Ferrari up into the lead.

As at Nurburgring in 1953, their first pit-stops seemed to break the Lancia spell. Not long after changing over, the Fangio/Castellotti car retired with transmission breakage, and then Ascari 'pushed it' too hard while displacing Phil Hill from the lead, and departed with a useless clutch.

With Valenzano/Rubirosa far back, Lancia hopes rested on No. 38, the Taruffi/Manzon car now leading, cheekily followed by the 1500cc Osca driven by Stirling Moss and Bill Lloyd and the lone Austin Healey. One after another the big cars had fallen out; the Cunningham, the Schell/Portago Ferrari, Phil Hill's Ferrari with that old Sebring transmission trouble, while the last Ferrari in the race, the Walters/Fitch 4.5, also retired with a 'bad connecting rod bearing' when holding second between the Lancia and the Osca.

With the race nine hours old, night fallen and headlights on, a Lancia victory looked certain, but a long, irritating stop ensued to remedy a faulty headlight, halving No. 38's lead of over 90 miles. Meanwhile the amazing Moss was haring round in the now practically brakeless Osca, slowing by sliding sideways up to the corners, skating past larger, lumbering opponents through Sebring's diverse bends, and driving like—well, like Moss at his superb best, at grips with adversity. It was the first time the Americans had seen 'the British boy' in action, and they were vastly impressed.

Came the eleventh hour, and Fate's most brutal blow to Lancia; a flying stone severed an oil pipe, and Taruffi's engine seized solid, out on the back straight. Hastily declutching, the forty-seven-year-old 'silver fox' coasted as far as possible, then began to push the 18-cwt Lancia to the pits. The veteran from Rome was fit and sturdy, but the pits were almost two-and-a-half miles away, while any assistance was forbidden by the regulations. He arrived totally exhausted and fit to drop.

The pit crew strove frenziedly to free the engine by pouring oil down the bores and other expedients, but to no avail. Out from the Cunningham pit went the signal to Moss: '38 Sick'; out went signals from Lancia to Valenzano in the sole surviving Lancia, still running despite having third and top gears only. The Italian responded magnificently, forcing the v6-Lancia round in the darkness at near-record speed in his efforts to close.

But Moss's Osca, remorselessly picking up laps on Taruffi's stationary car, soon passed into the lead, and at 10pm the little Osca 'took the checker', five laps ahead of the valiant Valenzano. Meanwhile the Chief Steward had given permission for the crippled Taruffi/Manzon Lancia to be driven over the finishing line on its starter motor—it would have finished third. But the starter could not turn the engine over, so Manzon pushed the car across the line, thereby precipitating a protest from the Austin Healey pit that the Lancia had not finished under its own power, as stipulated by the rules.

So all that Taruffi and Manzon got for their efforts was disqualification, and the sole consolation for the stricken Lancia équipe was second place—plus the fact that the winning car was at least Italian, albeit of less than half their engine capacity!

Moss and Lloyd averaged 73.6mph, contrasting well with the 5.4-litre Cunningham's 1953 average of 74.9mph. Stirling Moss drove most of the way save for the first three hours, in a car virtually clutchless and brakeless from the sixth hour; it was one of his greatest racing achievements, news of which sent the Maserati brothers, manufacturers of the Osca at Bologna, Italy, into transports of joy, especially as other 1500 Oscas were fourth, fifth and eighth, 1-2-3 on Index of Performance, and 1-2-3 in the 1½-litre class!

Third on three cylinders was the Macklin/Huntoon Austin Healey after an outstanding drive greatly aided by disc brakes, while sixth was a British 2-litre Kieft-Bristol driven by two Americans. With the best Jaguar eighth and no Ferrari in the finishing list, Sebring 1954 was indeed an exceptional race.

Now the Championship score read first, Ferrari and Osca, eight points each, second, Lancia, six points, third Aston Martin and Austin Healey, four points, fourth, Jaguar three points, fifth, Maserati and Kieft one point. And the Lancias which should have won at Sebring went back to Italy, licking their wounds and preparing grimly for the next round, the Mille Miglia.

VINDICATION FOR LANCIA

'The crowd went mad, swarming over the road despite the efforts of police and soldiers with rifle butts to keep them back. . . .' THE AUTOCAR, May 7th, 1954

In August 1953 the world's greatest racing driver, Tazio Nuvolari, died at the age of sixty-two at his home in Mantua. As a tribute to his memory, the Mille Miglia organizers decided that the route henceforth should deviate from Cremona to pass through *Il Maestro*'s home town, adding fifty-five miles to the total distance.

Race weekend, May 1st–2nd, was wet, misty and cold, after days of rain beforehand, but the public turn-out was as colossal as ever. The entry totalled 472 on paper, and 374 on the famous launching ramp in Brescia. Principal pre-race excitement concerned Mercedes-Benz, who were said to be entering three fabulous new cars capable of over 180mph; but the famous German firm confined their racing come-back to Grands Prix in 1954, leaving the annual scramble over Italy's roads and mountains to Ferrari, Lancia and Maserati, with three Aston Martins, three Austin Healeys and three Triumph TR2s, a lone H.W.M. Jaguar, and a Belgian-entered XK120 Jaguar to introduce some change of colour in a field preponderantly of Italian red.

Ferraris had built an even larger car, a savage 4.9-litre 12-cylinder, based on the 1951 Grand Prix car, and giving something like 345bhp; its handling qualities initially were not up to its power, as the veteran Giuseppe Farina found to his cost a quarter of an hour after starting. His car power-slid on a sharp left turn in Peschiera, skated off the road, knocked down a concrete post, and smacked into a tree. Farina broke an arm and hurt his nose, while his riding mechanic, Parenti, suffered a fractured pelvis. By a new concession introduced that year, Parenti need not have been there at all, as the carrying of a passenger was no longer obligatory. The 4.9-Ferrari was a complete wreck.

Maserati had an important new car too, a 3-litre six-cylinder which was hastily finished for the race. It lasted just one kilometre from Brescia, when Mantovani retired it with transmission failure. Meanwhile Taruffi, Ascari and Castellotti had taken their 3.3-litre Lancias out to a 1-2-3 lead, Taruffi being first into Ravenna at a 108.9mph average! The 4.9 Ferraris of Maglioli, Paolo Marzotto and his brother Giannino followed, but over wet, slippery roads, could make no impression on their Torinese rivals. The Lancias still ran 1-2-3 through Pescara, by which stage the 1953 race winner, Giannino Marzotto, had retired, as had Bordoni's 3-litre Gordini and Chiron's Austin Healey.

Taruffi was setting an amazing pace, pulling away from an

apparently subdued Ascari. The World Champion had not, in fact, expected to contest the Mille Miglia, his contract with Lancia specifically excluding this race, which he greatly disliked. But when his team mate Villoresi could not drive owing to an accident, fidelity to Lancia persuaded Ascari to take his place. Besides practising assiduously, he had talked beforehand with that master of the Mille Miglia, Clemente Biondetti, victor in 1938, 1947, 1948 and 1949, who counselled a steady pace, considerate of the mechanism.

'He whose foot is always hard down on the accelerator will not see the finish," said Biondetti.

On the difficult mountain section before reaching the Roman plain, two of the Lancias went out, Castellotti having mechanical trouble, and Valenzano crashing, breaking a collar bone. Also out, alas, went Reg Parnell, who had worked his DB3S Aston Martin up to sixth position, Louis Klemantaski again riding with him as passenger. They were cornering fast near Aquila when suddenly the wheels ran over a layer of loose stones, scattered around by an errant Fiat; the Aston skidded and crashed, being badly damaged. Reg's words on climbing out and viewing the wreck cannot, alas, be recorded, but Klemantaski assures us they were terse and expressive!

The flying Taruffi still led through Rome, thereby courting disaster if one accepts the 'he who leads through Rome never wins' theory. It certainly held true that year, for, as at Sebring, Taruffi's Lancia broke an oil pipe and was forced out of the race near Viterbo—wretched luck after a staunch attempt. Only one Lancia of the four which started now remained, with Ascari at the wheel, menaced by two 4.9-Ferraris. In pouring rain at Florence, the order was Ascari, Marzotto, Maglioli, followed by Scotti's 3-litre Ferrari, Musso's very fast 2-litre Maserati, Vittorio Marzotto's new 2-litre four-cylinder Ferrari of obvious Grand Prix derivation, called the Mondial, and Peter Collins in the sole surviving Aston Martin.

Rain pelted down during the crossing of the Appenines over the Futa and Raticosa passes to Bologna, and this section brought more eliminations, including both the big Ferraris! Collins's Aston and Scotti's Ferrari also dropped out, and thus Marzotto found himself second in a 2-litre car to the bigger Lancia, with Musso hot on his heels.

Ascari had been delayed in the mountains by a punctured tyre, but was aided by another competitor of herculean build, who raised the Lancia bodily while Ascari whipped the old wheel off and a new one on. The throttle spring had also broken, and the Lancia équipe, with all their 'eggs' now in the Ascari basket, were understandably 'on pins' at Bologna. But the sage Alberto passed a seemingly leisurely fourteen minutes there, having the car thoroughly checked before calmly resuming the race.

Soft-pedalling was against the Ascari nature, but although he topped 155mph along the very fast stretch near Mantua, and covered the Cremona–Mantua–Brescia section fast enough to win the Nuvolari Trophy for the highest average there, he nursed his Lancia skilfully and boomed into Brescia and the finish without incident, to run into a wildly enthusiastic reception. He won the Mille Miglia, the race he hated, in 11 hours 26mins. 10secs., by over thirty-five minutes from Marzotto's 2-litre Ferrari and Musso's 2-litre Maserati, this pair being only nine seconds apart after 992 miles!

Biondetti was fourth in a private Ferrari 3-litre, another 2-litre Maserati was fifth, and a new four-o.h.c. 1½-litre open Porsche sixth. The high mortality rate amongst the Championship class 3-litre runners was as surprising as the stamina and speed of the smaller capacity cars. Lance Macklin's 2.6-litre Austin Healey finished fifth in the unlimited sports class, to which it had been transferred from the Gran Turismo category through lack of a homologation certificate, and was twenty-third in general order. The H.W.M.-Jaguar of George Abecassis, and Tom Meyer's private DB3 Aston Martin both retired, but a talented Belgian rallyman-turned-racing-driver by the name of Olivier Gendebien drove his XK120 Jaguar coupé into twenty-first place, the highest-placed British car—after flying from Holland, where he had just won the Tulip Rally!

The points position in the Championship now showed Lancia dead level with Ferrari, each having fourteen points, well ahead of Maserati (five), Aston Martin and Austin Healey (four), Jaguar (three) and Kieft and Porsche (one).

MODENA VERSUS COVENTRY

'It was terrific, the cars were almighty fast, faster than grand prix machines. . . . The crowd was enormous and the sky full of heli-copters. . . . There is no race as good for as long.' MOTORSPORT (U.S.A), September–October 1954

After Italy's Mille Miglia, France's Le Mans. A very different race, and a very different entry. Numerically but an eighth of that received for the multi-class Mille Miglia, the sixty-car selection for the *Vingt-quatre heures du Mans* was packed with International talent, promising a colossal struggle.

As in 1953, Britain, America, France, Italy and Germany were all well represented, and in the Championship class were Jaguar, Aston Martin and Lagonda, Cunningham, Talbot and Gordini, Lancia, Maserati and Ferrari. But in this galaxy were stars bright and waning. The Talbots, already old, were now a year older, as were the two C4R Cunninghams; the Gordinis, always fast, were notoriously brittle; the Lagonda was an experimental 4½-litre V12 from the David Brown stable, looking like a well-built sister to the kindred 3-litre Aston Martins.

Soon it became known that the Lancias, which were new 3.8-litre models, would not be ready, while two new 2½-litre Maseratis arrived too late. On paper, then, and on practice form, another Jaguar–Ferrari duel for the lead appeared likely—and both had something special in the way of weapons.

Ferrari brought three of their ferocious 4.9s, very big, very 'hairy' machines, one of which had clocked 190mph in Italy! As for Jaguar, their 1954 cars were entirely new and highly exciting. Known as the D-type, and superseding the XK120C, they bore very smooth aerodynamic bodies of stressed skin construction, formed in magnesium alloy over a square-tube space-frame and an improved version of the famous six-cylinder twin o.h.c. 3442cc Jaguar engine. Dunlop magnesium racing wheels and disc brakes were fitted, the latter a vital weapon in the Jaguar attack, for whereas Ferrari planned to rely on the 4.9's immense torque and colossal acceleration to keep in front, Jaguar relied on deceleration as well to gain precious seconds.

Before the race there was a *brouhaha* of no small significance, when Donald Healey withdrew his three-car team of Austin Healeys in protest at the 'prototype' rulings within Appendix C, which permitted the building of sports-racing cars which in effect were Grand Prix cars with two seats, wider bodies, wings and lights. Makers such as Healey, seeking to race genuine production-based machines, had little chance against such specialized cars which, he contended, were making a farce of 'sports car racing'.

Donald Healey's was but a cry in the wilderness then, but the future was to hear the question raised again and again, before some small action was taken in an attempt to oust the disguised racer from sports car competitions.

But to Le Mans 1954. The course had been much improved (at the expense of its character) that year, with widening and resurfacing from Mulsanne to Arnage, corner improvements, and erection of stands. But one thing, which the Automobile Club de l'Ouest could not control, let them down—the weather.

Race day, June 12th, dawned with a downpour, stayed dry for the beginning of the race, then turned into a wettish evening, making the circuit tryingly slippery. More rain in the night, a damp dawn, and a morning of showers culminated in lashing rainstorms, overshadowed only by the intense drama of the race itself.

Baldly to record that the 4.9-litre Ferrari driven superbly by the portly Argentinian Froilan Gonzalez and the slender Frenchman Maurice Trintignant led the race practically from start to finish suggests a dull, processional race. It was anything but.

Robert Manzon catapulted into the lead at the getaway with his 4.9-Ferrari, his team mates Paolo Marzotto and Gonzalez at his heels, with the three D-type Jaguars of Moss, Ken Wharton and Rolt, moving up swiftly behind them. The warring sextet stormed past the pits on lap one at 130mph—Gonzalez, Marzotto Manzon, Moss, Rolt, Wharton—three reds, three greens, all nose to tail—a staggering spectacle and a shattering noise.

Moss tentatively forced the pace, edging past Manzon and Marzotto, while Rolt followed his example to pass Manzon— none of them fully extended at this stage, but simply 'trying it on' with the opposition. Behind came a bellowing string of Cunninghams, Gordinis, Aston Martins, Talbots, Porsches and the rest, cars of five nationalities and drivers of a dozen, all settling to *la ronde impitoyable*—'the pitiless round'.

Quickly there came the first casualties. A baby Panhard lost a wheel in the first minute, a Porsche was out after four laps, while Baggio buried Porfirio Rubirosa's Ferrari coupé in the sand at Tertre Rouge, to the dismay of Zsa Zsa Gabor and other glamorous adorners of his pit.

An hour and a half after the start, the rain came sheeting down, and Moss sprinted past Gonzalez to lead for Jaguar. The 'Pampas Bull', whose old, wild ways had given way in 1954 to magnificent control, promptly gave his great 4.9-Ferrari the gun and repassed the smaller Jaguar. So the tense 'game' went on until the first refuelling stops brought trouble.

Tony Rolt's Jaguar, suffering a slight misfire, was smartly refilled and taken over by Duncan Hamilton, who returned a lap later with the engine spluttering and spitting. Mechanics traced the trouble to choked fuel lines, filters were cleaned and off he went again. Then Peter Walker, in Moss's car, came in with the same bother, went off again, then stopped on the course with further blockages.

He blew the lines sufficiently clear to struggle back to the pits for further attention, finding Wharton there with the same trouble, while cries of 'sabotage' went up amongst the British contingent—but not from the level-headed Jaguar pit. Meanwhile, the Ferrari trio had gained a lead of over two laps, and with dusk falling and Le Mans taking on its unique 'night look', Britain's position, like the weather, did not look too good.

The V12 Lagonda had gone out when Eric Thompson skidded in the Esses, crumpling the tail and having to retire through damaged rear lights, while Jimmy Stewart's DB3S Aston Martin coupé did a swift *tête-à-queue* at White House when duelling with Meyrat's Talbot, overturned, and bounced and pounded itself into utter wreckage, the driver being thrown out, suffered a broken elbow, shock and bruises. Meyrat's Talbot hit the wreck hard and also vacated the race.

Ferrari's turn for trouble came in the eighth hour, when the Marzotto/Maglioli car retired with rear axle trouble, letting the

Whitehead/Wharton Jaguar up to second place. The infuriating fuel blockages on the other two cars had been cured by entire removal of the filters, and Rolt/Hamilton and Moss/Walker were now lapping with deadly purpose to regain time lost. For the latter pair it proved labour in vain, the Jaguar's brakes failing shortly after midnight, when Moss was rushing down to Mulsanne Corner at about 150mph!

By desperate use of the gears, handbrake and the escape road, he averted disaster, finishing up a mile from the course, en route for Tours! A pipe to the brake servo motor had pulled out irreparably. It rained on and off through the night, while Rolt/Hamilton moved up to third, and the Whitehead/Wharton car became afflicted with gearbox trouble which proved incurable. That left two Jaguars to two Ferraris, which Fate adjusted by forcing the Rosier/Manzon 4.9 out with gearchange trouble early on Sunday morning. By then two more works Aston Martins had gone; the Shelby/Frère car with a broken stub axle, and the Collins/Bira coupé, when lying fourth, in a repeat of Stewart's crash at White House—Bira miraculously crawling out of a virtual heap of scrap.

The morning brought more rain, but the Rolt/Hamilton D-type had closed considerably on the leading Ferrari, with Cunninghams third and fifth, a private Belgian-entered XK120C Jaguar fourth, and the Parnell/Salvadori Aston Martin DB3S, fitted with a supercharger, sixth. By 10am the Jaguar and the Ferrari were on the same lap. Then Blanc's old Talbot pulled across Rolt's path as he swept down to Arnage, the Jaguar careened into the sand and crumpled a front wing. The furious Rolt drove to his pit for a swift check-up of the damage; the car was pronounced O.K., but meantime Gonzalez had regained the Ferrari's full lap lead.

The pursuit continued. With the circuit occupied by numerous smaller cars, each concealed in clouds of spray, who but the respective drivers of the duelling Jaguar and Ferrari know how close, and how often, they came to disaster in such weather conditions? When the rain ceased again, both cars put on speed, and at around noon the Jaguar pit signalled 'flat out' to Hamilton, who had taken over from Rolt, and began carving off several seconds per lap, while the 4.9-Ferrari began to sound rough. Excitement mounted.

A swift pit-stop at 1.30 with Rolt taking over the Jaguar again, and the final battle began; a battle so tense that the unlucky departure of the last Aston Martin, Parnell's car with a blown gasket, was scarcely noticed—save by the David Brown pit! Despite further rain squalls, Rolt was carving off ten seconds per lap on the Ferrari. The rain worsened into a savage thunderstorm, forcing all to slow until it abated, then Trintignant, with a ten-minute lead, pulled in for the Ferrari's final stop and Gonzalez, who had neither eaten nor slept at all since the race began, leapt into the cockpit. He pressed the starter button—and nothing happened.

The tensed Ferrari pit crew exploded into frenzied action, a mechanic whipped the bonnet off, Gonzalez climbed out, another mechanic jumped down, and officials and cameramen seethed round the halted Italian car. Against Le Mans rules, a third mechanic also worked on the Ferrari, but Jaguar chief 'Bill' Lyons forbore to protest. Seconds passed, growing into minutes, and excitement swept the Jaguar pits. Then Rolt burst into view in a welter of spray and made for his pit, shouting for a vizor.

'Go on! Go on!' they shouted, and he accelerated viciously, only then realizing that the crowd massed at the Ferrari pit concealed the leading car! Blue-clad mechanics worked desperately on the Ferrari's ignition. Seven-and-a-half minutes passed, then the engine suddenly burst into life, Gonzalez jumped in, and was away, his car sounding ragged until he opened right out, now less than half a lap ahead of the Jaguar.

One hour to go, and still it rained; one minute, fifty-five seconds between Ferrari and Jaguar, and Gonzalez slightly widening the gap. Then Rolt, desperately in need of a vizor to replace his goggles, electrified everyone by rushing to his pit again, whereupon Duncan Hamilton, ready with helmet and vizor donned, leaped into his place instead, thereby saving valuable seconds, and shot back into the race.

That halt cost thirty-five seconds, plus the slowing and accelerating, and the gap was now over three minutes, with half an hour to go. Lapping at 112mph in pelting rain, Hamilton whittled it down lap by lap; 2.54, 2.35, 2.18, 2.2, 1.43, 1.26 . . . while 200,000 spectators stood, soaked but enthralled.

Suddenly the Ferrari pit awoke to the menace, speeding up the weary Gonzalez who, with the rain easing, now kept the gap constant between Italian and British cars. 4pm, the chequered flat at last; Gonzalez first on 4.9 litres for Ferrari, Hamilton second on 3.5 litres for Jaguar, with 1 minute 30 seconds and 2.54 miles between them after twenty-four hours of magnificent motor racing.

Third to finish was the American 5.4-litre Cunningham of Bill Spear and Sherwood Johnston; fourth the 'Belgian' Jaguar of Laurent/Swaters, fifth the Cunningham/Benett Cunningham, and sixth—joy for France!—the Guelfi/Pollet 2.5 Gordini. Only eighteen of the fifty-seven starters finished, the retirements including every Talbot, every Aston Martin, the Lagonda, a Cunningham-modified Ferrari, three Gordinis, and every Ferrari save one—the winning car.

That uncomfortable but enthralling Le Mans put Ferrari well into the Championship lead, with twenty-two points to Lancia's fourteen, and Jaguar's nine. With three rounds ahead, and Jaguars frankly not interested, only Lancia could now displace the 'Cavallino rampante' from a second Sports Car Championship victory.

'IT'S AN ILL WIND . . .'

'It is in no way our wish to run down this great British race . . . but all the same one cannot compare it to other events which also count for the World Championship of sports-cars. . . .' L'ANNUAIRE AUTOMOBILE, 1954–1955

Ferrari's Championship chances were strengthened still further when the A.D.A.C. announced the cancellation of the Nurburgring 1000-kms. race, due to be held on August 29th. The principal reason for this was the Mercedes-Benz decision not to run their new 300SLR sports car team originally entered. The German public are extremely partisan concerning motor racing, and unless there is a good entry of German-built cars having a good chance of success, then gate receipts show a marked fall. Without the magic name 'Mercedes' the organizers feared a loss such as they had sustained in 1953, and called the race off.

This annoyed Lancia considerably, since they saw in the German race a chance to close up on Ferrari in the Championship. Ascari/Villoresi, Taruffi/Manzon and Castellotti/Mieres were entered as drivers, and team cars were actually at the *Ring*, putting in intensive training, when the cancellation was announced.

But it is an ill wind that blows nobody any good, and in this instance the beneficiaries were the Ulster A.C., organizers of the Dundrod T.T. They received a magnificent entry, quite the best for the T.T. since the great old days of the Ards circuit. Ferrari entered, Lancia entered, Maserati and Osca entered, so did D.B. from France, while for Britain practically every competition-minded make was listed—Jaguar, Aston Martin, H.W.M., Frazer-Nash, Connaught, Cooper, Lotus, Kieft, Triumph. . . .

'Half of them won't turn up, old boy,' was the general consensus of opinion, based on past T.T. experience. But they did, every one of them!

'It'll pour like hell,' was the next gloomy prediction, and indeed it did—but only during practice. True, it rained on race day, September 11th, too, but those afternoon showers, heavy though one or two were, were mild by Dundrod standards.

There was but one fly in the ointment—the traditional handicap system by which the outright T.T. was determined. This was complex to competitors and baffling to the public, who after beholding maestros like Fangio and Ascari flash past, were told over the P.A. system that some diminutive 750cc flat-twin machine was 'leading the race'. The handicap was based on engine capacity, cars being granted a certain number of credit laps and a set average speed. In 1954 no less than twenty-eight capacity groups from under 750cc to over 6283cc were worked out, each with their own lap allowances and set averages.

Fortunately there was also a straightforward classification on distance covered for Championship contenders, and also class contests on distance, so that most foreign team managers (apart from D.B., the Index of Performance specialists) gazed perplexedly and mistrustfully at the handicap sheets, threw up their hands, and probably threw the sheets away, relying on the speed of their cars to clear the matter up as the race progressed. To the Italians the race is always to the swift, the fastest car wins the race, and no amount of paper work can make a smaller, slower car do so.

Apart from the miserable rain, practice was marred by the crash involving Froilan Gonzalez and his Ferrari. Dundrod's banks and bends caught the Le Mans winner out after a lap and a half, the Ferrari sliding badly at the Tornagrough S-bend under hard braking, and smacking the bank twice. Poor old 'Gonzo' was thrown out, sustaining a badly wrenched shoulder and, more serious, a spinal injury which was to strengthen his decision to retire from serious racing the following year.

News of his crash was followed by a wire from Italy for Umberto Maglioli, informing him that his mother had died, so that he left for home at once. Only two works Ferraris—both 750s four-cylinder 3-litre 'Monza' models rather than the unwieldy 4.9s—had been entered, and with two drivers gone the Italian team had no option but to pair Mike Hawthorn and Maurice Trintignant in the remaining car. A similar 750s, privately entered and painted green, was driven by the Dubliner Joe Kelly and Desmond Titterington, an Ulsterman who was consistently brilliant at Dundrod.

Driving the Lancias were Ascari/Villoresi and Fangio/Castellotti in the latest 3.8-litre cars, Taruffi/Piodi and Manzon/Valenzano in 3.3-litre models. Neither Fangio (who drove the 16-cylinder B.R.M. at Dundrod in 1952 and had a bad crash at Monza the following day) nor Ascari, whose first race it was at Dundrod, greatly liked the narrow, bank-bound 7.4-mile course, especially as the many blind bends all too often concealed smaller, slower cars such as TR2S or DB-Panhards. Even so, Ascari soon sent Walker's 1953 lap record tottering from 5mins. 1sec. to 4mins. 58secs., then reduced it further to 4mins. 54secs., while Titterington staggered everyone with a lap in 4mins. 55secs.

Jaguars aimed to exploit the handicap by reducing engine size on two of the D-types to 2482cc, using a shorter stroke; Moss/Walker and Whitehead/Wharton driving these, while Rolt/Hamilton took a normal 3442cc car. Aston Martins had three 3-litre DB3S, two of them having important engine modifications.

In all, the starters totalled fifty-one, the full distance for the largest cars in the race, excluding credit laps, being ninety laps or about 665 miles.

Right from the fall of the flag and the swift patter of feet across the road in the Le Mans start, Lancia, Ferrari and Jaguar were at each others' throats. Large, long-legged Tony Rolt fairly flew into his Jaguar and tore off, hounded by Ascari's Lancia, Hawthorn's Ferrari, the Belgian Swaters' independent XK120C, Abecassis's H.W.M.-Jaguar, Collins's Aston, Fangio's Lancia, et seq.

Hawthorn was up to second after the first wild round, fleeing before Rolt, Fangio, Collins and the rest, but by lap two the determined Mike had thrust past Ascari to lead. Fangio took Rolt, soon to be followed by Taruffi, so that by lap four Lancias were 2-3-4 behind the flying Hawthorn, who officially broke Walker's record on that round at 91.12mph. Ascari replied with 91.43mph though the Lancias obviously lacked the stability of the Ferrari when under cornering, and were harder to hold.

Fangio hit a bank at Wheelers' but sped on, while the lap record fell again, first to Hawthorn and Ascari jointly at 91.74 mph, and then at 92.38mph to Hawthorn, whose beautiful 750S 'four' seemed ideal for the course. Alas, Joe Kelly broke the gearbox in his own Ferrari before Titterington could show what he could do; and disaster next befell Fangio, whose Lancia wilted under pressure of the chase and vanished after fifteen laps with dire engine maladies betrayed by a long oil trail on the road and clouds of smoke.

That put Peter Collins up a place, but a round later a universal joint on his Aston Martin broke. It was finis, too, for the Sgorbati/ Macklin 2-litre Osca with ignition trouble, while Colin Chapman in his Lotus—two names destined for great fame—'hit a ditch' as a change from a bank and ended up in a field.

Ferrari pit-work was far superior to that of Lancia, and when Trintignant took over from Hawthorn, he found, a lap later, that their 32-second lead had grown to a comfortable 2mins. 25secs., a welcome gratuity from the opposition. Fangio took over Piodi's place in Taruffi's 3.3-Lancia, while Ascari's 3.8, trying to make up on the nimbler Ferrari, clocked 143.8mph through the measured kilometre despite blustering showers, but then spun at

Leathemstown and lost two minutes at the pits. Clearly Lancia, starting four to one against Ferrari, were badly rattled.

Jaguars were scarcely in the hunt at Dundrod, the Rolt/ Hamilton 3.5 losing its oil pressure and letting Moss in the 2.5 up into fourth place, well behind the Ferrari and the two Lancias' of Ascari/Villoresi and Taruffi/Fangio. Spurred by the Ferrari's facile lead, Ascari now forced his Lancia through the kilo. at 144.6mph, fastest of the day. A few laps later, however, a universal joint broke, and Alberto, the World Champion, had a narrow escape when the propeller shaft flailed up through the metal tunnel, an inch or so from his left thigh.

Next the Parnell/Salvadori Aston crashed into the bridge at Leathemstown, 'Salvo' limping it in to retire with damaged suspension. The Maseratis of Belucci and Perdisa also retired, and the next victim was Stirling Moss, his Jaguar's oil pressure going the way of Duncan Hamilton's. As in 1953, he coasted down from Quarry Corner to the finish, there to wait beneath an umbrella until the T.T. winner came through.

That winner was not the flying Hawthorn/Trintignant Ferrari. Over-generous handicapping of the smallest class, which were given twenty-one laps (155 miles) start over the 3-litre cars, made it impossible even for the Ferrari to catch the little French DB-Panhards on T.T. classification. When the handicap-leader René Bonnet's car crashed as a result of brake failure, the second team DB, neatly and unspectacularly driven by Laureau and Armagnac, moved up to win the T.T. at 68.75mph.

Hawthorn/Trintignant averaged 86.08mph—nearly 18mph faster—to take second place, although first on distance, first in class, and popular 'moral victors' after defeating the strong Lancia opposition. The Turin marque came in fourth and sixth on handicap, and won the over-3-litre class. On World Sports Car Championship classification Taruffi/Fangio were runners-up to the Ferrari, third were Manzon/Vallenzano/Castellotti (Lancia), fourth Abecassis/Mayers (H.W.M.), fifth Musso/ Mantovani (2-litre Maserati) and sixth Whitehead/Wharton (2.5-Jaguar).

So now Ferrari had thirty points, Lancia twenty, Jaguar ten, Maserati seven, Cunningham and Aston Martin four. In fact,

Ferrari had the Championship safely in their pocket, for with but one more qualifying race, outright victory could only raise Lancia's score to twenty-eight. The Turin concern's gallant effort had failed, despite their considerable expenditure on the *Competizione* models. Better cars and the 'know how' acquired by Ferrari in years of racing had defeated them.

It was not surprising that Lancia, with a new Formula 1 G.P. car under development, were not amongst the starters for the final Championship-round in Mexico. Their cars were 'not ready.'

THE LAST CARRERA

'Boy, I really enjoyed that race!' Phil Hill; MOTOR RACING, April 1959

Lancia, Mercedes, Ferrari, Maserati and Talbot between them could have made a magnificent struggle of the fifth *Carrera Panamericana*, Mexico. The withdrawal of Lancia and Mercedes, and the inability of Talbot and Maserati to fulfil early hopes of competing, made the race largely a Ferrari *fiesta*, but a memorable one withal.

No official works Ferraris were entered, but two of the big, brutal 345bhp 4.9s which beat Jaguar at Le Mans had swiftly been sold for dollars in the U.S.A., and appeared under private sponsorship, works driver Umberto Maglioli driving Erwin Goldschmidt's entry, and Jack McAfee of California being entered by John Edgar. Seven other private Ferraris competed, comprising three 4.5s (Chinetti, Cornacchia and Phil Hill), two of the new 3-litre 'fours' (Bracco and de Portago), an older 3-litre (Bonomi) and a 2-litre Mondial for Rubirosa.

The opposition was of varying potency, but considerable interest. There was a Spanish Pegaso, a rare, highly expensive and technically advanced 3.2-litre supercharged v8, entered by the President of the Dominican Republic, and driven by the Pegaso chief tester, Joaquin Palacio, a racing veteran. There were two of the new 130bhp, 2.6-litre Austin Healey 100s models— the first (and last) British entries in the 'Pan-Am', with Lance Macklin/Donald Healey and Carroll Shelby driving them. There were two Kurtis-Kraft, one Lincoln-engined, the other with a supercharged Nash unit; a Chevrolet Corvette for U.S. driver Bill von Esser, a Packard Special for the Mexican-domiciled Frenchman, Jean Trevoux and, for the second year, that astonishing 'Hot Rod' Special of Akton Miller. This homely vehicle with its Oldsmobile engine, Ford chassis, Nash gearbox and Model T Ford bodywork, carrying a deep screen in unknowing anticipation of the 1960 Appendix-C requirements, was dubbed the *Ensalade*—the salad—by the Mexicans, and became one of the most talked-of cars in the five-day race.

Unmoved by the urgent entreaties of Stirling Moss, the Jaguar Company declined to send any works cars to Mexico, despite the Moss/England 'recce' of the previous year. But Francisco Ibarra entered an XK120C, supported by one Oscar Fano Bush in an XK120. In all there were 149 starters, contesting numerous sports and touring car classes.

Six a.m. was damp and surprisingly chilly at Tuxtla Gutierrez on November 19th, when car No. 1, Jack McAfee's big 4.9-Ferrari, lined up for the start. '*Cinco, quatro, tres, dos, uno*'—down went the flag, the big red 12-cylinder car gathered itself, and rocketed away. Behind it, at one-minute intervals, 148 cars were despatched singly, their destination Ciudad Juarez on the Rio Grande, eight stages, five days and 1,908 miles away.

But barely one hundred miles north of Tuxtla, McAfee's Ferrari was out of the race, sadly bent and broken after skidding over an embankment near Rio Hondo at about 120mph and somersaulting. McAfee escaped serious injury, but his co-driver, Ford Robinson, died instantly from a broken neck.

Four other Ferraris failed to complete the first 329.4-mile stage to Oaxaca. The Marquis de Portago had started one minute after McAfee, closed on him over the twisting mountain roads, outside Tuxtla, then duelled fiercely at around 150mph on the twenty-five-mile straight over the Tehuantepec Isthmus. The Spaniard's black 3-litre held the 4.9 until an oil pipe broke, a piston seized, and the car's race was run. The Ferraris of Bonomi Bracco and Rubirosa were all disqualified for finishing the stage outside the time limit after encountering trouble; the same fate, alas, forced out Macklin's Austin Healey, delayed with condenser trouble.

With the wisdom of long experience, Maglioli did not over-extend his 4.9-Ferrari so early in the race. Even had he done so, he would have had to work hard to match the pace of Phil Hill in his smaller, older, but very nimble 4.5-Ferrari—on the mountain roads. The slim twenty-seven-year-old from Santa Monica and his fellow Californian co-driver Richie Ginther travelled at electrifying speed in their blue-and-white car, formerly the actual 4.1-works Ferrari driven to victory by Ascari and Farina in the 1953 Nurburgring 1000-kms. race, 'stroked' out to $4\frac{1}{2}$ litres and fitted with a distinctive finned tail, *à la* D-type Jaguar.

Phil Hill won stage one from Maglioli, Cornacchia and Ak Miller, was second to Maglioli in stage two, won stage three from Maglioli and Palacio's Pegaso, was second to Maglioli in stages four, five, six and seven, and won the final, full-throttle slam across the desert to the finish at Juarez 137.6mph, crossing the line at an intimidating 174mph, to finish second overall in the race. This was a remarkable performance by an amateur entry, and not surprisingly it focused the attention of Signor Ferrari himself on the Californian's talents.

But where the mountains give way to the incredibly fast highways across the flat Mexican plains, nothing could approach the sheer velocity of the 4.9-Ferrari in Maglioli's capable hands. He won stage four at over 109mph, stage five at over 115mph, stage six at over 111mph, and stage seven at a staggering 120mph. On aggregate performance he won the fifth Pan-American Road Race at the record average of 107.93mph, half an hour quicker than Fangio's Lancia in 1953.

Of the rest of the unlimited sports car class, Cornacchia's Ferrari coupé took third, Chinetti's was fourth, the incredible Hot Rod of Akton Miller fifth—a wonderful feat indeed—and Trevoux's much-modified Packard sixth. The Pegaso went well and very fast, and lay fourth in the unlimited class until it rounded a bend during stage four and found Karl Bechem's $1\frac{1}{2}$-litre Borgward stuck on the corner after misjudging in heavy mist. The Pegaso struck it, bounced off, careered off course, caught fire, and was reduced to virtual scrap.

Shelby's Austin Healey crashed into a huge boulder and was written off, while its driver broke both his arms. The two Kurtis-Kraft, the Corvette and the two Jaguars all retired, and the final placings looked very rosy for Maranello, being one, Ferrari (Maglioli), two, Ferrari (Hill), three, 1.5-Porsche (Herrmann), four, 1.5-Porsche (J. Juhan), five, Ferrari (Cornacchia), and six, Ferrari (Chinetti).

Thus Ferrari confirmed their status as the Championship marque in no mean manner, Maglioli enhanced his reputation as one of Italy's finest sports car pilots, and Phil Hill put his feet firmly on the ladder to international fame. Yet the 1954 *Carrera* was a race tinged with bitter tragedy, marred, as a hazardous 1,900-mile road-race contested by drivers and cars of widely varying capabilities, and won at over 107mph, must be, by too many accidents, too many of them fatal.

Of the 149 starters, eighty-five finished, over thirty were involved in crashes and eight people were killed and seven injured just prior to and during the race. That part of the Mexican press which viewed the race unfavourably 'made hay' of the accidents, and with encouragement from political factions, worked up an emotional furore over 'the race to death'.

Eventually a Government ban was imposed on this great but ill-starred race, and although several efforts have since been made to revive it, Mexico's unique road race has never been held since 1954.

Interviewed during the winter of 1954, Enzo Ferrari expressed his pleasure at winning the Sports Car Championship for the second successive year. 'But', he said, 'a third success will not be easy for us to achieve, for bigger commercial factions than mine are bidding for this—and other—honours in motor racing'.

By 'bigger commercial factions', the Commendatore meant Mercedes-Benz of Germany, whose 3-litre 300SLR sports/racing model—the car entered for, then withdrawn from, several 1954 events—had not only been timed at over 180mph, but had also disported its sleek shape at Monza—practically in Ferrari's own backyard—where, without undue effort, it lapped steadily at speeds half a second faster than Gonzalez' record lap, made in the 1954 Italian G.P. in a Formula 1 Ferrari.

1955 promised to be very interesting indeed.

CHAMPIONSHIP SCORE-SHEET 1954

Make of Car	Buenos Aires 1000-km., Argentina	Sebring 12-hour, U.S.A.	Mille Miglia Italy	Le Mans 24-hour, France	Tourist Trophy, Gt. Britain	Carrera Panamericana, Mexico	Total Score	Best Four Performances
Ferrari	8 (1st)	—	6 (2nd)	8 (1st)	8 (1st)	8 (1st)	38	32
Lancia	—	6 (2nd)	8 (1st)	—	6 (2nd)	—	20	20
Jaguar	3 (4th)	—	—	6 (2nd)	1 (6th)	—	10	10
Osca..	—	8 (1st)	—	—	—	—	8	8
Maserati	1 (6th)	—	4 (3rd)	—	2 (5th)	—	7	7
Porsche	—	—	1 (6th)	—	—	4 (3rd)	5	5
Aston Martin ..	4 (3rd)	—	—	—	—	—	4	4
Cunningham ..	—	—	—	4 (3rd)	—	—	4	4
Austin Healey ..	—	4 (3rd)	—	—	—	—	4	4
H.W.M.-Jaguar ..	—	—	—	—	3 (4th)	—	3	3
Gordini	—	—	—	1 (6th)	—	—	1	1
Kieft..	—	1 (6th)	—	—	—	—	1	1

SCORING: First 8 points; second 6pts.; third 4pts.; fourth 3pts.; fifth 2pts.; sixth 1pt.

C

CHAPTER 3

ENTER THE SILVER ARROWS

GERMANY'S onslaught on Formula 1 fields with the highly advanced 2½-litre, eight-cylinder, fuel-injection W196 Mercedes-Benz, made the year 1954 a memorable one in Grand Prix racing. For 1955, it became known that, in addition to an extensive Formula 1 season, the world-famous Stuttgart marque were to take part in major sports car races, using the 3-litre 300SLR which was largely based on the G.P. design, and which had already appeared in prototype form.

As their primary target was the Coupe des Constructeurs for the World Sports Car Championship, it was anticipated that Mercedes would 'kick off' with Round one, the Buenos Aires 1000-kms. race in Argentina on January 23rd. But they didn't, being fully occupied with their Formula 1 team for the two Grands Prix included in the *Temporada*. Significantly, however, the Germans brought three 3-litre 300SLR engines with them, which were installed in the G.P. cars for the Free Formula G.P. of Buenos Aires, thus gaining some invaluable experience of running the engines under racing conditions, and incidentally scoring first, second and fourth places with the W196–300SLR 'compounds'.

LOCAL BOYS MAKE GOOD

'*Menacing heat and the mixed quality of the entry contributed to keeping the stands half empty.*' Dr Vicente Alvarez; AUTOSPORT, February 11th, 1955

Scuderia Lancia had now entirely abandoned sports car racing to concentrate on Formula 1, and as neither Jaguar nor Aston Martin were prepared to make the long trip to South America, Ferrari, the reigning Champion, was left as principal contender

66

in the 1000-kms. race, with Gordini the only other European representative.

A revised and somewhat faster permutation of the Autodrome-cum-Motorway theme was used this time. The lap length was 10.56 miles, and the duration fifty-eight laps, which, in the soggy heat of race day, was far too long to sustain spectator-interest, even though the embodiment of the local highway into the course meant a free show for all.

It was a dull race. Two official Ferraris took part, one a new 3.7-litre six-cylinder model for Trintignant and the Argentinian Gonzalez, who decided that his 'retirement' from racing excluded home events; the other a 3-litre 750s for Maglioli and another Argentine, Clemar Bucci. Both cars, amazingly, were disqualified during the race, the 3.7 because 'Gonzo' took a short cut off the circuit to his pit when the fuel pump gave trouble, and the 3-litre when Bucci's engine died, and he accepted help from several over-enthusiastic countrymen in restarting.

But there are generally a few private Ferraris around in any major race, and in this case one of the ex-works Le Mans 4.9s, very competently handled by 'local boys' Saenz Valiente and Jose Ibanez, went on to win the race on behalf of the 'prancing horse', with the Najurieta/Rivero 4.5 following home. The sole excitement, after Gonzalez' lamented departure, came when Ibanez smote a large dog when motoring smartly down the Avenue General Paz at about 140mph, damaging the radiator and nose of the Ferrari and temporarily losing it the lead while some rather gruesome repair work was effected. The dog, it seems, was past repair.

The final order after over six-and-a-half hours of driving was 4.9 Ferrari, 4.5 Ferrari, 2.0 Maserati (Grandio/Faraone), 1.5 Porsche (F. Juhan), 3.0 Gordini (Schell/Bayol) and 2.5 Ferrari (J. and O. Cameno), so that, once again, Ferrari headed the Championship after the opening round, score: Ferrari eight, Maserati four, Porsche three, Gordini two.

PROTESTS FLY IN FLORIDA

'If this year's Sebring International 12-hour Grand Prix of

*Endurance turned into a royal racing rhubarb, the emphasis should,
in fairness, be placed on the adjective "royal".* John Bentley; THE
AUTOCAR, April 1st, 1955

Sebring, 1955, was notable for several things; various circuit
improvements, a new bridge over the track near the start, a new
timing box, new fencing. . . . For the record entry of one hundred
and eight cars, of which twenty-nine had to go on reserve. . . .
For Ferrari actually sending a works entry, prize money or no
prize money. . . . For Mercedes-Benz *not* running, thereby missing a second Championship round. . . . For Officine Maserati's
first serious bid in the Championship class with a formidable
new 3-litre 'six'. . . . For u.s. contender Briggs Cunningham's
entry of a lone disc-braked Jaguar, driven by 'Jag's' new No. 1
driver, Mike Hawthorn and talented Phil Walters. . . . For the
Jaguar's narrow victory over the best of many Ferraris competing.
. . . And for the monumental mess-up in official lap scoring, which
soured the victors' victory and sent protests and counter-protests
flying. . . .

As Mike Hawthorn said, it was 'quite a motor race'! Driving
the Ferrari, a 3-litre 'four' entered by Texas oil magnate Allen
Guiberson, were those two fine American pilots, Phil Hill and
Carroll Shelby. Five other Jaguars and over a dozen Ferraris
were competing, the works entry being a 3-litre for Taruffi and
Schell. Briggs Cunningham also fielded a beautifully compact
and shapely new model, the C6R, built around a 3-litre four-
cylinder Mayer-Drake engine—the famous Indianapolis track
racing unit, while Austin Healey were still pitting moderately-
priced, near-production 100S models against the sports-racers,
but reducing the disadvantage by having Stirling Moss and Lance
Macklin at the wheel.

Eighty cars in a long, long line in front of Sebring's rather
sketchy pits, eighty drivers lined up opposite, tensed and silent
as 10am neared and the starter's flag was raised, made an impressive sight on March 13th, 1955. The flag swept down, there
was the rush of feet, the whirr of starters and the roar of engines.
'Sprinter' Moss was the first to move off in his Austin Healey,
but the larger displacement cars at the forward end naturally

had the advantage on getaway. Ensley's Kurtis-Cadillac was first over the line, but it was green-helmeted, vizored Mike Hawthorn, 'the lanky tow-headed Englishman', who swiftly 'barrelled into the lead' (*vide* the American press) chased by seventy-nine hard-accelerating cars, tight-massed on Sebring's broad tarmac.

Just how many phenomenal avoidances, slight brushes, and heartier contacts there were during the first mile or so, nobody knows, but drivers and organizers must have sighed with relief as the field gradually spread out. Hawthorn and his co-driver Phil Walters consolidated a lead which they held for ten out of the twelve hours, and only Taruffi/Schell in the works Ferrari passed the disc-braked Jaguar, leading for two brief spells before falling back again.

Behind, the field was decimated as cars crashed, became bogged in sandbanks, or had their insides chewed up by Sebring's relentless demands on transmissions, brakes and engines. Bob Said's 3-litre Ferrari lasted a lap, unavoidably smashing into an ambulance standing *on the circuit* tending to Redélé who had overturned his Renault. Jack McAfee's Ferrari caught fire on the fourth lap, race leader Hawthorn being somewhat surprised to encounter a large fire engine racing him on the circuit, bells clanging gaily as it sped to the blaze. As the Ferrari was causing much obstruction, McAfee valiantly drove it, with tail and rear tyres well alight, down an escape road.

'Gentleman' Jim Kimberly's 4.9-Ferrari broke its differential; the new C6R Cunningham's flywheel flew to pieces, the Portago/Maglioli Ferrari jammed its gearbox; Rubirosa's Ferrari spun on spilt sand at a corner and went backwards into straw bales which unfortunately concealed a very hard fire hydrant; Cesare Perdisa, lying third in the works 3-litre Maserati, lost third gear, vital at Sebring; he signalled his loss to the pit, who unsympathetically replied 'Use the other three'. When he finished, he had but two left.

Between 8 and 9pm, when darkness had fallen and cars slammed past in a glare of headlights, the leading Jaguar came through trailing a smoke screen and running on five cylinders. To a chorus of 'Oh-oh, this is it', Phil Walters brought the car in for a plug change, although the real trouble was a warped cylinder

head. Several stops ensued for water, oil and fresh plugs, while
Carroll Shelby, one arm still in plaster after his Pan-American
accident the previous November, flogged the second-place Ferrari
round, to cancel out the Jaguar's two-lap advantage and snatch a
narrow lead.

Then Walters speeded up despite his troubles, caught the
Ferrari, and led it over the finishing line by a margin of 25.4secs.
Uncertainty marred the finish. P.A. announcements had given
confusing and contradictory reports, putting the Jaguar two laps
ahead of the Ferrari and then *vice versa*, finally stating that the
Jaguar had won by ten seconds. The Cunningham pit sent
Walters off for an extra lap 'just in case', whereupon he ran out
of fuel, while Nello Ugolini from Scuderia Ferrari, who was
also controlling the Hill/Shelby pit, declared that by his lap-
scoring the Ferrari had won.

Luigi Chinetti, Ferrari's New York representative, therefore
entered a protest against the Jaguar victory on behalf of Allen
Guiberson, the Ferrari entrant, who declared 'We won it. Our
pit slowed down the car during the last five laps after our timer
told us we were ahead by three minutes fourteen seconds'. Then
Briggs Cunningham counter-protested that his Osca 1500, driven
by Lloyd/Huntoon, had won the Index of Performance class
instead of the Hill/Shelby Ferrari.

In the end the scoresheets of the Cunningham and Ferrari
pits, together with the official race sheets, were taken to New
York for examination at a special meeting of the A.A.A., held
eight days later. The Jaguar victory was then officially confirmed,
with the Ferrari 25.4secs. behind in second place, but still winner
of the Index of Performance class from the Osca and the Jaguar.
It was established that a scoring error had apparently crept into
the Ferrari's pit chart during the seventh hour and this, combined with the misleading P.A. broadcasts, had lulled the Guiberson pit into a false sense of security. Thus a good race spoilt, and
an irritating aftermath, ended in handshakes all round.

Apart from this regrettable *brouhaha*, an interesting point in
the Sebring placings was the performance of the two new 3-litre
Maseratis, which finished strongly in third and fourth places,
driven by Bill Spear/Sherwood Johnston and Valenzano/

Perdisa respectively. Fifth was the Taruffi/Schell Ferrari, and sixth the remarkable Moss/Macklin Austin Healey 100s, which outpaced many faster cars and headed an Austin Healey 1-2-3 success in the series production class.

The Championship score now read Ferrari fourteen points, Maserati and Jaguar eight, Porsche three, Gordini two, Austin Healey one, with the Mille Miglia next ahead, as a probable source of further points for Ferrari and possibly Maserati, if not for the others.

A KISS FROM NEUBAUER

'Winning a race is 90 or 95 per cent preparation. Luck is only 5 per cent.' Alfred Neubauer, Mercedes-Benz team manager

Stirling Moss's Sebring drive with Lance Macklin in the Austin Healey was but an interlude to several weeks of arduous training in Italy for the Mille Miglia at the end of April. At the beginning of the year the British driver had signed a contract to drive for Mercedes-Benz in all major Grands Prix, and also in four sports car races. These included the Mille Miglia, to his regret, for the prospect did not enthral Moss at all. He had already driven in it three times, each time without success, concluding that, not only was Italy's classic 1000-mile race the most dangerous in the calendar, but also that no British driver had a chance of success owing to the impossibility of learning the 992-mile course properly, unless he lived in the country.

However, Mercedes required him to drive in the 1955 race, so that was that. He could only practise hard and memorize the route as much as possible, and to assist him he enlisted the aid of that well-known journalist, Denis Jenkinson, who rode with him as passenger and guide. Together they covered five complete laps of the entire Brescia–Rome–Brescia course, three of them in Moss's private 220 Mercedes saloon, one in a 300SL, and one in a 300SLR, 'Jenks' making copious notes on the nature of the course as they motored.

His notes were finalized, checked and rechecked, typed out, and mounted on a roller map device in the cockpit, so that as

Moss drove, his passenger unrolled the eighteen-foot-long 'route card', conveying his information to the driver by various pre-arranged hand signs. Moss's five laps of practice were modest; of his team mates, Karl Kling (who so nearly won for Mercedes in 1952) did fifteen; Juan Manuel Fangio (who so nearly won for Alfa Romeo in 1953) did eight, and Hans Hermann did six. Such extensive practising was unprecedented, but merely in the tradition of Mercedes-Benz, who only did things one way—thoroughly.

Ferrari turned out in force to defend the home colours, fielding five cars in all. These comprised a 4.4-litre 'six' for the 'firebrand' Castellotti, on loan from Lancia, and four 3.7 'sixes' for the astute Piero Taruffi, Paolo Marzotto, Maglioli and Sighinolfi. There were sundry private Ferraris as well, a single 3-litre Maserati for Perdisa, and a lone DB3S Aston Martin for Peter Collins.

In the ballot for starting positions, Ferrari were luckier than Mercedes in drawing late numbers, it being easier to pursue and to know one's opponent's position than to set the pace from an invisible pursuit. Moss started seventh from last, followed by Castellotti, Sighinolfi, Marzotto, Gordoni (3-litre Gordini), Perdisa (Maserati) and 'the silver fox' Taruffi last of all.

Castellotti set a tremendous opening pace with the 4.4-Ferrari averaging Brescia to Ravenna—188 miles—at 119mph, and passing Moss's Mercedes. But the Italian car quickly broke up under the strain, and as Marzotto had tyre and suspension trouble, it was Taruffi who led the race at Pescara—by just fifteen seconds from Moss. Then a quick stop for fuel and a snack cost the Mercedes twenty-eight seconds only, whereas Taruffi's Ferrari was delayed for almost one and a half minutes. This gift of a minute from Ferrari, plus the virtuosity of Moss and the invaluable aid of 'navigator' Jenkinson, took the Mercedes into first place by 1min. 49secs. at Rome, despite a spectacular charge through a barrier of straw bales just outside Pescara.

To lead through Rome was asking for trouble, but Moss, though superstitious, wasn't hanging back to give Taruffi the privilege, and defied the legend. Just outside Rome he passed Kling's wrecked Mercedes, from which the driver escaped with three broken ribs. Maglioli's Ferrari was slowing with trouble and then poor Taruffi's 3.7-Ferrari expired through oil pump failure near Viterbo. Other retirements included the Aston Martin of Collins with engine trouble, and Perdisa's 3-litre Maserati.

The inspired Moss led through Florence, his average so far a rousing 97.5mph, with Hermann and Fangio next up, all in Mercedes! But Fangio had to stop to repair an injection pipe, and then Hermann's engine suddenly expired on the Futa Pass— a stone had ripped through the fuel tank. Now two Ferraris and two Mercedes remained in the fight for first place. But it was Moss ahead at Bologna; Moss ahead at Modena; Moss ahead at Parma and Piacenza—an Englishman in a German car leading Italy's greatest road race!

He covered the final 85-mile stage, Cremona to Brescia via Mantua and Verona, at an average of 123mph, slamming across the finishing line at over 100mph to take the chequered flag. The Mercedes had started from Brescia at 7.22 on the morning of May 1st; it returned just before 5.30pm, having covered 992 miles of open Italian roads in 10 hours. 7mins. 48secs., at the staggering average of 97.9mph. The previous best by any Mille Miglia winner was Marzotto's 88.39mph two years before.

Fangio was the runner-up, thirty-two minutes behind; Maglioli's Ferrari was third, Giardini's very fast 2-litre Maserati fourth, the American John Fitch in a factory-entered Mercedes-Benz 300SL coupé fifth (and GT class winner) Sighinolfi's Ferrari was sixth, while the Austin Healey 100S of George Abecassis was the highest-placed British car, taking eleventh position over-all, and fifth in the unlimited class.

Stirling Moss, black of face, withstood a kiss from his delighted team manager Herr Neubauer, and far from tottering to bed utterly exhausted after almost 1000 miles of racing, drove to the Stuttgart works that same night, thanks to 'keep-awake' pills! It was a great victory for Mercedes, but a greater one for Moss, rating amongst the finest of his many fine achievements.

As for Italy, Germany's triumph left her somewhat dismayed. The last time a foreign car won the Brescia–Rome–Brescia classic was in 1931—and it was a Mercedes! Now the *Tedeschi* were back with a vengeance. But Ferrari's Championship lead remained substantial with eighteen points to Maserati's eleven, and Jaguar and Mercedes' eight, although with Le Mans coming up as round four and Mercedes going the way they did in Italy . . . who could say? And as early as January 1955, Mercedes had announced a three-car entry for the French classic. . . .

DISASTER

'*Motor racing is dangerous.*' Warning to spectators appearing on tickets issued at British speed events, also prominently displayed on notices by order of the Royal Automobile Club.

Le Mans, 1955, is a race which all would like to forget, but which, like Paris–Madrid 1903, stands out blackly in motor racing history.

Prospects were so bright beforehand. Full teams from Ferrari, Mercedes-Benz, Jaguar, Aston Martin and Maserati, two Gordinis, one Lagonda, one new C6R Cunningham, plus the best of International talent in the smaller capacity classes, all added up to the promise of a brilliant manifestation. Ferraris had their new 4.4-litre, 370bhp 'sixes' (with the American Phil Hill recruited as one of the drivers) and Mercedes their intimidating 3-litre 300SLRs, equipped for this race with novel flap-type air brakes on the tail, greatly minimizing the load on the drum brakes, and matching the retardation of Jaguar's disc-brakes.

Jaguar fielded a trio of D-types, sleek, purposeful and superbly ready, while Maserati had their new 3-litre cars, though deprived at the last moment of their No. 1 driver, Jean Behra, due to a practice accident in which he was struck by a D.B. when an innocent bystander.

The first two hours of the race on June 11th–12th fulfilled all pre-race promise, a veritable battle of the giants developing between Ferrari, Jaguar and Mercedes, after the fiery Castellotti had rocketed into the lead. He was caught by Hawthorn's Jaguar on the sixteenth lap, but Fangio—who, of all men, had muffed his Le Mans start by getting the gear lever up his trouser leg!—forced his Mercedes past Mike two rounds later. Then those two great protagonists fought it out at over 120mph average, lap after lap, until at the close of the second hour Hawthorn had raised the lap record to 122.39mph, nearly 5mph better than the Maglioli/Marzotto 1954 record of 117.53mph.

Half an hour later, when Hawthorn was completing his thirty-fourth lap, now several seconds ahead of Fangio, the magnificent awe-inspiring skill of the battling leaders became a topic subjugated by the appalling shock of the world's worst motor racing accident. So much has been said and written about the Le Mans catastrophe of 1955 that it is better to record the facts as they are known, as briefly as possible, and pass on.

Three cars were involved: Hawthorn's Jaguar, Lance Macklin's Austin Healey 100S, and Pierre Levegh's 300SLR Mercedes-Benz, which Hawthorn had just lapped. On lap thirty-four, by pre-arranged signal, the Jaguar driver pulled into his pit to refuel and hand over to his relief, Ivor Bueb. Coming up the straight towards the pit, he passed Macklin's Austin Healey on the left, then extended his right arm to indicate his intention of pulling over, and made for his pit.

Macklin braked momentarily and eased out to his left, and at the same instant, Levegh's Mercedes, coming past at about 150mph, moved slightly to the right and struck the Austin Healey's nearside front wheel. Instantly the Mercedes ricocheted on to the protective earth embankment on the left of the road, then bounced back again, rode up the tail of the Austin Healey, and launched itself over the top of the bank.

The Mercedes scythed through a small enclosure and finished up ablaze on top of the bank with such impact that the engine mass and the front suspension were torn out and projected forward into the main enclosure, packed with spectators gathered to watch pit activities. Red flames changed to intense, glaring white as the magnesium bodywork ignited, and there came two explosions, one when the fuel tank, almost empty of fuel but full, of course, of petrol vapour, blew up. Thick, oily smoke rose high in the blue sky.

It seemed incredible that one disintegrating car could wreak such havoc, but eighty-two people were killed that day and over a hundred injured. Pierre Levegh was killed instantly, while the

Austin Healey spun round and charged the pits. knocking down and injuring three people, though Macklin himself was unhurt.

Fangio was coming up behind Levegh, travelling about 5mph faster, when he saw the Frenchman raise his left arm as a signal; he braked and came through the mêlée unscathed. It has been said that Levegh saved Fangio's life but lost his own through that signal. Levegh knew that Fangio was behind, and was no doubt anxious not to impede his chase of the Jaguar. When the Frenchman raised his arm—no easy feat against the terrific air blast encountered at 150mph—did he mean to convey to Fangio that it was safe for him to pass? Or to indicate that he was about to pass Macklin? Or to warn him of trouble ahead?

Many witnesses confirmed that Levegh's car was occupying the 'centre lane', allowing room for the faster Fangio to come through, and that it moved to the right as it approached the Austin Healey, occupying the 'right hand lane.' Was this movement to the right made in anticipation of Fangio's passing, or was it, perhaps, a muscular reflex action on Levegh's right arm after signalling at 150mph with his left?

None of these questions could be answered with certainty, poor Levegh meeting violent death seconds later.

The immediate impulse was to stop the race, and when the full news of the catastrophe filtered through, the public wondered why this was not done. The great decision rested with Charles Faroux, Clerk of the Course, but that shrewd old doyen of motor racing resisted the impulse. Swiftly he foresaw that the movements of ambulances and medical aid would only be impeded by a sudden exodus of the 300,000 people gathered at Le Mans. Further, human nature being what it is, many would inevitably make straight for the scene of the disaster and add to the confusion and congestion. Better, he reasoned, to continue the race and keep the public mind absorbed in it; Faroux was doubtless also conscious of the tradition of carrying on, while even he cannot have known how appallingly large the death roll was until later, by which time he felt there was little to be gained in stopping the race.

Hawthorn's co-driver, Ivor Bueb, was a well-known Formula 3 and small sports car driver, and a new recruit to the Jaguar team;

it was his unenviable task to take over the Jaguar just after witnessing that horrifying accident, and strive to hold Fangio's Mercedes, now driven by Stirling Moss.

By midnight the Mercedes had gained a two-lap lead over Bueb and a shocked, dispirited Hawthorn. At 1.45am the two Mercedes of Fangio/Moss and Kling/Simon were flagged in and withdrawn from the race by a grim-faced Neubauer, on orders from Stuttgart. With them departed such interest in the race as remained.

The Hawthorn/Bueb Jaguar boomed on through pouring rain on Sunday to a sombre, hollow victory, averaging 107.07mph to the 105.09 of Gonzalez/Trintignant the previous year. Second came Peter Collins and the Belgian driver-journalist Paul Frère in an Aston Martin DB3S, third the Belgian-entered Jaguar of Claes/Swaters, and fourth, fifth and sixth three astonishing 1½-litre Porsches. All the Ferraris, the Maseratis, the Gordinis, the Lagonda and the Cunningham retired; two of the Jaguars did likewise, but Aston Martin's 'Le Mans luck' had broken at last with that gratifying second place.

With Mercedes forfeiting an obviously good chance of augmenting their Championship score, Ferrari's lead of eighteen points was now narrowed by Jaguar with sixteen; Maserati still had eleven, Mercedes eight and Porsche and Aston Martin joined in with six points each. But nobody cared about Championship points just then, being too chastened by so savage and brutal a demonstration of the fact that 'motor racing is dangerous'.

★ ★ ★

Inevitably blame was cast upon the drivers concerned. "Hawthorn cut too sharply across Macklin's path. . . . Macklin braked and swerved out unnecessarily. . . . Levegh moved too far to the right and misjudged his speed. . . ." The indictments flew hotly. Mercedes-Benz didn't help by rather too quickly issuing a statement containing several errors, while France's partisan press naturally tended to blame the British rather than the French driver.

By tragic irony, Levegh had sportingly been offered his place in the Mercedes team at Le Mans in token of their admiration for his efforts in 1952 with a 4½-litre Talbot when, driving alone, he led the race until after the twenty-second hour when sheer fatigue caused him to overtax his engine, thereby giving victory to Mercedes-Benz.

Yet it must be said that, of the three drivers involved, Levegh alone was handling a car he was not fully accustomed to. The 300SLR Mercedes could top 180mph, whereas his former mount, the Talbot, might have managed 145mph, while Levegh himself had not raced at all since Le Mans the previous year, when he finished eighth.

As was later confirmed at the official investigation by a Governmental Tribunal, blame for the accident could not be pinned on any one person; it was the result of freak circumstances which did, however, accentuate the extreme dangers of sports car racing with mixed fields and a wide speed differential, 180mph cars driven by Grand Prix masters sharing the course with small cars incapable of more than 100mph, handled in many cases by far more inexpert drivers. And at Le Mans up to 1955, such mixed fields had to race past the vital pit area on a road scarcely adequate for three cars abreast at a point where the fastest were exceeding 150mph, i.e. over 70 yards per second.

That the road was too narrow was conceded, first by the emergency rules imposed by the F.I.A. on future racing events concerning approach to the pits, and later by the A.C. de l'Ouest, when announcing plans for completely rebuilding the pit area. Stringent 'safety measures' became a dominant factor in motor race organization after Le Mans 1955, as was inevitable if the sport was to survive. Even then, its survival was touch and go.

GREEN VERSUS SILVER

'*People who thought about such things felt strongly on behalf of the organizers, the Ulster Automobile Club, that they had laid on a first-class race with a wonderful entry. Fate, perhaps assisted by the narrowness of the roads, had seen fit to remove all the glory.*' THE AUTOCAR, September 23rd, 1955

In reaction to Le Mans, many race cancellations ensued, including all French events, the German, Swiss and Spanish G.P.s, and the Nurburgring 1000-kms. race, which was to have been Round Five of the 1955 Championship. The organizers, the A.D.A.C., declared in a statement, '. . . *During the past few weeks the notion of responsibility to be assumed by the organizers has been extended in the public opinion to such an unreasonable degree that, while this crass and unconventional attitude is being maintained, the organizers will not possibly be in a position of carrying out great competitions . . .*'

Soon the tidal wave of reaction crossed the Atlantic to Mexico where, despite urgent petitions, President Adolf Ruis Cortinez banned all motor racing on Mexican roads, pending the issue of new International safety regulations. That set the final seal on the fate of the *Carrera Panamericana,* which had been listed, rather optimistically, in the Calendar for November.

Two qualifying events out. That meant only two left—the T.T. at Dundrod, and the Targa Florio in Sicily. Daimler-Benz took action, wiring an entry of three 300SLRs for the T.T. to the Ulster A.C. Ferrari, Maserati, Gordini, Porsche and Osca also entered, while Aston Martin and Jaguar, plus many smaller capacity British marques, were naturally represented. Far less naturally, Jaguar entered just one D-type for Mike Hawthorn to meet such mighty opposition—a decision hard to comprehend, since either it was worthwhile for a concern like Jaguar to support racing fully, i.e. with a full team, or not at all, rather than to field a single, unsupported car.

As the 1955 T.T. was the Golden Jubilee event, commemorating the fiftieth birthday of Britain's—and the world's—oldest motor race, the heavily oversubscribed entry list, containing all the 'big guns' of sports car racing, was worthy of it. Further, the organizers had at last scrapped the old, unsatisfactory handicap system, the Trophy now going to the fastest finisher in the eighty-four-lap, 623 mile race, while an Index of Performance category was introduced, carrying equal prize money (£500) for the winner.

None love a good motor race more than Ulstermen and the Irish, and an enormous crowd came out to Dundrod on Saturday, September 27th to watch the cream of British and Continental sports-racing cars in action. Nor were they disappointed.

When the forty-nine-car field was released and had unravelled itself a little around the 7.4 sinuous miles of Dundrod, it became clear that the Jaguar–Mercedes battle which had been cut short at Le Mans was to be resumed.

Moss and Hawthorn, two masters of Dundrod, shot out ahead, the silver Mercedes leading the green Jaguar and pulling away slightly each lap. But Mike, though handicapped on the interminable bends in roadholding and acceleration owing to the Jaguar's Le Mans-bred rigid rear axle, never let go, and Fangio, lying third and trying hard, just could not pass.

Then, intruding on this great battle, and on subsidiary disputes between Aston Martin, Maserati and Ferrari, came more grim tragedy, as if 1955 had not already had enough. Two British drivers, Jim Mayers and Bill Smith, lost their lives in a multiple mêlée near Cochranstown, six cars in all being eliminated from the race. Mayers' Cooper-Climax had struck a stone gateway, flew to pieces, and caught fire. Blazing fuel gushed on to the roadway, which unfortunately was concealed beyond a brow past the Deer Leap, and several cars hurtled one after the other into the wreckage.

Soon a thick, evil cloud of black smoke marked the scene of tragedy, and other cars picked their way through smoke and flame and continued the race. No spectators were involved, however, that being a forbidden area.

The race went remorselessly on. After ten laps Fangio tired of the shapely green tail of Hawthorn's Jaguar and forced his way past, only to be promptly repassed. Fangio repeated the act, and again Hawthorn re-took the Mercedes, setting a new lap record at 94.61mph, and this time pulling out a fair margin before stopping on lap twenty-five at his pit for a refuel, handing over to the Ulsterman Desmond Titterington. And when Fangio made his pit stop, the Jaguar moved back into second place.

Then came the unexpected. Leader Stirling Moss's offside rear tyre flung a tread and burst at about 140mph, and after fighting the disabled car down to a controllable pace, during which he clouted the bank at Wheeler's Corner, he limped to the pits, where the battered rear wing had to be cut right away, and the wheel changed. Meantime Titterington had roared past into the lead, to the undisguised joy of the Ulster crowd, and when the Mercedes rejoined the race, it had the American John Fitch, not Moss, at the wheel.

Fitch did not know Dundrod as Moss did, and inevitably lost ground, particularly when some real Dundrod weather began to brew up and heavy rain fell. Soon the Jaguar's lead grew from seconds into minutes, and by lap thirty-six Titterington lay some four minutes ahead of Fitch, now third behind the Fangio/Kling car. At this deterioration of the German position, a frowning Neubauer brought Fitch in, and Moss, rested or not, was in and away like lightning to retrieve the situation.

Moss in the wet was masterly, although it may well be said that, but for the rain, a Mercedes might never have caught the Jaguar, since the German cars were consuming far more tyres in the dry. On rainy roads, however, the rigid axle of the D-type meant excessive wheelspin, and soon Moss had cut Titterington's lead down to just over two minutes, when the Jaguar swept into its pit and Hawthorn took over.

Still it rained, and by lap fifty-five Moss had the Jaguar in sight; two laps later a Mercedes was leading the T.T. again, Stirling piling on the seconds in preparation for his next pit stop. On lap sixty-one he came in, taking on fuel and changing the rear tyres, while the Jaguar again snarled past into the lead, to immense excitement in the stands, which rose to fever heat the next round, when Hawthorn and Moss swept through, two lengths apart.

The Mercedes overhauled the Jaguar as both vanished from sight, and now nothing could hold the flying Moss. Behind was Fangio, motoring magnificently to make up time lost by *his* co-driver, but he could not gain on Hawthorn, and it looked as if the Jaguar would score second place—a magnificent showing for a single car against the might of Mercedes. Alas, had Mike Hawthorn the support of two other Jaguars, he might yet have defeated the German cars; as it was, the D-type chose lap eighty-three, the very last round, to blow up, the crankshaft breaking at Quarry Corner, almost within coasting distance of the finish. The car spun in its own oil and stopped, Hawthorn climbed out and walked back, cheered to the echo for his heroic effort.

Stirling Moss won magnificently, Fangio was second, and Count von Trips, emerging successfully from a pitched battle with the Aston Martins and Maseratis, finished third—Mercedes 1-2-3 after all, and Jaguar out after so valiant a fight. Neubauer was amongst the first to commiserate with Hawthorn and Titterington, the heroes of the day.

Of the rest, the Ferraris performed poorly. Weakened by the loss of Gendebien, who had crashed the third car in practice and went to hospital, Castellotti/Taruffi and Maglioli/Trintignant could only manage sixth and eighth places, headed by an Aston Martin DB3S, splendidly driven by Peter Walker and Dennis Poore into fourth position, and Musso's 3-litre Ferrari. Jean Behra crashed heavily in his 3-litre Maserati, being thrown out and losing an ear, while another accident in the later stages brought a third fatality in the 1955 T.T. when Richard Mainwaring overturned his 1100cc Elva and was trapped beneath when it caught fire.

But for the triple tragedy, that Dundrod race fought out so stirringly by the leaders would have been outstanding amongst 1955 Championship events; instead, the accidents all too drastically stressed the limitations of Dundrod, with its narrow roads and unsympathetic banks. Thus, in that black year for motor racing, one more casualty was to be added—the Dundrod T.T., which has never been held since.

TENSION IN THE TARGA

'I shunted the wall fairly hard. Fortunately it was a very poorly built wall—it seemed to crumple away, and I finished up with the front wheels poking very, very near the edge.' The late Peter Collins: THE AUTOCAR, November 4th, 1955

Mercedes-Benz now had a fighting chance, sixteen points to Ferrari's nineteen, for the Championship, with one round to go. Jaguar also had sixteen, but if the Coventry concern could only whisk up one car for the T.T., they were hardly likely to enter for the Targa Florio in distant Sicily—which was scarcely 'D-type country' anyway!

The attitude of Daimler-Benz was vastly different. Fangio had clinched the 1955 World Drivers Championship with his victory in the Italian G.P. for Mercedes; Werner Engel had won the 1955 European Grand Touring (or Rally) Championship, using Mercedes 220 and 300SL cars; now the Germans wanted the 1955 World Sports Car Championship to complete the trilogy.

Thus Stirling Moss was whisked away from holidaying on a boat at Cannes to the Mediterranean island of Sicily, while his racing manager, Ken Gregory, 'chased up' and recruited two other British drivers, Peter Collins and Desmond Titterington, for the Mercedes team for Vicenzo Florio's famous race. It was the thirty-ninth of a classic series, held over the most testing and hair-raising circuit ever used for racing—the forty-five-mile Madonie mountain circuit, formed of roughly metalled roads and abounding in corners of every kind. Rocky masses, boulders, gulleys and sheer precipices awaited the incautious, to say nothing of frequent landslides, or the washing of masses of mud or gravel on to the road from the hills.

It was wonderful, fantastic, and as ruthless a test of driving skill as could ever be devised; accidents were plentiful, yet Madonie was not stupidly, pointlessly dangerous, as were some modern courses; it was a challenge to any driver worth his salt, and its mortality record stands as the smallest of any of the classic racing venues.

To comply with Championship regulations, the length of the Targa Florio for 1955 was increased from the usual eight laps to thirteen, making the total distance 580 miles, with nearly 10,000 corners to negotiate. That meant two drivers per car, and Mercedes paired Moss/Collins, Fangio/Kling and Titterington/Fitch to drive the 300SLRs. The team were practising three weeks beforehand, and the equipment they brought along was staggering —eight lorries, eight sports cars, seven other cars, and three short-wave radio stations to set up supplementary pits around the long course, to say nothing of forty-five mechanics and other personnel.

For 'home defence', Ferrari put in two works cars, a $3\frac{1}{2}$-litre 'four' for Castellotti/Manzon and a 3-litre for Maglioli/Sighin-olfi. Taruffi had been nominated with a third car, but apparently withdrew after a quarrel. Carroll Shelby and Gino Munaron shared a privately entered 3-litre Ferrari, and several others ran. Maserati were present too, the popular veteran 'Gigi' Villoresi sharing a 3-litre with Musso, while the Trident also had some potent new 2-litre 'fours'. The complete entry, split into various classes down to 1100cc, totalled sixty cars, of which forty-seven started.

After endless rain in practice, race day dawned with warm Mediterranean sunshine. Cars were dispatched, one every half-minute from 7am, the Championship disputants being last in the procession. That Stirling Moss was on his mettle was indicated by his opening round, completed in forty-four minutes flat—which was 2mins. 23.6secs. faster than Castellotti's lap record of 1954—and this on a standing lap!

This staggering feat placed Moss easily first, followed by Castellotti's Ferrari, 1min. 15secs. back, Fangio, Musso, Titterington, and Shelby. But Moss's second lap took a mere 43mins. 39secs., placing him still farther ahead, while round three he accomplished in 43mins. 7.4secs.—a speed of 62.2mph! That put Castellotti four minutes in arrears, and Fangio five minutes three seconds back, with ten laps—450 miles—yet to cover.

Was the British boy overdoing it this time? That odious phrase 'I told you so' was uttered in more than one language on the fourth lap, when Moss's Mercedes failed to come round, and Eugenio Castellotti's Ferrari roared triumphantly past in the lead, hailed gleefully by the partisan *Siciliani*.

About six miles from Collesano, Moss's back wheels had picked up some mud and the car suddenly slewed sideways at nearly 100mph, striking a bank with a wallop; the Mercedes bounced back, spun, then plunged down a six-foot drop into a sloping field, its engine still running. It took twelve minutes and over thirty spectators for Moss to find a way back to the circuit, his battered, boiling car resuming the race in fourth place, behind Fangio/Kling, Castellotti/Manzon and Titterington/Fitch. He swept into the pits, where mechanics fell upon the car, beat the body straight, opened out the flattened exhaust pipe ends, and poured ten quarts of water into the radiator, which had almost boiled dry while Moss tried desperately to climb out of his field up a forty-five degree slope.

Peter Collins, assuming the '*Maintenant, c'est a moi*' role immortalized by Jean Chassagne in the Bentley days of sports car racing, now swiftly took over and put in four brilliant laps, his fastest only twenty-one seconds slower than Moss, who knew the 300SLR inside out. First he caught Fitch, now driving the Titterington Mercedes, next Kling in Fangio's car, and then Manzon, relief for Castellotti. But Collins, too, had his prang to add to the drama and uncertainty, charging through a four-foot-high stone parapet and stopping with his front wheels close to a sheer drop. He hastily reversed and shot away again, completed his four-lap stint, then handed back to Moss.

Meantime, there was further drama in the Ferrari pits. The race rules required that no driver should cover more than five laps at one go, and with thirteen laps overall, that meant at least two stops for change of drivers by each car. Ferrari seemingly made a tactical error, for Castellotti, their fastest man, had handed over to Manzon after four laps, then took over again *three* laps later, leaving six to cover. This meant an extra stop to change drivers yet again, scarcely the way to fight opposition as tough as Mercedes-Benz.

Yet second place behind a Mercedes in the Targa could bring Ferrari equal on Championship points with the German marque —twenty-four points each—ample incentive for Ugolini to urge Castellotti to 'give his all'. This was the kind of order Castellotti enjoyed. He drove like a demon, the Ferrari tail slewing this way and that through the endless bends, the wheels kicking up showers of dust, stones and mud as he viciously accelerated, braked, slid and slithered his way around the Madonie.

With three laps to go the Ferrari was one minute thirty-four seconds behind Moss, but Fangio was uncomfortably close behind when Castellotti skittered into the pits for Manzon to drive that essential lap, a babble of high-powered Italian speeding the Frenchman on his way. A painful tension ensued in the Ferrari pit, and the agitated Castellotti could scarcely contain himself when Manzon failed to come round on time. The unhappy Frenchman had struck a rock, breaking a front wheel, and had to change it by the roadside. When at last he reached the pits, much demented shouting ensued and Castellotti leapt into the car, nearly setting the tyres alight in the frenzy of his get-away, and driving most of the last two laps sideways on.

But it was all in vain, for Fangio by now had a five-minute lead on the Ferrari, and the incensed Castellotti had to rest content with third place behind two silver German cars. Moss/Collins magnificently first at 59.80mph (previous fastest, Taruffi's Lancia at 55.88mph in 1954), Fangio/Kling second, Castellotti/Manzon third, Titterington/Fitch fourth—that was the finishing order of this remarkable race, with a pair of 2-litre Maseratis next in.

So Mercedes-Benz had done it! Thanks to the brilliance of two young British drivers, and the tremendous performance and ruggedness of the 3-litre 300SLR Mercedes, they had clinched the 1955 World Sports Car Championship by two points. As for Ferrari, the losers by two points, they had split the German's beloved 1-2-3 victory formation, although that was poor compensation for a lost Championship.

CHAMPIONSHIP SCORE-SHEET 1955

Make of Car	Buenos Aires 1000-km., Argentina	Sebring 12-hour, U.S.A.	Mille Miglia, Italy	Le Mans 24-hour, France	Tourist Trophy, Gt. Britain	Targa Florio, Sicily	Total Score	Best Four Perform-ances
Mercedes-Benz ..	—	—	8 (1st)	—	8 (1st)	8 (1st)	24	24
Ferrari	8 (1st)	6 (2nd)	4 (3rd)	—	1 (6th)	4 (3rd)	23	22
Jaguar	—	8 (1st)	—	8 (1st)	—	—	16	16
Maserati	4 (3rd)	4 (3rd)	3 (4th)	—	2 (5th)	2 (5th)	15	13
Aston Martin ..	—	—	—	6 (2nd)	3 (4th)	—	9	9
Porsche	3 (4th)	—	—	3 (4th)	—	—	6	6
Gordini	2 (5th)	—	—	—	—	—	2	2
Austin Healey ..	—	1 (6th)	—	—	—	—	1	1

SCORING: First 8 points; second 6pts.; third 4pts.; fourth 3pts.; fifth 2pts.; sixth 1pt.

CHAPTER 4

A PROD FROM THE TRIDENT

TWO ANNOUNCEMENTS of vital importance to the World Sports Car Championship were made at the close of 1955. The first came from Prof. Fritz Nallinger, Technical Director of Daimler-Benz A.G., on the occasion of a ceremony at Unterturkheim to celebrate the marque's remarkable triple victory in the three International Championships of 1955.

To a distinguished gathering which included Neubauer, Uhlenhaut, Fangio, Moss, Kling, Herrmann, Collins, Tittering-ton, Fitch, Gendebien, Engel and Taruffi, he announced that Mercedes were to withdraw, not only from Grand Prix racing, as was already known, but also from sports car events.

'We have all profited greatly by the experience gained in racing car competition', he said. 'Now further development of our production programme makes it advisable to employ our highly qualified personnel in the manufacture of production cars. . . .'

No Mercedes in racing for 1956 meant a hasty reshuffle of drivers. Fangio and Collins signed with Ferrari, and Moss with Maserati, also with Aston Martin for certain sports car events.

The second announcement concerned Le Mans. In the light of the 1955 tragedy, rigorous and expensive new safety measures were to be enforced, the circuit was to be materially altered in the pits area, a new, wider road laid, and new double-decker pits erected. In addition, much revised race regulations were introduced, the most important point, so far as the C.S.I. Championship was concerned, being the restriction of manufacturers' prototypes to a maximum capacity of $2\frac{1}{2}$ litres. Cars above that capacity had to be of series-production type, with at least one hundred examples built or laid down by mid-February, 1956.

This served to eliminate several of the most blatant 'sports-racers' from the entry, but it also eliminated Le Mans from the

Championship contest, since the new rulings were devised not by the F.I.A. but by the A.C. de l'Ouest for their famous 24-hour race only.

That cut the list of qualifying events down from seven to six—the Buenos Aires 1000-km., Sebring 12-hour, Mille Miglia, Nurburgring 1000-km, Dundrod T.T. and *Carrera Panamericana*, although the last two were listed more in hope than anything else.

A BATTLE OF AXLES

'This race showed that a good 3-litre can better the performance of larger engines. The previous race record was well beaten.' AUTO ITALIANA, December 10th, 1956

So to Argentina, land of beef—and of Fangio!—for Round One of the Fourth Constructors' Cup contest on January 29th. The organizers of the Buenos Aires 1000-km. chose the shorter of their *circuit routier* layouts again that year, 5.88 miles round as in 1954, but run clockwise, just for a change. No David Brown or Ecurie Ecosse entries were forthcoming this time, but that didn't mean an unchallenged win for Ferrari. Officine Maserati had really got their 3-litre six-cylinder sports-racing car *going*, besides having drivers who could really *go*. Stirling Moss teamed up with that tough and very versatile 'local boy' Carlos Menditeguy (pronounced something like 'Mahnditaygee'!), and Froilan Gonzalez shared with Jean Behra.

Even so, the odds against the Trident were heavy, for Ferrari had two of their great 4.9-litre cars for new team member Fangio and Castellotti, and for two other new members of the Scuderia, Peter Collins and Luigi Musso, late of Maserati, plus a 3.5-litre 'big-four' for the new Belgian member Olivier Gendebien and new American member Phil Hill. In addition, there were two 4.5s and a 4.9 driven by private *Ferraristi*, while amongst the makeweights was a C-type Jaguar, an Allard and a 300SL Mercedes driven by two Chileans.

The Ferrari 4.9s soon gobbled their way into the lead, and barring pit-stops for fuel, tyres and changes of driver, looked as if they meant to stay there. Peter Collins showed his mettle and the pace of his car by whipping round at 103.11mph—fastest lap of the day, but Castellotti in Fangio's car hit some straw bales when leading, bent a wheel and dropped to fifth position, while Moss and Behra on 2 litres less gave the Musso/Collins car no peace.

Mensiteguy took over from Moss at around half-distance, keeping up the pressure on the leading Ferrari, and at the same time holding off the Hill/Gendebien 3.5. Then the leader went out with a broken rear axle, and for the first time a 3-litre Maserati was leading a Championship race. Ferrari's new racing manager, Eraldo Sculati, moved fast, flagged in Castellotti, now lying third, and bade Fangio take over.

El Chueco now began a spectacular chase of the smaller Maserati, clipping four to five seconds per lap from its one-lap lead. But Maserati's new team manager, Nello Ugolini, ex-Ferrari, countered by putting Moss in Mensiteguy's place, although the stop narrowed the gap between the Maserati and the pursuing Ferrari, promising a dramatic finish. Moss fled as before 'a frightful fiend', and the exciting, intimidating spectacle of Fangio the master, all out in the brutish, bellowing 4.9, suddenly ended in anti-climax when its rear axle broke, as had the other big Ferrari's.

Ugolini gave Moss what the Americans call the 'EZ' signal, the Maserati now holding a two-lap lead over Gendebien/Hill in the works 3.5-Ferrari, and motoring smoothly on to win at 96.13mph. It was a veritable joy day for Maserati, as Behra/Gonzalez were third in the other 3-litre car, with de Tomaso's $1\frac{1}{2}$-litre 'four' fourth and a class winner. A 2-litre Ferrari was fifth, and—you can't keep a good make down—the Mercedes-Benz 300SL from Chile was sixth, so that the new Championship scoreboard looked refreshingly different after the opening race, reading: first, Maserati (eight points), second, Ferrari (six), third, Mercedes (one).

Obviously Ferrari had to watch the 3-litre Maserati very carefully; it was fast, handled beautifully, and held the road better than their 4.9s or even the 3.5. Sebring on March 24th promised much interest.

A BATTLE OF BRAKES

'But there on the list, virtually rubbing elbows with the world's top-ranking sports car brass, was a team of 1956 Chevrolet Corvettes, looking as awkwardly out of place as a girl in her first high heels'.
MOTOR TREND, June 1956

Few Sebring 12-hour races could match the 1956 event for quality of entry, or of racing. Maybe the introduction of a modest $10,000 prize fund, plus 'expenses' for foreign contestants, helped, but the fifty-nine-car line-up was an organizer's dream, with serious British, French, German, Italian and American competition and all the big names amongst the drivers.

Ferrari and Maserati were there to re-fight their Buenos Aires battle, and this time the 4.9s stayed behind and Maranello ran three new 3½-litre 'big fours'. Maserati had two 3-litre machines, as in Argentina, while a very welcome Anglo-American entry of three D-type disc-braked Jaguars came from the New York Jaguar distributorship. Work's team drivers Hawthorn/Titterington and Hamilton/Bueb steered two of them, and the Americans Johnston/Spear the third.

Aston Martin returned to Sebring with a team of three disc-braked DB3S cars, Stirling Moss driving his first race for the Feltham team, paired with Peter Collins, both these drivers having prior agreements to drive the British cars in their respective Maserati and Ferrari contracts.

Highly interesting was the entry of three factory-supported series-production Chevrolet Corvettes, the first time in a generation that a Detroit manufacturer had backed motor racing. John Fitch also entered a Corvette, bored and stroked to raise the V8 engine's capacity from 4.4 to 5.2 litres and bring it into the 5–8 litre class. There were also two Ford Thunderbirds entered by the former Indianapolis racing driver Peter de Paolo, plus several U.S.-entered private D-type Jaguars.

Race day was hot, as was the pace right from the 10am start. Fitch's special Corvette at the top of the line led momentarily, but Moss's Aston Martin wheels were actually the first to roll, while Hawthorn was first into the first bend. His blue and white

Jaguar was fitted with fuel injection, giving it a performance of which Mike made full use, striving to outpace the tenacious Moss. And in third position sat 'old man' Fangio, playing the waiting game and hoping for the leaders to wear themselves out, with something in reserve if they didn't.

When the first pit-stops for fuel and change of drivers came round after about two hours, Stirling Moss's Aston lost nearly three minutes for adjustments, dropping to eighth place when Peter Collins took it back into the race. Desmond Titterington took over from Hawthorn, and Castellotti from Fangio, their Ferrari now a very menacing second.

The 3-litre Maseratis were disappointing this time, for though spasmodically fast, they seemed unable to match the pace of the 3.5-Ferraris, besides suffering a serious blow when Menditeguy crashed dramatically in the Esses, his car overturning and the driver suffering a double skull fracture and other injuries. The crash was attributed to an over-zealous official who, on observing how cars were brushing the straw bales on the S and gradually easing the corner, decided to push several back, whereupon Menditeguy came through on his regular line and found, too late, that it had been altered.

Stirling Moss was another casualty with what the pit marshal called a 'frozen' transmission; solid it may have become when it seized, but not 'cold'! Next out was the Hamilton/Bueb Jaguar with a broken brake line after lying fifth, and in the fifth hour the leading Jaguar also met braking bothers, making a lengthy pit-stop which let Castellotti's Ferrari up into the head of affairs.

Now Hawthorn took Titterington's place at the wheel and put in some hard driving to re-take the lead as Castellotti handed back to Fangio. But by the eighth hour Ferrari were out in front again, for the Jaguar was in serious distress, much time being lost at the pits while large quantities of brake fluid were poured in. The anxious Mike then put in another lap, only to return to have the hydraulic system bled, though with little improvement.

The Jaguar bolt was clearly shot, and the Ferrari was never again headed. Not lack of speed, but lack of deceleration before Sebring's punishing turns, had defeated the Jaguar after another gallant battle. Fangio and Castellotti ran out the comfortable victors at a record 84.06mph, being the first to cover over 1000 miles in the twelve hours at Sebring. Their team-mates Musso and Schell were runners-up with another 3.5-Ferrari, while Jack Ensley and the Indianapolis driver Bob Sweikert saved Jaguar's prestige by finishing a fine third in their private D-type.

Despite having only first and top gear left, Roy Salvadori and Carroll Shelby brought their DB3S Aston Martin home fourth, while fifth was the surviving 3-litre Maserati of Behra/Taruffi, which had lost much time at the pits, but showed its teeth with the fastest lap of the race in 3mins. 29.8secs. by Behra. A works 1.5-litre Porsche was sixth, also winning the Index of Performance as a change from the French DB, which ran out of fuel and had to make do with fourth in the class.

Three of the Chevrolet Corvettes survived the long race, to general satisfaction of the crowd, John Fitch/Walt Hangsen winning their class and placing ninth overall. Just how hard that 5.2-mile airfield circuit in Florida is on cars was revealed by the list of retirements—thirty-six cars out of fifty-nine, one of the last and unluckiest being the Tony Brooks/Reg Parnell Aston Martin, which lay fourth until the final hour, when the engine seized.

So it was back to the Championship *status quo*, with Ferrari back in the lead with fourteen points to Maserati's ten, while Jaguar, Aston Martin and Porsche now joined in with four, three and one points respectively.

CASTELLOTTI'S GREATEST DRIVE

'He is usually reckoned to be rather wild in his driving but he was now disproving this idea. . . .' MOTOR SPORT, June 1956

April 29th was Mille Miglia day, and a singularly unpleasant one, moreover, the race being run in pelting rain. For the first time in the history of the race, the roads were completely closed to outside vehicles, while in a further effort to minimize the accidents which blighted this famous race, the entry was cut from 600 to a 400 maximum, and the slowest classes eliminated, while drivers were 'screened' for their ability.

There were, in fact, 367 starters, and of the Championship contenders, Ferrari and Maserati were the main protagonists, the former fielding a very strong quartet in Fangio and Castellotti with new 3.5-litre 24-plug V12s, and Collins and Musso with 3.5 'fours'. Officine Maserati had a new, larger 'six' of 3½ litres—actually a hasty substitute for a new 4½-litre V8 which was far from ready—for Stirling Moss and passenger Denis Jenkinson, plus two 3-litres for Taruffi and Perdisa. None were in good trim for a 992-mile race, suffering from hasty and inadequate preparation, whereas in contrast the Ferraris were in superb form. So were a surprisingly large contingent of Mercedes-Benz 300SL coupés from Germany, running in the Gran Turismo class, and backed by the works with Neubauer, Uhlenhaut, Kling and many mechanics in attendance.

No Jaguars or David Brown entries competed this year, but ironically, two of the Le Mans 4½-litre twelve-cylinder Lagondas, which would have made worthy Mille Miglia contestants, were out in Italy for filming purposes, complete with team manager John Wyer; a waste of talent which many Britons deplored.

The hero of the race, without any shadow of doubt, was twenty-five-year-old Eugenio Castellotti. He jumped into the lead very quickly, leading into Verona at 120.7mph, and extended his lead through Vicenza and Padua despite increasingly heavy rain. Beyond Ravenna, Taruffi made a determined bid for Maserati, catching the Ferrari before Forli, only to crash into a stone post near Rimini when saturated brakes failed to check his pace. Another who crashed early in the race was that notable figure in British racing, John Heath of H.W. Motors, whose Formula 2 H.W.M.s put Moss and Collins on the road to fame. Heath's H.W.M.-Jaguar went off-course near Ravenna, and unfortunately his injuries proved more serious than anticipated, and he died in hospital.

Castellotti next met unexpected opposition from the young German, Count Wolfgang von Trips, snugly protected from the raging elements in his 300SL Mercedes. The audacious Trips took the lead between Rimini and Pesaro, only to be caught again on the rapid run to Ancona and down to Pescara. Then Trips crashed when passing a '1900' Alfa Romeo, and Peter

Collins moved up into second place, dogged by Fritz Riess's 300SL.

Cocking a snoot, like Moss in 1955, at the 'he who leads through Rome' adage, Castellotti stormed into the Eternal City and out again with a ten-mile lead over Collins, Riess and Fangio, and stayed out in front for the rest of the way, defying violent storms, heavy mist in the mountains, torrential rain and flooded roads. As for Moss, the 1955 victor, he never saw Rome this time, the Maserati getting right out of control on the slippery mountain roads at Antrodoco, near Aquila, and plunging down a steep slope, to be halted by the only tree in the area. Juan Fangio, last man to leave Brescia, stopped to ensure that Moss and 'Jenks' were safe and sound, even offering them a lift to the next control in his passenger's seat.

Now Luigi Musso seemingly awoke to the fact that his great rival Castellotti was stealing his thunder, and put on speed to pass, first Fangio, then Riess, taking third place before Florence, and remaining there to the welcome finish at Brescia, where already thousands of umbrella'd spectators had cheered Castellotti to the echo for his heroic drive to victory. As one noted for driving 'on the edge' in G.P. cars, and sometimes overdoing it, his delicate handling of the ultra-powerful 3.5 v12-Ferrari in such appalling conditions was all the more praiseworthy. It was indeed Castellotti's *capolavoro*—the masterpiece of his racing career.

Second in the four-cylinder 3.5 was Peter Collins, third was Musso, fourth Fangio, fifth (and first in the GT class) Gendebien, all in Ferraris—the highest placed 300SL was that of Metternich/Einsiedel, in sixth place, with others seventh, eighth and tenth, the latter the unlucky Riess, delayed en route.

The bad weather brought several accidents besides that of poor John Heath, and unfortunately the co-drivers in two cars, a Mercedes and an Alfa Romeo, were killed after leaving the road, the Alfa also killing two spectators and injuring five. The death roll rose to six, when a Stanguellini crashed avoiding a dog and struck a group of watchers, killing one.

Many drivers blamed the unchecked enthusiasm of the spectators for the Mille Miglia accidents, Fangio speaking of the crowds near Rome forming 'human fences' on some of the most dangerous bends. Ever since the Le Mans tragedy, opposition to the Mille Miglia had mounted in influential Italian circles, and now, despite the A.C. di Brescia's laudable efforts to improve safety conditions for the spectators, the race had gained another black mark.

MOSS VERSUS FANGIO

'The sight of Hawthorn and Frère with the D-types broadside on in the wet during practice was most inspiring. Two very brave men.' D. S. Jenkinson; MOTOR SPORT, July 1956

Round Four took place at the Nurburgring in Germany, where the A.D.A.C. ran their 1000-km. race again, after a three-year lapse. The entry included a surprisingly strong British contingent, joining in battle with the Ferraris and Maseratis. Aston Martin sent three cars, which meant that Ferrari lost Peter Collins for this race by prior contract; in his place they recruited another Englishman, the versatile Ken Wharton. Jaguar entered two D-types, with Hawthorn/Titterington in the fuel injection car, and Hamilton/Frère in a carburetter model.

Keen to regain the Championship they had lost to Mercedes in 1955, Ferrari sent no less than eight cars to Nurburg for their drivers to try, Fangio/Castellotti and de Portago/Gendebien taking 3.5-litre 'fours', and Musso/Trintignant and Phil Hill/Wharton 3.5 V12s. Officine Maserati pitted three 3-litre 300s models against their Modena rivals, with Moss/Behra, Taruffi/Schell and Perdisa/Manzon at the wheels.

During practice Paul Frère inverted his Jaguar, so that Norman Dewis of Jaguars had to drive out a replacement from Coventry, arriving too late for practice. This 'Jag' and Perdisa's Maserati, which had also not practised, took up fifty-sixth and fifty-seventh positions, at the tail-end of the long Le Mans line-up at the start.

The Nurburg starting scene, set on the broad apron in front of the pits, with the crowds packing the stands and enclosures in their thousands, and the P.A. commentators working them up into a state of tense expectancy as zero hour nears, is always

Above: The American 5·4-litre Cunningham with which Phil Walters and John Fitch won the 1953 Sebring, Florida. *Right:* Stirling Moss with his disabled Jaguar at the 1953 Dundrod T.T. *Below:* After the Jaguar victory, Le Mans, 1953; Duncan Hamilton and Tony Rolt with their wives.

Above: Piero Taruffi pushes his Lancia two miles to the pits, Sebring, 1954, after leading the race. *Below:* Reg Parnell surveys the wreck of his Aston Martin in the 1954 Mille Miglia.

Duncan Hamilton in the first D-type Jaguar, Le Mans, 1954. *Below:* Ascari, Lancia's No. 1 driver, heads the field at the start of the 1954 Dundrod T.T.

Above: Umberto Maglioli in his big Ferrari crossing the line at Durango, the fifth stage of the 1954 Carrera Panamericana, Mexico, which he won. *Below:* Le Mans, 1955, showing the comparatively narrow road and a small proportion of the crowd, where Pierre Levagh's Mercedes-Benz crashed, wreaking grim tragedy.

Above: Moss, the winner, follows Musso during the 1955 T.T. race, the last to be held on the Dundrod circuit. *Below:* Winning the 1955 Targa Florio and clinching the Championship for Mercedes-Benz goes the 300SLR of Peter Collins and Stirling Moss (at the wheel).

Castellotti in his
Ferrari sweeps into
Brescia to win the
1956 Mille Miglia.

Maserati drivers
Jean Behra, Stirling
Moss, Piero Taruffi
and Harry Schell
share the victory
laurels at the 1956
Nurburgring.

Moss's Maserati,
Hawthorn's Jaguar
and an Aston Martin
are first off at the
1956 Nurburgring.

Akton Miller's
American 'Caballo
II' at the final
Mille Miglia, 1957.

Winner of the 1957
Nurburgring, the
Aston Martin of
Tony Brooks and
Noel Cunningham-
Reid.

Stirling Moss's
ultra-low Maserati
coupé at Le Mans,
1957, laying an
ominous trail of
smoke.

Ivor Bueb at full chat in the Ecurie Ecosse D-type Jaguar which won at Le Mans, 1957.

Partners in victory at Le Mans, 1957; Flockhart, Bueb, chief mechanic Wilkinson and Ecurie Ecosse team chief David Murray.

Rear wheels spinning, Mike Hawthorn motors his Ferrari through a field during the 1957 Swedish G.P. at Rabelöv.

Shock is recorded on Harry Schell's smoke-blackened face after emergency medical treatment for burns during the 1957 G.P. of Venezuela.

Blazing fiercely, Schell's 4½-litre V8 Maserati was completely gutted.

Aerial view of the 1957 Swedish G.P.; Rabelöv village where Mike Hawthorn and others ran off the road (two Ferraris can be seen parked off the corner).

Above: Peter Collins and Olivier Gendebien in their 3-litre Testa Rossa Ferraris during the 1958 Sebring race won by Collins and Phil Hill. *Below:* The start of the 1958 Goodwood T.T., with the swift-footed Stirling Moss first to his car (Aston Martin No. 7).

A burst tyre on his Ferrari brings Mike Hawthorn's No. 4 to the pits at Nurburg, 1958.

Above: Out goes Fairman, in goes Moss—an ultra-rapid pit-stop for the winning Aston Martin at the Nurburgring, 1959. *Below:* Ambition achieved—an Aston Martin wins at Le Mans; Carroll Shelby gets the chequered flag in the classic 24-hour race of 1959.

Above: The Aston Martin team at Goodwood had special nitrogen-operated permanent jack to speed up tyre changes during the 1959 T.T. *Below:* Roy Salvadori's Aston Martin on fire in the pits at Goodwood, 1959.

Above: Dan Gurney's 'Birdcage' Maserati No. 5 leading the Nurburg 1000-km, 1960, run in gloomy conditions of fog and damp. *Below:* The Camoradi car at Le Mans, 1960, showing the Maserati interpretation of the unpopular 25cm. windscreen-height regulation.

Above: Briggs Cunningham's prototype E Jaguar leads through the Esses at Le Mans early in the 1960 race. *Below:* The same race a few hours later, with the winning Frere/Gendebien Ferrari sweeping past the stands in pouring rain.

Above: The ugly but effective 'Birdcage' Maserati Type 61 in which Stirling Moss (seen here) and Dan Gurney won the Nurburg 1000-km in 1960. *Below:* Following G.P. trends, Ferrari put their 2·5-litre V6 engine behind the driver on the 1961 type 246, with which Wolfgang von Trips won the Targa Florio after shattering the lap record.

impressive. The last seconds were counted out harshly over the loudspeakers: '*Funf, vier, drei, zwei, ein*', down swept the starter's flag, and across the concrete rushed fifty-seven drivers, one of them, Peter Walker, stumbling and falling partly under his Aston Martin. He scrambled up with cut and grazed arms, leapt into his car and joined the mad exodus. Stirling Moss had effected his usual lightning getaway, only to be passed by Hawthorn's blaring Jaguar. Then Fangio appeared out of the blue, and shot past both, galvanizing the pair into counter-action, first Hawthorn whipping back into the lead, only for Moss to pass both again, making the first lap order Maserati, Jaguar and Ferrari.

But this preliminary sparring soon abated, Moss establishing a firm lead while the Jaguar's outdated rear axle design, no handicap on the Le Mans billiard table surface, now cost Hawthorn vital seconds on each lap of the bumpy, serpentine *Ring*. So Fangio caught him again, this time pulling away, and next Luigi Musso essayed to pass on the South Turn. But the Ferrari lightly touched the Jaguar, was deflected in the turn, slid off into a narrow ditch and overturned, trapping the Italian in the cockpit. Several hefty marshals lifted the car and got Musso out, soaked in petrol and with a broken arm and rib.

That meant two Ferraris out, for 'Fon' de Portago had overdone it at the Karussel, smiting a remarkably substantial hedge which closed up the radiator grille. A dozen German *polizei* restored the car to terra firma, but their assistance meant its eventual disqualification. Fate's frown next settled on Peter Collins, driving his DB3S splendidly in fourth place, until a blocked jet forced him right back. Then Paul Frère's Jaguar had dire clutch trouble when a piece of starter housing broke away, compelling its retirement, after the Belgian had worked up from fifty-sixth to seventh position within six laps. Perdisa's Maserati was a further casualty, suffering rear suspension trouble.

On lap ten Mike Hawthorn was black-flagged (meaning 'come in at once') and told to pass cars on the left only, as per A.D.A.C. regulations. Twice, it seems, he had encountered Porsches occupying the nearside at crucial points and dived past on the right, as several others were doing, this being accepted practice in British races.

D

Came the first pit-stops at around one-third distance, but smart pitwork kept Moss's Maserati in the lead, now driven by Jean Behra, who headed Castellotti in Fangio's car, de Portago, who was transferred to Hill's Ferrari, depriving Wharton of his first Ferrari drive, Schell in Taruffi's Maserati, and Titterington in Hawthorn's Jaguar. Alas, Behra was quickly back to the pits, the Maserati drooping forlornly at the rear. The transverse leaf rear suspension had broken on the nearside, and the leader was out, Castellotti slamming past into first place.

Ugolini acted quickly. Out went the 'come in' signal to Harry Schell, the gay Franco-American glumly handing over to Behra after driving only four laps. Taruffi was scarcely more pleased, for the regulations allowed the *two* drivers of a retired car to transfer to another of the same team, but not one, so that obviously Moss would relieve Behra, and Piero and Harry were unemployed.

By half-distance (twenty-two laps) the order was Castellotti, de Portago, Behra, Titterington, but Behra moved into second place three rounds later, and the brilliant Frenchman then began to close on the leading Ferrari, now driven by Fangio again. On lap twenty-eight there were 23½ seconds between them; by lap thirty-one only 10 seconds.

Then the Maserati tore into the pits for its final stop for tyres and fuel; seconds slipped by, Fangio's lead extending to 67 seconds before Moss, the fourth man to drive that car, slammed back into the race. Twelve laps to go; 6 seconds per lap to make up; could Moss do it?

Meantime, Hawthorn's Jaguar came in with a battered front, after contacting a Porsche which obstinately held the left of the road at an awkward spot. But further trouble followed in a leaking fuel tank, which brought a rush of anxious officials with fire extinguishers at the ready. The Jaguar mechanics plugged it with two rubber grommets, but fourth place was irrevocably lost before Titterington was able to drive off.

Then '*Achtung, achtung—Fangio kommt*!' brayed the pits' loudspeakers, and to tremendous excitement the race leader stormed into the Ferrari pit a mere four laps from the finish, took on a few litres of fuel and tore off again. But during the

25 seconds he was at the pits, Moss's Maserati had burst past leader once again and, what was more, extending that lead. Fangio slammed his Ferrari through Nurburg's unending corners with magnificent desperation, but had to give way; Moss in the Maserati was his match, and took the winning flag 26.2 seconds ahead of the Argentinian.

It was Maserati's second 1956 victory in a Championship race with the 3-litre, credit at Nurburg being shared by four drivers, Moss, Behra, Taruffi and Schell, the Briton and the Frenchman each driving twelve laps, the Italian sixteen and the Franco-American four.

Malignant fate chose that final lap to strike at the unfortunate Jaguar, now back in tenth place, for a half-shaft broke with just half a lap to go. And Salvadori's Aston Martin broke its de Dion tube on the last round also, when occupying the Jaguar's former fourth place. Over 600 miles around the Nurburgring and then that—could luck be worse?

Behind Moss and Fangio across the line came de Portago/ Gendebien in the Hill/Wharton Ferrari, the indecently fast $1\frac{1}{2}$-litre Porsche of von Trips/Maglioli, the Collins/Brooks Aston Martin, and another Porsche in sixth position. Maserati had won, but Ferrari still led the Championship comfortably, now with twenty-eight points to Maserati's eighteen. Aston Martin were third with only five points, Porsche and Jaguar had four, and Mercedes-Benz two.

The situation was now extremely interesting. By c.s.i. regulations, with only five qualifying events that season, placings would be based upon the three best performances of each marque. That gave Ferrari two wins (eight points for each) at Sebring and the Mille Miglia, and six points for second place, either at Buenos Aires or Nurburg; total twenty-two. Maserati also had two wins (Buenos Aires and Nurburg) plus two points for fifth at Sebring; total eighteen.

Thus there were four points between the rival Modenese makes, and just one race to go. This was the Swedish G.P., an event new to the Championship series, but certain of a full entry of Italian cars!

SWEDISH MUSICAL CHAIRS

*'This must surely stand as the first major European race victory by
an American driver for very many years, shared on this occasion by
a crafty French co-pilot.'* MOTOR MUNDIAL, September 1956

International motor racing on a major scale was comparatively
rare to the Swedish public. The Swedish Grand Prix itself had
been revived as a sports car race only the previous season, after
a lapse of several years, but so successful had the 1955 event
proved (it was run at Råbëlov, and won by Fangio's 300SLR
Mercedes) that the organizers, royally encouraged by Prince
Bertil of Sweden, pressed on with preparations for 1956.

Then came cancellation of the T.T., and F.I.A. sanction to
incorporate Sweden's race in the Sports Car Championship
series. The Råbëlov circuit, some five miles from Kristianstad—
a very pleasant lakeside resort in south-eastern Sweden—was
widened in many places, and several bumpy sections smoothed
off by resurfacing. Measuring 4.04 miles to the lap, the course
was composed of local roads giving one fast, one medium and
two very slow corners, all joined by shortish straights; 140mph
could be attained at points, but brakes had a very hard time of
it at Råbëlov, especially over the F.I.A.'s stipulated distance of
1000 kilometres.

Just how serious Ferrari and Maserati were about the Championship was revealed by their entries of *five* cars each. This
brought acute driver-problems to both teams, but Ferrari solved
theirs by inviting Mike Hawthorn back into the Maranello fold,
since Jaguar were not competing, and also engaged Duncan
Hamilton, whose high-spirited victory against team orders in the
Rheims 12-hour race a month earlier caused him to become an
ex-works Jaguar driver. That talented young German from
Cologne, Graf von Trips, was also recruited to the team as
Hamilton's co-driver, the other pairings being Fangio/Castel-
lotti, Collins/Gendebien, Hawthorn/de Portago and Trintignant/
Hill, with Robert Manzon also on call.

Besides their 'regulars'—Moss/Behra and Taruffi/Schell,
Officine Maserati secured some highly cosmopolitan talent,

pairing the Italians Villoresi and Maglioli, the Swiss Benoit Musy with the Frenchman André Simon, and the Spaniard Francisco Godia with the Swede Joakim Bonnier. Musy and Godia actually owned the 3-litre cars they were driving, but were operating under the factory 'wing' in this important race. Maserati also brought with them a prototype of formidable aspect and specification—a raucous 4½-litre, four-camshaft, four-carburetter V8, reputedly giving 375bhp, which appeared during practice only in various drivers' hands, finally shed some oil around, and then was put away for a later day.

Against the phalanx of Italian red stood two Ecurie Ecosse D-type Jaguars in dark blue, for the 1956 Le Mans winners Ron Flockhart and Ninian Sanderson, and Titterington/Lawrence, while there was a third D-type, Duncan Hamilton's own car, driven by the Whitehead half-brothers Peter and Graham. To widespread disappointment there was no David Brown entry, the Aston Martins which could cross the Atlantic for Sebring being unable, for some reason, to cross the North Sea to Sweden. Several private Ferraris and Porsches completed the entry of twenty-seven cars.

Drivers who had been to Råbëlov in 1955 still found the course narrow and somewhat bumpy despite the improvements, but all was set on Sunday, August 12th for a brilliant manifestation, with the Swedish public still pouring into the enclosures at zero hour, 12 noon. By then several drivers were almost in their cars from the Le Mans start, for the use of a large clock device marking off the final 10 seconds seemed to invite 'jumping' the start. Peter Collins was one of the culprits, being first on the move, followed swiftly by Moss, Hawthorn and the rest, preponderantly red. One more Ferrari–Maserati battle had begun.

From the start the pendulum of fortune swung against the Trident. Taruffi's 3-litre Maserati came into collision with Flockhart's Jaguar on lap one, being too damaged to continue, while several laps later, Godia's car charged off-course at the difficult corner in Råbëlov village, limping back and later retiring when Bonnier had taken over. Collins's bellowing 12-cylinder Ferrari, however, went out to lead the race, remaining there for forty-seven laps, by which time a third Maserati, that of Musy, had also retired.

Then Collins handed over to the Belgian Gendebien, who was overtaken by a welter of Italian red as he accelerated back into the race, Stirling Moss's Maserati now leading from von Trips. Then both made routine stops, giving Fangio/Castellotti a turn out in front until they, too, pitted, which let Behra in the Moss car take back the lead for Maserati.

Surprise and confusion followed when Collins took over—not Gendebien's car again—but that of von Trips! Yet the race regulations permitted such switchovers, and when the leading Maserati returned pitwards with brake trouble after six laps, Collins found himself first again. Now Manzon in Gendebien's car blew up at Råbëlov corner, and Collins and Hill hit the resultant oil patch and danced a Ferrari duet off-course, Hill vanishing into deep corn, but emerging again unharmed to resume the race. Four Ferraris, two Maseratis left.

Then Collins smote a sandbank and dropped behind Fangio and Hawthorn, who had also explored the Råbëlov cornfield when pressing the brake pedal produced negative results. Moss now suddenly appeared driving the Maglioli/Villoresi Maserati, and shortly afterwards his 'other' car met real trouble when Behra was refuelling at the pits. Slaphappy pit work caused fuel to spill over the tail, the hot exhaust ignited it, and a great column of flame and smoke shot skywards. The blaze was smartly controlled by expert fire marshals, but the car's race was over. Four Ferraris, one Maserati left.

Moss was forcing Villoresi's practically brakeless car round, holding fifth place but ever hopeful of coming up with a lagging Ferrari, when suddenly, on the 117th round, his engine locked up and caught fire near the Fredrikslund corner. That meant more practice for the highly efficient Swedish firemen and a walk home for Moss. Four Ferraris and no Maseratis left.

The race now looked a foregone conclusion for Ferrari, although the field had thinned elsewhere. Both Ecurie Ecosse Jaguars had gone, the Flockhart/Sanderson Le Mans winner with rear axle trouble, and the Titterington/Lawrence car with a rod through the side of the engine. But the Whiteheads' car still boomed steadily on, climbing up the leader board as faster but less consistent rivals fell by the wayside.

Fate's last blow was at Ferrari, Castellotti's engine breaking up when leading on lap 123, shortly after taking over from Fangio, who had built up a two-lap advantage over the Trintignant/Hill and Hamilton/von Trips/Collins Ferraris.

But the remaining three Ferraris slammed round and round unassailably until the 153rd and last lap, a calm, shrewd little Frenchman and a tense, talented Californian piloting the winning car. It took Trintignant and Hill 6hours, 33mins. 47.7secs. to win at 94.69mph, clinching the Sports Car Championship for Ferrari. Second came the Hamilton/Trips/Collins Ferrari, third the Hawthorn/de Portago/Hamilton Ferrari—what a mix-up for the race recorders!—and fourth, fifth and sixth came three series-production class Ferraris, the Swedish private entries of Kvarnstrom/Lundgren, Borgefors/Hammarlund and Nottorp/Andersson, heading the lone Jaguar of the Whiteheads, which, however, placed fourth in the sports class.

Ferrari 1-2-3-4-5-6!—a grand finale indeed for the *Cavallino Rampante*, worthily establishing them as the World Sports Car Champions.

CHAMPIONSHIP SCORE-SHEET 1956

Make of Car	Buenos Aires 1000-km. Argentina	Sebring 12-hour, U.S.A.	Mille Miglia, Italy	Nurburgring 1000-km. Germany	Swedish G.P.	Total Score	Best Three Perform-ances
Ferrari	6 (2nd)	8 (1st)	8 (1st)	6 (2nd)	8 (1st)	36	24
Maserati	8 (1st)	2 (5th)	—	8 (1st)	—	18	18
Jaguar	—	4 (3rd)	—	—	3 (4th)	7	7
Aston Martin	—	3 (4th)	—	2 (5th)	—	5	5
Porsche	—	1 (6th)	—	3 (4th)	—	4	4
Mercedes-Benz	1 (6th)	—	1 (6th)	—	—	2	2

SCORING: First 8 points; second 6pts.; third 4pts.; fourth 3pts.; fifth 2pts.; sixth 1pt.

CHAPTER 5

THREE-PRONGED ATTACK

AT THE close of 1956, the *Commission Sportive* of the F.I.A. announced their revised Appendix C—the 'sports car racing Formula', so to speak. There was little of the straightforward simplicity of the racing Formula 1 and 2 about Appendix C. It was long and complex, and in its 1957 form was almost a carbon copy of the 1956 Le Mans regulations of the A.C. de l'Ouest. There were sundry omissions, however, notably that of the 'prototype' clause which restricted such machines to $2\frac{1}{2}$-litres maximum engine capacity, and thereby excluded Le Mans from the 1956 Sports Car Championship.

Cars now had to have two doors at least, hoods were obligatory for scrutineering but might, by supplementary ruling, be removed for racing; windscreens now had to be full-width, measuring at least 100cm. wide and 15cm. high. There were other dimensional requirements, most of which had been tried at Le Mans already, so that several manufacturers were already 'blooded'. The full-width screen occasioned much grumbling—and some ingenious compromises in plastic or perspex to minimize the drag effect.

In sum, the new appendix was a very limited attempt to bring the competition sports car to a closer resemblance of the genuine article as used by the public, but the loopholes were many, and the 'two-seater Grand Prix car' or 'sports-racer', exciting vehicle though it was, continued to differ all too greatly from its production 'brothers'. This was largely attributable to the F.I.A.'s 'prototype' clause, introduced in order that design would not stagnate, but which enabled manufacturers who were out for victory in the bigger, better-paying sports car races, to build 'specials' without having to lay down a certain number for production. And factories such as Ferrari and Maserati, which already had racing car designs at hand, naturally tended to embody their proven features into a competition 'sports cars'.

One of the most formidable of these fascinating beasts was the 4.5-litre V8 Maserati, which played a major part in 1957 Sports Car Championship events, beginning with the opening round, the Buenos Aires 1000-km. race in the Argentine.

MANY HANDS MAKE LIGHT WORK

'Moss unintentionally discovered that it would move off from rest (with a bit of coaxing) in fifth gear—giving a 0 to 170mph range in fifth! What more could you want?' Peter Garnier *re* the 4.5 Maserati, THE AUTOCAR, February 8th, 1957

For 1958 sports car events, Stirling Moss and Juan Manuel Fangio found themselves driving for the same firm once again. Not Daimler-Benz Aktiengesellschaft this time, but Officine Maserati s.p.a., who were armed with a formidable new weapon in the new 4½-litre four-o.h.c. V8 Tipo 450S to challenge their Modenese neighbours and rivals, Scuderia Ferrari.

When the first V8 had appeared in practice at Kristianstad the previous August, it was not yet *au point*, and the drivers preferred the older, more tractable 3-litre 'six'. But by January 1957, after a hard winter's development, they sang a different song. The 450S, now giving 400bhp, proved so explosively fast during practice at Buenos Aires that the *Argentinos* dubbed it 'the Bazooka', and Ferrari drivers, equipped with twin-cam 3.5 V12s, were somewhat disgruntled at being so thoroughly outpaced. Their manager, Eraldo Sculati, consoled them by reminding them that there was safety in numbers.

The Buenos Aires organizers switched circuits for that year, abandoned the road-cum-track affair at the Autodrome which was so easy for gate-crashers to get in without paying, and reverted to an earlier circuit, the Costanera on the sea-front, which had been used for racing before the Autodrome was built. The Costanera layout was 6.3 miles long, and drivers were horrified to find that it included a two-way stretch down a boulevard where cars travelled opposite ways at over 160mph, with just a line of white paint and an occasional straw bale to separate them!

The course, moreover, was extremely bumpy, and spectator 'barriers' at some points consisted of wires stretched between the trees just at drivers' head height! Despite these hazards, Fangio screamed round in the Maserati 'Bazooka' at an average of almost 110mph, whereupon the Ferrari équipe demanded the inclusion of a chicane along the dual roadway to cut speeds. The organizers concurred, installing a diamond-shaped chicane where previously had been a roundabout, carefully removed to raise speeds! But Fangio still got round at 106mph!

More trouble ensued. The F.I.A. naturally required competing cars to comply with the new Appendix C, but the Argentine A.C. declared that, as they had only received the official text of the new appendix from Paris at the end of November, many Argentine entrants had insufficient time to modify their cars. In an exchange of cables, however, the F.I.A. was adamant, and faced with Appendix C or no race at all, the organizers yielded, precipitating a frantic scramble by competitors to devise Heath Robinsonian hoods from sheets of perspex, sticks of wood, tubing, wire and canvas. The results were laughable but 'complied', although in one or two cases cars would have needed total rebuilding to meet the new dimensional requirements, and were not permitted to start.

Then the method of start itself brought further bother, the track by the pits being rather narrow for the time-honoured Le Mans run-and-jump. The suggestion of a grid line-up with dead engines, then a 'start engines, on your mark, get set, go!' sequence was dismissed, and a Le Mans start decided upon after all.

But when it came to race day, drivers found that the organizers had changed their minds again, and would employ a massed start with engines running. The twenty-six car line-up included four works Maseratis—the big v8, a 3.5 'six' and two 3-litre 'sixes'—and four works 3.5-Ferraris, various independents using these marques, and some welcome opposition all the way from Merchiston Mews, Edinburgh, in two D-type Jaguars of the Ecurie Ecosse. But alas, the two became one when Ron Flockhart hit, first a kerb, then a concrete lamp post during practice, which meant extensive repairs for the 'D' but not, fortunately, for Flockhart. The surviving Scottish car was driven by Ninian Sanderson and the Argentinian Roberto Mieres.

Stirling Moss took first spell in the big, bellowing 4.5-Maserati, rushing away from the 'pursuit' by six to nine seconds per lap until the thirty-third round. Then he handed over to Fangio, who continued the good work, well ahead of several panting Ferraris. It was a newcomer to the Scuderia, Masten Gregory of Kansas, U.S.A., who was heading the chase very capably in his 3.5, until he handed over to Castellotti, who actually displaced Cesare Perdisa, listed as Gregory's co-driver. The old game of motor racing musical chairs had begun again.

Musso, who had taken over Castellotti's own Ferrari on lap two as the latter was unhappy about the back end, now gave it to von Trips. Then Musso hopped into de Portago's car which von Trips should have shared, but which Peter Collins took over when his own seized up after three laps; all very baffling but of no moment in a Championship contest for *cars*, not drivers.

For all Ferrari's driver-switching, it looked like a Maserati win, so obviously superior was the V8, until Fangio, leading Castellotti by a lap, made curious signs as he passed the pit. A withdrawal pin in the clutch had, it transpired, fallen out, but Fangio was motoring on without a clutch until, on the fifty-seventh lap, the crown wheel broke and the 'Bazooka' was out.

Now Ugolini called in Menditeguy, who was driving Behra's 3-litre Maserati in fourth place, replacing him with Moss, who drove flat out to retrieve Maserati fortunes. His meteoric drive from the sixty-fifth to the ninety-eighth and final lap, made Moss the hero of the day; breaking Fangio's nice new lap record by .1 of a second, Moss ripped round, first catching Castellotti, who had been put into de Portago's car, much to the latter's indignation, then haring after Musso the leader.

The British driver was picking up 10 seconds per lap on the Ferrari, sending the 100,000-strong crowd delirious with excitement, but time was against the Maserati, and Musso was still over a minute ahead when the chequered flag went out for another Ferrari victory. Three drivers—Gregory, Castellotti and Musso shared the honours; three drivers, Behra, Menditeguy

and Moss, shared second place; three drivers, Collins, de
Portago and Castellotti, shared third!

Fourth came the Scottish Jaguar of Sanderson/Mieres, to the
huge delight of team 'Chieftain' David Murray and chief
mechanic 'Wilkie' Wilkinson; Bonomi/Piotti in the 3.5-Maserati
were fifth, and a 1½-litre Osca sixth.

Marring the excitement of the Maserati-Ferrari battle, were
two serious accidents. On lap one Oscar Cabalen's 3-litre Maserati
went out of control and into massed spectators, six being injured,
while a few laps later, Oscar Camano's 2-litre Maserati hit one
of the much criticized bumps, leapt into the air, and struck a
tree head on at over 100mph, the driver being seriously injured.
As a result, the Costanera circuit received a real 'slamming' in
the Argentine press, and a return to the Autodrome for 1958
seemed a certainty.

A KICK AT THE HORSE

'*The car? Magnificent! We just stroked it. . . .*' J. M. Fangio
after winning at Sebring.

So to Sebring once again. The U.S.A.'s qualifying event for the
Championship had drawn another excellent entry, although Aston
Martin and the Ecurie Ecosse, both billed to go, failed to do so.
That left the main British attack vested in three Cunningham-
entered D-type Jaguars, one a fuel injection job bored out to
3.8-litres, driven by Hawthorn and Bueb. In view of the depressing fact that the Jaguar Company themselves had now withdrawn
from racing, this American-sponsored effort was doubly welcome.

Naturally Maserati's 'Bazooka', to be driven by Fangio and
Behra this time, was a big source of attraction, but the sensation
of Sebring was the new competition Chevrolet, officially the
Super Sport Corvette SS, designed by Zora Duntov, who was at
one time with the Allard concern of London.

The Corvette SS had a fuel injection 4.6-litre pushrod o.h.v.
V8 engine of production basis, but embodying much light alloy
in its construction, and giving 300bhp. This engine was set in a
tubular space frame, while other features of this startlingly un-
American 'research project' included de Dion rear axle, cast

magnesium racing wheels, servo-assisted inboard rear brakes and a low-drag body of magnesium sheeting, pleasingly free of American 'styling' gew-gaws.

Both Fangio and Moss tried out this car during practice, returning laps of 3mins. 28secs., only 3 seconds slower than Fangio's best with the 4.5-Maserati. Each was considerably impressed, but the Corvette's promising performance was countered by many teething troubles inevitable in a new design.

A full complement of Ferraris, their 3.5-litre twin-cam engines now 'stretched' to 3·8 litres, turned out for Sebring, but the team was decidedly the poorer for the loss of Eugenio Castellotti, who had been killed a few days before when practising on the Modena Autodrome with a Grand Prix Ferrari. They fielded Collins/Trintignant, Musso/de Portago and Trips/Hill, whilst among the independents, Masten Gregory had the fast 3.5 single-cam Ferrari entered by Temple Buell.

Stirling Moss, driving a 3-litre Maserati six, performed his usual 'first away' act at the start, but Collins 'gunned' his 3.8-Ferrari into the lead, and remained there for twenty-five searing laps. Then Jean Behra, taking first turn in the 4.5-Maserati, went past with maddening ease, the Frenchman and Fangio thereafter driving as on a high speed tour, never resorting to the engine's full 7000rpm, but using the car's prodigious acceleration to stave off the opposition without overstressing the machinery.

Behind, Moss in the 3-litre Maserati 'mixed it' spiritedly with the Ferraris, while Mike Hawthorn and Ivor Bueb were up there too, their 3.8-Jaguar going strongly, its 1956 disc brake defects cured by using new-type quick-change pads. By half-distance the 'Bazooka' led by ten miles from the Musso/de Portago Ferrari and the Jaguar. The Moss/Schell Maserati had dropped back, and the sister Maserati of Salvadori/Shelby had been disqualified for making too early a refuel.

The Ferraris were now becoming both brakeless and breathless, giving their drivers a hard time. By about three-quarter distance, when night had fallen and headlights were on, the Hawthorn/Bueb Jaguar had prised the de Portago/Musso Ferrari out of second place, but by then the Moss/Schell Maserati was moving back on to the leader board. With one hour to go, Hawthorn had a 3-minute lead over Moss, but the Jaguar had lost much of its brake fluid owing to a disintegrating seal, and was now braking on the front wheels only (the lessons of troubles such as these, it should be stressed, are embodied in the production models—one of the great benefits of motor racing).

So Moss caught the Jaguar and took its second place, Hawthorn nursing his car along until, on the very last lap, the rear axle ran dry of lubricant. Fearing that the headlights of a car looming in the mirror were those of Masten Gregory's Ferrari, lying fourth, Hawthorn then risked all in a 'do or die' dash to the finish, the axle obliged by not seizing, and the Jaguar took a hard-earned third place. The headlights were not, in fact, Gregory's, but Fangio's, who was just prevented from lapping the Jaguar for the fifth time!

First with the 4.5, second with the 3-litre—a very satisfying result for Officine Maserati. As for the works Ferraris, they were right off form, Hill's car retiring, and Collins/Trintignant and Musso/de Portago placing sixth and seventh, six laps behind the Gregory/Lou Brero 3.5-Ferrari which took fourth place, heading the second Cunningham-entered Jaguar driven by Hansgen/Boss.

The new Chevrolet Corvette ss, cynosure of all eyes, suffered *quo* in Championship racing was round four, the Nurburgring departments. As driver John Fitch ruefully remarked, 'After three laps every ruddy thing fell apart!' but there were high hopes for the car's future, with Le Mans as its particular target.

Now the Championship score sheet showed Maserati ahead with fourteen points, Ferrari having eleven, Jaguar seven and Osca one, with the Mille Miglia coming up, and promising another tense fight between the rival Modena marques.

THE LAST MILLE MIGLIA

'With its great speeds, its high hopes, disappointments and sudden disaster, the Mille Miglia is over again—possibly for ever.' THE AUTOCAR, May 17th, 1957

The atrocious weather which marred the 1956 Mille Miglia decided the A.C. di Brescia to hold their 1957 race in May rather than April, in the hope that the spring rains would have abated. There were rumours of drastic changes, of entries restricted to one hundred only, of a new, shorter, enclosed circuit, of drastic screening of cars and drivers, but in the end it became the same romantic, desperately exciting and frankly perilous race over Italian roads, narrowed by the massed humans on each side.

Chief protagonists in the 'big' class were inevitably Ferrari and Maserati, with added interest from an Ecurie Ecosse Jaguar, a Cooper-Jaguar and an American entry from Akton Miller of Panamerican Road Race fame in 'Caballo II', a 400bhp fuel-injection Chrysler-engined Special of low build, carrying twin head fairings reminiscent of Moss's 1955 Mercedes. So often such entries were talked of but never materialized, but to the huge joy of the *Bresciani*, this one did, and the blue and white car was warmly cheered as it joined the queue early on Sunday morning, May 12th, for Renzo Castagneto's traditional send-off from the starting ramp in the Viale Rebuffoni.

Maserati had a remarkable machine for those two remarkable Mille Miglia motorists Moss and Jenkinson—one of the 4½-litre v8s with a 5-speed gearbox and 2-speed reduction gear, giving a choice of ten ratios to meet all conditions over the 992 miles. Hans Hermann the ex-Mercedes man had another strange Maserati, fitted with a 3½-litre edition of the experimental 2½-litre v12 G.P. engine, while Scarlatti and Bordoni had 3-litre 'sixes'.

The opposing Ferraris comprised two new 4.1-litre cars, their v12 engines giving 380bhp, crewed by Collins/Klemantaski and Taruffi, unaccompanied. 'Fon' de Portago and von Trips had 3.8-litre 'twelves', as at Sebring. Notable absentees were Fangio and Hawthorn, neither of whom was keen on the race, Behra, who was to have driven a 5-speed v8 Maserati but crashed it in practice, breaking a wrist, and Musso, who was laid low with a stomach ailment.

Last of the cars to leave was the Moss/Jenkinson Maserati No. 537, which rolled down the ramp and was away with a raucous bellow at 5.37 in the grey dawn. Half an hour later, sleepy *Bresciani* who had stayed up all night watching the start were startled to hear the harsh exhaust note of a returning car.

It was Stirling Moss, his big v8 already out of the race with a broken brake pedal, after covering just seven and a half miles! Meanwhile Peter Collins led through Verona; Trips led through Ravenna; Collins through Forli, getting nicely warmed up. Behind sped four more Ferraris, but what of the feared Maserati opposition? Not only Moss, but now Hermann in the v12 was out with mechanical trouble, leaving Bordoni and Scarlatti to uphold the Trident with their more reliable 3-litre cars.

Collins was driving superbly, and looked well on the way to becoming the second Englishman to win the Mille Miglia. He led through Ancona, Pescara, Rome (bettering Moss's 1955 time by three minutes). He led across the Radicofani to Siena, averaging 100.66mph overall, against Moss's 99.81 of 1955. He led through Florence, racing on through rain and sleet over the Futa and Raticosa passes—but now he and his intrepid passenger Louis Klemantaski were hearing nasty grinding noises in the rear axle as the limited slip-differential gear began to give trouble.

On through Bologna, Modena, Reggio Emilia and Parma they went, hoping against hope that the drive would last. Eighty miles from the finish, and the nasty noise became nastier, all drive to the wheels suddenly ceased, and Peter Collins uttered several words better understood in his home town of Kidderminster than at Maranello; a great British driver had lost his greatest victory.

Now the silver-haired veteran, 51-year-old Piero Taruffi, took over the lead, though his final drive, too, began making noisy protest while descending the Raticosa. Skilfully nursing his car along, he was passed briefly near Mantua by von Trips' smaller Ferrari, but he regained the lead and swept home to Brescia and to victory at last, after fourteen drives in the Mille Miglia. He won at 94.82mph, and few victories were more popular. Behind followed two more Ferraris, the 3.8 of von Trips and the 3-litre GT saloon of Gendebien. But the Marquis de Portago's 3.8 was missing.

Flockhart's Scottish Jaguar, alas had to retire when the chassis-cum-body structure began to break up when going strongly in fifth place before Rome, while Dick Steed's Cooper-Jaguar and Akton Miller's thunderous Miller-Chrysler were also casualties.

Then chilling news began to circulate in Brescia of a terrible accident involving de Portago and his passenger Eddy Nelson. Not only were they both dead, but eleven spectators were also killed when a wheel of the Ferrari locked up and the car careered wildly off the road at over 150mph. The accident was near a hamlet called Guidizzolo only thirty miles from the finish. A burst tyre was at first suspected, but later it was thought the final drive had failed, as on Collins's car.

Whatever the reason, the result was grim. There was an immediate outcry from Italian M.P.s, the press and other influential bodies. The Mille Miglia's unfortunate past, its long record of accidents and deaths was assiduously sorted over and cited, and this time the persuasive powers of the organizers, and of Castagneto and Count Maggi, 'fathers of the race', could not check the reaction. The Italian Government banned motor racing on public roads thereafter, and the classic Mille Miglia suffered the bitter humility of becoming a rally.

Clouded by the Guidizzolo tragedy and its aftermath, Ferrari could derive little joy from their triple victory, while the subsequent impounding of the Mille Miglia cars for the official enquiry so enraged Enzo Ferrari that he threatened never to race his cars again on Italian soil.

But Ferrari were now back in the Championship lead, having nineteen points to Maserati's seventeen. Scarlatti had driven his 3-litre very well to take fourth position, defying the dictum that 'no Maserati ever lasted out the Mille Miglia'. Jaguar still had seven points, and now Porsche moved on to the scoresheet with two points for fifth in the Mille Miglia, earned by erstwhile Ferrari driver Maglioli.

THE GREEN MUSCLES IN

'*Reg Parnell was almost lost for words, and two Feltham mechanics performed a little dance of victory in front of their pit. . . .*' Maxwell Boyd: AUTOSPORT, May 31st, 1957

In motor racing, few things are more pleasing than the surprise victory. An event which brought a welcome rupture of the *status quo* in Championship racing was round four, the Nurburgring 1000-km. on May 26th, when the confident Italians came up against new and unexpectedly strong British opposition.

A fortnight before, a new Aston Martin competition 3-litre, the space-framed, 5-speed DBRI–300, had enjoyed a successful dress rehearsal on the very fast Spa circuit in Belgium, when Tony Brooks and Roy Salvadori took the first two places in the 180-mile Spa Grand Prix. No works Ferraris or Maseratis had run there to provide a yardstick of performance, however, and the two British cars faced infinitely tougher opposition at Nurburg, one of Europe's hardest circuits.

There were, for instance, two v8 'Bazooka' Maseratis and two 3-litre 'sixes'; while Ferrari, despite the continued retention of two of their cars by the Italian authorities, fielded a 4.1, a 3.8, and a new, experimental 3-litre. The dauntless Ecurie Ecosse were there again with a trio of D-type Jaguars, despite their built-in handicap on the rough, ever-undulating *Ring*, of rigid rear axles and no limited slip differentials. Another Jaguar D was entered by Murkett Bros. to be driven by young Henry Taylor and the redoubtable Archie Scott-Brown, the one-handed driver who scored so many British successes, but was all too often prevented from racing abroad because of his handicap.

Fangio's contract with Maserati stipulated Grands Prix only, but with Behra still unfit, the *Weltmeister* agreed to drive at Nurburg, taking the savage-noted 4.5 round during practice in 9 minutes, 43.5 seconds, fastest of all. Then came Britain's first surprise, when Tony Brooks lapped in an effortless 9 minutes 48.2 seconds, second fastest and 4 seconds quicker than Moss's v8 Maserati. That this was no flash in the pan, Brooks and his co-driver, Noel Cunningham-Reid—nephew of Lord Mountbatten —proved on race day.

The brilliant Brooks was first away at the Le Mans start, Moss being way behind for once. With a strident bellow from its exhaust, the svelte green Aston Martin went out to lead the first eight laps from a storming string of red cars, until Moss's Maserati detached itself from the pack and passed Brooks to lead—and to pull away. With 160bhp less beneath his bonnet, and thirty-six laps yet to cover, Brooks kept his head and spared his car. Two laps later the unfortunate Moss was out of the race, the 4.5 breaking a half-shaft and shedding a wheel.

That put Fangio out of a job, and Brooks back into the lead, so when Harry Schell brought the second-place v8 Maserati in for fuel and tyres, Hans Herrmann had to yield place to Fangio. But instead of picking up on the leading Aston as might be expected, Fangio himself was passed, first by Collins, then by Hawthorn, both in Ferraris. Pit-stops by his rivals put him up to third place on the sixteenth lap, when he brought the car in for a lengthy pit-stop. Mechanics worked on the rear suspension and leaking oil cooler, then Moss took over, now lying seventeenth. One lap later he retired with a split oil tank and other troubles!

With both v8s gone, Ugolini's next move was to pop Moss into the Bonnier/Scarlatti 3-litre, but after a lap he gave it back to them, as the suspension was giving trouble. So the last Maserati was brought in, the 3-litre belonging to Godia but running as a team car. Out jumped co-driver Horace Gould and in jumped Moss—his fourth Maserati that day! to spend the rest of the race climbing up from eleventh to sixth place.

Then Fangio took over and moved the Maserati up another place before Tony Brooks crossed the line, the taut roar of his green DBR1 as clean and healthy as on lap one, to score as fine and convincing a British victory as had been seen for years. Over four minutes behind came the first Ferrari, that of Collins/Gendebien; the Hawthorn/Trintignant car was third, a further one and a half minutes back, then came the fabulous 1½-litre Porsche of Maglioli/Barth, on the *same* lap as the Ferraris of almost three times the engine size! Fifth was the Godia/Gould/Moss/Fangio Maserati, and sixth the other DBR1 of Salvadori/Leston.

Yet another Aston Martin, the older, private DB3S of Peter and Graham Whitehead was ninth, while all three of the Ecurie Ecosse Jaguars finished this long, hard race, taking eighth, eleventh and sixteenth positions. The Murkett Bros. Jaguar was less fortunate, Henry Taylor crashing early on, so that Archie Scott-Brown never got his Nurburg drive after all.

In any survey of British motor racing achievements, much is inevitably said of the brilliant Vanwall victory of Moss and

Brooks in the European G.P. at Aintree in July 1957, this being 'the green's first' classic Grand Prix win since the Sunbeam days of the 'twenties. Yet Aston's success at Nurburg six weeks earlier surely ranks equally in merit. It was disputed with the finest Continental sports car teams over one of Europe's hardest courses; its duration was 623 miles compared with the 270 miles of the Aintree circuit, and it took Brooks and Cunningham-Reid 7 hours, 33 minutes, 38.2 seconds to cover the distance.

It compares equally well with a Le Mans victory, admittedly of longer duration but over easier terrain, yet ironically, though success at Le Mans earns the full blast of world publicity, Aston Martin's success at Nurburg brought comparatively little publicity. Tony Brooks drove the first sixteen laps and the last sixteen, Noel Cunningham-Reid driving the interim twelve with praiseworthy skill, lapping consistently at speeds little slower than Brooks, and never imperilling their first place—yet this was his first race in the Aston Martin team, and his first race abroad! They averaged 82.4mph.

So Britain came on to the Championship scoreboard with eight points, placing Aston Martin third behind Ferrari (twenty-five) and Maserati (nineteen). Jaguar's seven points remained unimproved, but with Le Mans—favourite Jaguar country—coming up, there were hopes of adding to the score over the weekend of June 22nd–23rd.

BETTERING BENTLEY'S BEST

'*Although the new lap record stood to the credit of my 4.1-litre Ferrari ... I am sure I could have got round faster on the 3.8 Jaguar purely by virtue of its better braking ...*' Mike Hawthorn, "*Challenge Me the Race*"

The situation at Le Mans called for very different mechanical characteristics than Nurburg. Power at the wrong place on the *Ring* could be an embarrassment, whereas at Le Mans it was welcome almost anywhere. Good roadholding at Nurburg was vital; at Le Mans it was less important than quick pick-up and a high maximum down the long straights. Bhp, low frontal area and stamina, they were the chief requisites on the Sarthe, and with the A.C. de l'Ouest's 1956 2½-litre prototype ruling now dropped, the fuel consumption restrictions relaxed, and the F.I.A.-stipulated full-width screen now 15cm. deep instead of 20, Le Mans was back in the Championship, the cars were less like real sports cars than ever, and the big teams sent their biggest 'bangers' to do battle.

Sensational was Maserati's latest effort, devised to exploit streamlining to the *n*th degree—a 4½-litre V8 with coupé top, designed by Frank Costin, the aerodynamicist of Lotus fame, and all too hastily produced. It was incredibly low, unusually ugly, but doubtless efficient, its main handicap being the usual Maserati inability to have a car properly ready in time. Stirling Moss and Harry Schell were to drive the car, both rather envying Jean Behra his open V8 when race day brought hot sunshine. A third Maserati entry was the Scarlatti-Bonnier 3-litre.

Scuderia Ferrari's foursome comprised two 4.1s, a 3.7, and a new 3-litre model with single-cam 12-cylinder engine, an elegant new line in bodywork produced by Scaglietti, and a rigid rear axle—a design retrogression anywhere but at Le Mans, as Jaguar had a habit of demonstrating. The Coventry marque, though now out of racing themselves, were strongly represented by the 1956 victors, Ecurie Ecosse, with a 3.8 and a 3.4 D-type, by Duncan Hamilton/Masten Gregory in the former's 3.8, and by two further D-types, one Belgian, the other French-entered.

Aston Martin, hopeful after their Nurburg triumph of breaking their 'Le Mans luck', had two 3-litre six-cylinder DBR1–300s, and a new, larger derivative, the DBR2/370, with 3.7-litre engine. Prominent on the first entry list were three Chevrolet Corvettes, nominated by General Motors themselves! Alas and alack, on June 6th mutual agreement was reached in Detroit between members of the American Automobile Manufacturers' Association to withdraw from sponsorship or active participation in motor racing events.

This shattering decision killed Zora Duntov's Corvette SS project stone dead, and no Chevrolets were seen at Le Mans that year. Such a narrow-minded policy might have brought quick repercussions in Europe, but imagination and enterprise

have clearly suffered for many years in the United States under
the dead hand of the big combines which control their automobile industry.

From Britain's point of view, Le Mans 1957—celebrating its
twenty-fifth anniversary, and the fiftieth of its organizers—was
historic. Italy, however, would no doubt prefer to forget it.
With an open car to leap into instead of a very shallow coupé,
Peter Collins out-Mossed Moss in the traditional run-and-jump
Le Mans start, his Ferrari screaming off into an immediate lead,
heading Brooks's Aston, Moss's Maserati, Gendebien's and
Hawthorn's Ferraris and Flockhart's Jaguar on round one.

Down the Mulsanne straight Collins recorded 154mph without fully extending his car, but the experimental pistons in the
Ferrari took exception to such speeds, and poor Collins's race
was run after a mere three laps. His team-mate Hawthorn then
took over the lead, breaking the first four-minute lap ever at
Le Mans at 125.62mph, while Behra's open-air Maserati passed
Moss's claustrophobic coupé into second place. The '200mph'
Maserati was down on revs., and fastest so far through the flying
kilometre was Masten Gregory's 3.8-litre Jaguar at 178.88mph—
a chastening velocity for a sports car.

A pit-halt after one and three-quarter hours killed Hawthorn's
lead, when sheer bhp had its brief say, the two big Maseratis
taking command until they, too, made pit-stops which were but
the prelude to disaster for Officine Maserati. Moss's coupé began
to lay an ominous smoke trail which, after further stops, brought
retirement after 2 hours 10 minutes with both a broken oil pipe
and a wrecked final drive, through failure of a potjoint cover and
consequent seizure.

Then, calamity on calamity, André Simon took over the open
v8 Maserati from Behra, but failed to cover two laps before his
final drive also broke and the car was stranded at Mulsanne.
Simon walked unhappily in, whereupon an agitated Behra casti-
gated his partner unmercifully before Simon could get in a word
of explanation.

Into the lead, then, went Ron Flockhart's fuel-injection Jaguar
of the private Ecurie Ecosse stable, never thereafter to be displaced by its rivals. The Brooks/Cunningham-Reid 3-litre Aston

Martin motored magnificently into second place by the fifth hour, by which time the Hawthorn/Musso Ferrari had gone out with piston trouble. Four hours later the Trintignant/Gendebien 3-litre Ferrari also retired with piston failure after lying third, leaving but one Ferrari, the 3.8 of Lewis Evans/Severi to combat the British cars.

Aston Martin, however, were visited with their typical 'Le Mans luck'. The Whiteheads in the big 3.7 went out with gear-change trouble after six hours; the Salvadori/Leston 3-litre had but fourth gear left in its 5-speed gearbox, and gave up with an overstressed engine in the ninth hour, while Tony Brooks in the second-place car, also lapping on fourth gear only, did a most un-Brooks-like thing just after taking over from Cunningham-Reid, by crashing at Tertre Rouge early in the twelfth hour when trying to make up time on one gear.

That consolidated the Ecosse Jaguars in first and second positions, and with all opposition save one Ferrari now elimin-ated, all they had to do was to slog it out to the finish, heading a string of other Jaguars. Scoring a remarkable victory for private enterprise over factory teams, the two dark blue D-types crossed the line in close company, Flockhart and Bueb the winners at a record 113.85mph, and Sanderson/Lawrence second, eight laps behind, while—*coup de théatre*—a helicopter dropped masses of rose petals all over the finishing scene and pretty French girls kissed the victors heartily!

Behind came Jaguar after Jaguar, the French blue car of Lucas/Jean Marie third, the Belgian yellow car of Frère/ Rouselle fourth, and the British green car of Hamilton/Gregory sixth, separated from its fellows by the sole surviving Ferrari, the Lewis-Evans/Severi 3.8 in fifth place.

Five cars started, five finished, in first, second, third, fourth and sixth positions! To this staggering demonstration of Jaguar speed and stamina, and Ecurie Ecosse efficiency, was added victory on Index of Performance by Lotus as well as two class wins, and a further class win by a French-owned Aston Martin, making the Jubilee Le Mans of 1957 a tremendous British occasion, surpassing in glory the famous Bentley days of old.

It raised Jaguar's Championship score to fifteen points, placing them third behind Ferrari (twenty-seven) and Maserati (nineteen), although with the glories of Le Mans to sustain their reputation, the Coventry concern could not have cared less about the c.s.i.'s contest just then. But Ferrari and Maserati cared very much.

TABLES TURNED

'*By hard concentration Collins began to close on Behra, but the Frenchman just opened his throttle a little wider, for a little longer, and the Maserati left its pursuer out of sight.*' MOTOR

By now all hopes of reviving the Dundrod T.T. had been abandoned by the Ulster A.C., as the costs of incorporating the safety measures required by the R.A.C. were beyond their means. It appeared, then, that the Swedish G.P. on August 11th would settle the destiny of the c.s.i.'s Cup for 1957. Taking their four best performances so far, Ferrari and Maserati were six points apart, so naturally both were strongly represented at Kristianstad.

Two open V8 4.5s and a 3-litre represented Maserati; two 4.1s, a 3.1 and a 3-litre made up the official Ferrari strength, several private entries adding weight to the 'Prancing Horse' attack, while two Ecurie Ecosse Jaguars in their distinctive dark blue, and a yellow Belgian-entered D-type made it look less like an Italian national event. Regrettably no Aston Martins ran; admittedly they were too far behind to do any good in the Championship, but their superb DBRIs might well have disturbed the Italian monopoly.

The 4.05-mile Råbëlov circuit set amidst heathland and dark, lofty pines, was unaltered since 1956, which meant that it was still rather bumpy and narrow here and there, hard on brakes, but highly interesting. So was the race (of six hours duration this time instead of 1000 kms.) with Ferrari going swiftly into the attack on the Maseratis. Mike Hawthorn jumped into the lead at the fall of the Swedish flag, driving with all his splendid fire, Moss and Phil Hill hard in pursuit. The Ferrari led for six laps, when Moss's 4.5 Maserati went past, while Behra in the other V8 was menacing Hill's third place. It was a grim tussle, with no let-up, but Behra closed inexorably, passed Hill on lap ten, Hawthorn on lap fifteen, and his own team-mate Moss on lap seventeen!

Behra was in great form. Three times he bettered Fangio's lap record, and soon the two v8s had shaken off the Ferraris, already running short of brakes. Moss and Behra chopped and changed for the lead until refuelling time, when Moss handed over to Harry Schell, and Behra, a few laps later, handed over to—Moss! Rain was now falling, sending spectators scampering for shelter, but those around the pits soon rushed out again to see what had brought Schell back so soon. A pot joint in the transmission had seized, and one 'Bazooka' was out.

Keeping up the game of musical chairs amongst his drivers, Ugolini now stopped Giorgio Scarlatti's 3-litre Maserati six and put Schell into that. Meantime the blustery rain became heavier, and as it fell an unexpected adversary came out of the ruck to challenge the Italian cars—valiant little Archie Scott-Brown in the 3.8 Ecurie Ecosse Jaguar, which moved right up from seventh to third place. Moss now gave Behra his v8 back, and took over Schell's 3-litre, and soon it was seen that the remarkable Scott-Brown was even closing on Collins, in second place!

The Jaguar's disc brakes were in far better fettle than the drum type on the Ferrari, but the exciting chase ended when Archie spun in the wet in a big way, and dropped back. Yet the Jaguar's intrusion was a warning both to Maserati and Ferrari, who could easily lose vital Championship points to this usurper from Scotland. Both pits increased the pressure, Collins/Hill being spurred into closing the gap on Behra, while Moss closed on the Musso/Hawthorn Ferrari, lying third.

This car had had an adventurous race, exploring the Swedish countryside more than once as the brakes deteriorated. It also burst a tyre, then burst a brake pipe, leaving it three brakes only, so that Stirling Moss's 3-litre Maserati soon moved up into third place. The Jaguars had now begun to feel the pace too, Jack Fairman in the 3.4 of Ninian Sanderson having chronic gear-change trouble, while Scott-Brown's car, taken over by Lawrence, broke an oil pipe sixteen laps from the end, and ran out of oil and off the road simultaneously, when the driver got a faceful of hot lubricant. The car hit a bank and split its fuel tank, a poor ending to a great effort.

So the race ran out, Behra taking the chequered flag for Maserati, having driven 116 laps of the 145 covered by the car in the six hours, and averaging 97.88mph. Phil Hill and Peter Collins were second for Ferrari, and Moss third for Maserati in the 3-litre also driven by Scarlatti, Bonnier and Schell. Hawthorn/Musso were fourth, the Belgian-entered Jaguar of de Changy/Dubois came fifth, a Finnish-driven Ferrari 750s sixth, and the Fairman/Sanderson 'one-speed' Jaguar was eighth. Retirements included the Gregory/Seidel live-axled 3-litre Ferrari and the Gendebien/Trintignant 3.1 Ferrari.

Now the Championship situation was highly intriguing. Ferrari had thirty-three points in all, and Maserati had twenty-seven, but by C.S.I. regulations, the four best performances only would count out of six events, or even out of seven; that reduced Ferrari's score to twenty-eight, and Maserati's to twenty-five— just three points between the rival marques. The issue remained in doubt until three weeks later, when the F.I.A. confirmed that the Venezuelan G.P. at Caracas would rank as the seventh and final round in the 1957 Championship. That gave Officine Maserati their last chance to defeat Ferrari.

VENEZUELAN ALARMS AND EXCURSIONS

'I ... *kept going and going and just about the point when I really began to wonder where the hell I was, all of a sudden there was a bunch of cars coming* TOWARD *me !* SEDANS *! So I made a big U-turn and went back the way I came and finally found the "circuit" again !*' Phil Hill, MOTOR RACING, May 1959

Venezuela is, of course, a country at the Northern end of the South American continent, specializing in strange things like asphalt, balata, tonka beans and an occasional revolution. But in recent years it has also produced oil in large quantities, thus becoming very wealthy. Caracas, the capital, is naturally the centre of this prosperity, and amongst its indulgences, this lavishly modern city decided, in 1955, to include an international motor race. The first prize included a substantial number of *bolivars*, the national currency, duly collected by one J. M. Fangio.

For 1956 General Marcos Perez Jimenez added a large cup of solid gold, with which that year's winner, Stirling Moss in a Maserati, staggered off gleefully. Now the third Venezuelan G.P., run on a new circuit at Caracas, had been granted World Championship status.

When the drivers first saw the 6.2-mile circuit they were horrified. It was formed out of the road system leading into Caracas, made use of a fly-over to link two sides of a dual highway, went into and out of a park, incorporated some very fast bends, a lengthy 160–170mph straight, and a dead slow hairpin. Marking of the course was extremely poor, it being all too easy for drivers to go the wrong way, as Phil Hill found when he drove five miles down one road and met traffic coming the other way, during practice!

In the end, the drivers, all members of that controversial 'racing drivers' union', the U.P.P.I., went *en masse* to the organizers and insisted on various improvements—'or else'! They had their way, alterations including the levelling of a ramped pavement traversing a two-way highway, which cars were expected to take at 140mph or so. One hazard which could not be remedied, however, was that of slower cars sharing the course with 400-plus bhp *bolidos*, and amateurs with G.P. aces. Apart from the Championship circus, the entry included Osca, Porsche, A.C.-Bristol, Mercedes-Benz 300SL and other cars, also some very large, U.S.-entered Chevrolet Corvettes of production type.

Championship contenders were Ferrari and Maserati only, both out to settle that three points difference. Ferrari put in two 4.1s and two 3.0s; Maserati entered *three* v8 4.5s (the third car actually Temple Buell's newly acquired property, driven by Masten Gregory) and one 3-litre. Engaged to co-drive a v8 with Stirling Moss was Tony Brooks—his sole drive in a works' Maserati.

Maybe it was the Venezuelan climate, but the Le Mans start was distinctly sluggish, a Chevrolet Corvette making the best getaway! But it was soon overtaken by a storm of Italian red, led by the mercurial Moss, Behra, Hawthorn, Gregory and von Trips. Then Gregory whipped past Mike Hawthorn, and Collins closed on both as they took the fly-over crossing.

Seconds later the v8 Maserati was flying in the air, having failed to take the turn; it hit the sandbags, bounced, then landed with a harsh metallic crunch on its back. Incredibly, Gregory crawled out little the worse, apart from facial cuts, saved by the crash-bar which he had insisted on Maserati's fitting the previous day.

That left three works Maseratis. Behra's v8 now challenged Collins and Hawthorn for the lead, the trio fighting it out until Stirling Moss settled the issue by storming past the lot. Next Peter Collins had to dodge a Porsche at an awkward spot, and wiped off the end of the Ferrari's four-tailpipe exhaust system, when charging over several displaced sandbags. 'It's an ill wind . . .', however, and his engine promptly found another 400 revs. or so on the shorter pipes!

Moss settled down in the lead, with Behra holding a watching brief for Maserati on Collins and Hawthorn. But on lap thirty-three Moss flashed down the return leg of the dual motor road preceding the pits at his customary 165mph when an American, A. P. Dressel, swung his 2-litre A.C.-Bristol across into his path, just before his braking point. With some 65mph speed differential between the two cars, the impact when the big Maserati hit the A.C. was terrific. Dressel's car was projected into the air, then struck a lamp post which virtually bisected it, Mike Hawthorn, seeing the drama from behind, believed at first that the two flying halves were separate cars. The Maserati charged on and over-turned, Moss very luckily being cast out, suffering a severe shaking only. Dressel's injuries were remarkably light, and his escape little short of miraculous.

That left two works Maseratis. The plucky Moss walked back to the pits, arriving just in time to see Behra's car catch fire while refuelling. The blaze was smartly extinguished, but Jean's hands were badly burned, so Moss hopped into the seat and drove off. He hopped out of the seat almost as quickly, for it was one part of the burning car which the firemen had neglected! He endured a lap then came in, his overalls and person painfully scorched. Harry Schell then inherited the 'hot seat', but made sure the fire was really out before setting off!

Schell was gaining rapidly on the now-leading Ferraris, when he came up on the outside of Joakim Bonnier's 3-litre Maserati on a very fast right-hander. Both cars were doing over 120mph, when suddenly a rear tyre burst on Bonnier's car, which lurched and skidded into Schell's with appalling effect.

The 3-litre cannoned across the road, smack into a concrete telegraph post, which broke and fell straight across the cockpit, bare seconds after Bonnier had leapt out. The 4.5 slammed against a wall, then bounced off, the fuel tank burst and the car caught fire, blazing into a heap of scrap. Bonnier and Schell picked themselves up, one cut and bleeding, the other burned, both dazed with shock, but alive.

That left no works Maseratis, after as disastrous a day of racing as the Trident had ever experienced. The Ferraris went on and on in procession to finish the 1000-kilometre race in the first four places, Collins and Hill driving the winning car, and making the Sports Car Championship a certainty for Automobili Ferrari —their fourth in five years.

Runners-up were Hawthorn and Musso, and next home came Trips/Seidel and Trintignant/Gendebien. Fifth, ironically for Officine Maserati, came a private 3-litre Maserati driven by Marcotulli and Chimeri, and sixth was a 1600 Porsche. But Fate wouldn't even give Maserati fifth place—a mistake in timing was discovered, reversing its position with the Porsche!

The aftermath of this incredible chapter of Maserati accidents at Caracas was calamitous. Not only had they lost the Championship; they had virtually lost two £8000 cars, with another badly damaged. Officine Maserati rocked on its foundations, and when the F.I.A. decided that winter to amend the Championship rulings and restrict engine size to 3 litres for 1958 onwards, it was the final blow to the Modena concern. They had expended several thousands of pounds in developing that magnificent V8 four-camshaft power unit for the 450S competition car, and now it was rendered obsolete.

In January 1958, Commendatore Omer Orsi, President of Officine Maserati, announced the official withdrawal of his concern from motor racing, thereby following in the footsteps of Daimler-Benz and Jaguar.

CHAMPIONSHIP SCORE-SHEET 1957

Make of Car	Buenos Aires 1000-km., Argentina	Sebring 12-hour, U.S.A.	Mille Miglia, Italy	Nurburgring 1000-km., Germany	Le Mans 24-hour, France	Swedish G.P.	Venezuelan G.P.	Total Score	Best Four Performances
Ferrari	8 (1st)	3 (4th)	8 (1st)	6 (2nd)	2 (5th)	6 (2nd)	8 (1st)	41	30
Maserati ..	6 (2nd)	8 (1st)	3 (4th)	2 (5th)	—	8 (1st)	1 (6th)	28	25
Jaguar	3 (4th)	4 (3rd)	—	—	8 (1st)	2 (5th)	—	17	17
Aston Martin ..	—	—	—	8 (1st)	—	—	—	8	8
Porsche.. ..	—	—	2 (5th)	3 (4th)	—	—	2 (5th)	7	7
Osca	1 (6th)	—	—	—	—	—	—	1	1

SCORING: First 8 points; second 6pts.; third 4pts.; fourth 3pts.; fifth 2pts.; sixth 1pt.

CHAPTER 6

FELTHAM FORCES THE PACE

FOR 1958, the F.I.A. fixed a 3-litre top limit on engine capacity
for World Sports Car Championship events, in a belated attempt
to reduce maximum speeds. Without the imposition of other
restrictions to eliminate the highly-expensive 'two-seater Grand
Prix car', however, most authorities were sceptical of whether
speeds would be reduced sufficiently, knowing well how, by the
laws of progress, makers invariably contrive to extract more
performance from less engine as the years pass.

There were those who asked, 'If 175–180mph on 4.5 or 4.9
litres was "dangerous", would 155–160mph on 3 litres be "safe"?'
And others thought back to the 300SLR Mercedes-Benz, which
comfortably managed its 170mph on 3 litres back in 1955; the
general consensus of opinion was that 'there would be little in
it', so far as speed was concerned, and that all the F.I.A. had
done, in effect, was to put an extra nail or two in Maserati's coffin.

Certainly competition was now narrowed to the point of dullness. Ferrari, of course, would be there, and David Brown's
Aston Martins also, but who else could put up a good fight for
Championship points? Not Maserati, alas, apart from some old
3-litre sixes in private hands. Not Jaguar, their 3½-litre D-type
now a five-year-old design anyway. Nobody, in fact, except
Porsche of Germany with their fantastic little 'flat fours' of 1½
and 1.6 litres. Prospects, in fact, looked far from bright.

TESTA ROSSA TRIUMPH

*'The Moss/Behra Porsche . . . like a dachshund nipping at the heels
of a bird dog.'* AUTOMOBILE YEAR

The first Championship round of 1958, as usual the Buenos
Aires 1000-km., was almost forgotten in the tremendous *brouhaha*

surrounding the on-off-on Argentine Formula 1 Grand Prix, for which potential European participants were given such short notice that it would actually take place, that some declared they couldn't, and others that they *wouldn't* go. But Scuderia Ferrari somehow managed to send cars across the South Atlantic in time, not forgetting to bundle a team of three new 3-litre single-cam 12-cylinder Type 250 sports-racing cars on the boat for the *mil kilometros*.

Generally termed the 'Testa Rossa' or TR Ferraris, these cars were developed from two 3-litre prototypes which appeared during 1957; they had long noses with large air vents each side for brake cooling, and cutaway sections behind the wheels to discharge the heated air. Not the most handsome of Ferrari sports cars, they were undeniably efficient, the 12-cylinder engines giving 300bhp—i.e. 100bhp per litre. Testa Rossa means 'red head'—cylinder head in Ferrari's case, the name deriving from an earlier 2-litre sports model with rigid rear axle, the chassis of which provided the basis of the 1958 3-litre competition model. Ferrari's TR was, in fact, one of the more reasonable of sports-racing cars, having a genuine link with normal road car designs.

Although the field for the Buenos Aires 1000-km. totalled twenty-six, the only apparent opposition to the Ferraris came from several private 3-litre Maseratis, including one belonging to Francisco Godia of Spain, whose co-driver was to be Fangio himself. Stirling Moss also arranged to drive a 3-litre Maserati, but this car broke its crankshaft in practice, so he transferred to a 1.6-litre four-cam RSK works Porsche, co-driving with Jean Behra.

After their 1957 experiences at Costanera, the organizers reverted to the old Autodrome *circuit routier*, the race duration being 106 laps, 628 miles. Peter Collins jumped ahead at the start, but Luigi Musso came smartly into collision with Trintignant's G.T. Ferrari on the second lap, his Testa Rossa being too badly bent to race further, much to co-driver Hawthorn's relief—he having considerably overdone the sunbathing, and being scarcely able to sit down! Fangio began to force Godia's Maserati through the pack, and

E

soon fastened on to Collins's tail. Then Homer nodded; trying to overtake the leading Ferrari on lap four, the Maestro overdid it, crushing the nose of his car against the sandbags. Mechanics tried to repair the damage but the jagged ends of the crumpled nearside front wing repeatedly cut the tyre under cornering stresses, and eventually Fangio had to retire. Another 3-litre Maserati crashed on the eighth lap, the driver, Jorge Magnasco, unfortunately being killed.

The two remaining Ferraris of Collins/Hill and Gendebien/von Trips now appeared to have things all their way, but with the fighting spirit both of a Behra and a Moss in one small but extremely fast silver Porsche, nothing was certain. The redoubtable pair prised von Trips out of second place early in the race, staying put until the bigger Ferrari dislodged them again, only four laps from the end. The Briton and the Frenchman, animators of an otherwise dull race, finished third, 9.8 seconds behind.

The effective Collins/Hill combine won the race at 98.57mph, the American making the fastest lap at 102.93mph. Fourth behind the heroic Porsche came another Ferrari driven by Drogo and Gonzalez (a Dominican driver, not the famous Froilan), fifth were Mieres/Barth (Porsche) and sixth Munaron/Mantovani (Ferrari).

Thus, in this not very bright opening to the Championship season, Ferrari had the lead as usual with eight points, Porsche were next with two points, and nobody else had any points at all.

STROKING JAGUARS IS DANGEROUS

'Sitting right up there in fourth position like a happy ferret among a bunch of geese was Team Lotus No. 56, an 1100, no less.' SPORTS CARS ILLUSTRATED, June 1958

Sebring looked much more promising. Ferrari and Porsche were joined by Aston Martin, Jaguar (two entered by Ecurie Ecosse, one by Cunningham) and Lister-Jaguar (entered by Briggs Cunningham), the 3.5-litre Jaguar power units being 'de-stroked' to 3 litres.

Numerically, Ferrari had things nicely their way, with three factory TRs, three private TRs and six other private entries, against two Aston DBRIs, three Jaguars, two Listers and two works Porsches. There was also a team of three Climax-engined Lotuses from Britain, very fast, reputedly fragile, and only 1100s, therefore hardly expected to figure amongst the Championship placings. Stirling Moss was driving one of the Aston Martins, he having signed with the Feltham team for major 1958 sports car events. 'Lister-meister' Archie Scott-Brown was making his first appearance in the United States, driving one of the Cunningham-entered Listers.

At 10am, March 22nd, the cars lined up on the broad, breezy acres of Sebring's start/finish straight; sixty-five cars of nineteen makes, ranging from big blue-and-white Chevrolet Corvettes to 750cc Abarth-Fiats and DBS. And first away was the Corvette driver who had led the Venezuelan race the previous November —'Honest John' Kilborne they called him ('he must have been in the motor trade' said Peter Collins!). But Kilborne's glory was brief, Moss and Hill bursting past, while simultaneously the Corvette's fuel injection gave trouble, so that its driver earned the unusual distinction of both leading and tailing on the first lap.

Stirling Moss was fairly blasting ahead of the field, pulling out a 90-second lead in the first hour over a battling trio consisting of Salvadori's Aston, and Hill's and Hawthorn's Ferraris. By then the opposition had already thinned drastically. Either because he accelerated too hard, or the Lister momentarily hung back, Gendebien's Ferrari rode straight up the back of Scott-Brown's blue-and-white Lister during lap four. Archie suddenly found his already cramped cockpit full of Englebert tyre and Ferrari wheel, which came to rest on his right shoulder, after rolling a neat trench up the light alloy tail of the Lister! Neither driver was hurt, but the Lister had to retire, while the Ferrari dropped thirty-five minutes on repairs.

Then the second Lister, driven by Crawford, lasted only seventeen minutes longer, when the 'stroked' Jaguar engine, running at higher revs. and with modified camshafts, suffered valve-spring breakage which was to affect every Jaguar running. Next to go was the Cunningham-entered D-type with a hole in at least one piston, and after about two and a half hours of racing

E*

the Sanderson/Bueb D-type of Ecurie Ecosse also went out—more broken valve-springs.

An hour or so later, and the last Jaguar, driven by Flockhart/Gregory, had died of the same malady. Not that trouble was exclusive to the Coventry marque. The lone 3.0 Maserati of Dale Duncan/Joakim Bonnier faded away with undisclosed trouble, the Behra/Barth works Porsche did in its gearbox, and then Carroll Shelby brought the Salvadori Aston Martin in while lying third, with an infuriating trouble. A universal-joint linkage at the aft end of the gearchange-rod had broken, and although the Feltham mechanics sweated to devise a repair, it broke again and the car was forced out of the race.

Worse was to come. Not long after setting a new lap record in 3 minutes 20 seconds—96.00mph—Moss burst a tyre. He hobbled round for over half a lap on the flat, then handed over to Brooks, still 50 seconds to the good on the Collins/Hill Testa Rossa. But now the DBR1's transmission was giving trouble, and when Brooks came in and handed back to Moss at 2pm, Collins was only 12 seconds behind.

A long pit-stop of 3 minutes 40 seconds ensued for repairs, the Ferrari getting well away before Moss rejoined the fray and went like a bomb to make up the loss. The gap narrowed lap by lap, but Stirling had a shock on one round when his bonnet flew off, just catching a corner of his full-width screen and scoring his helmet. Then, after 5 hours 16 minutes of racing, the transmission cried 'enough', and the only British cars left in the running were now the sleek little 1100cc Lotuses.

The rest of the twelve hours was a Ferrari procession, although the Hawthorn/Trips and Richie Ginther/von Neumann Testa Rossas dropped out after three-quarter distance, while the survivors were very short of brakes—as usual at Sebring. Once again the Collins/Hill combination proved the winning one, Phil pulling in for Peter to drive the last few rounds to victory at 10pm, both then driving up a portable ramp to be fêted, laurel-hung and kissed by the Race Queen.

Second in was the Musso/Gendebien Ferrari, and a highly popular third came one of the amazing 1600cc Porsches, that of Schell/Seidel. Even more amazing was the Lotus performance, one 1100 finishing fourth overall, driven by two U.S. amateurs, Weiss and Tallaksen, the other two cars being sixth (designer Colin Chapman and Cliff Allison) and ninth. One hundred per cent finishers in a twelve-hour race over a notoriously hard circuit was something of which the London concern could be very proud.

RETURN TO THE TARGA

'*The competitors have to learn this difficult circuit on the open roads with hundreds of scooters, cars, trucks and the gaily painted Sicilian chariots, cows, sheep, mules and goats, not to mention chickens, cats and dogs.*' Bernard Cahier, ROAD AND TRACK, August 1958

After Sebring, Ferrari was well away on Championship points, having sixteen to Porsche's eight and Lotus's three. The next round was in Italy, but now that the traditional Mille Miglia was no more, that older and even more famous race, the Targa Florio, returned to the Championship series for the first time since 1955. The Italian Government had relaxed its ban on road racing for this Sicilian event with its excellent accident record, although confirmation that the Targa would count for the Championship was not made official until a few weeks beforehand.

On paper it promised to be another Ferrari–Porsche contest, until a hasty entry of a single works DBRI Aston Martin came in for Stirling Moss and Tony Brooks. This cheered things up, although it seemed a somewhat forlorn hope against four official Ferraris on their home ground.

On the opening lap Moss went haring off, but hit a kilometre stone and lost half an hour at the pits, changing the wheel and effecting other repairs. Meantime Luigi Musso had taken command of the race, turning his first lap in the Ferrari at 43 minutes 56 seconds (Moss's 1955 record 43 minutes 7 seconds) and getting well away from team-mate Collins.

Moss blatted back into the race, breaking his own lap record with a ferocious round in 42 minutes 19 seconds—63.4mph around Madonie's mountains! On lap four he bettered the figures to 42 minutes 17 seconds, and had worked back to sixth place when the Aston Martin's transmission—a weak point on the DBRI—broke under the strain, and Ferrari was left ruling the 3-litre roost.

But on this wild and woolly course, where the only straight is three-and-a-half miles long, and there are over seven hundred bends in the forty-five mile lap, compact size and nimbleness have their advantage, and the Italian 1½-litre Oscas and the German Porsches were putting up a magnificent fight against cars of double the engine size. Two Oscas actually lay second and third in the opening stages, but one retired and the other dropped back. But then Porsche took up the cudgels, Jean Behra's RSK passing the Hawthorn/Trips and Collins/Hill Testa Rossas to take second place, until a sixth-lap halt to hand over to Scarlatti dropped the little silver bomb to third.

Out in the lead, Musso and Gendebien were unassailable, driving a beautifully co-ordinated race. Musso experienced an eleventh lap drama, however, when he came late to the pits, completely minus brakes as the fluid had all boiled away! The reservoir was hastily replenished, the brakes checked, then Gendebien took over the car, to maintain its lead until the fourteenth lap and a very fine victory.

Jean Behra and his Porsche were in tremendous form. Resuming the wheel from Scarlatti, he closed remorselessly on Hawthorn, who was finding the Targa very tiring indeed. Three laps from the end, Ferrari's team manager Tavoni hung out urgent signals, one warning Hawthorn to 'Watch Behra', the other telling Wolfgang Seidel, whose Testa Rossa lay fourth, to 'Catch Behra'. But the tough little *Niceois* with the famous chequered helmet was driving with all his pugnacious skill, and nothing that Hawthorn did could hold the Porsche off. Behra swept past into second place on the last lap but one, while farther back, a fruitless chase by Seidel ended in a blown-up Ferrari.

Thus, though Ferrari emerged the victors thanks to splendid work by Musso and Gendebien, Porsche were scarcely the 'gallant losers'. On half the engine capacity, Behra had bearded the Ferrari lion in its own den. Another lap and the six-minute gap between his car and Gendebien's could have been narrowed considerably, and indeed, had a Moss shared the driving of the Porsche with Behra, victory might well have been within its grasp.

The final order, behind the Ferrari and the Porsche showed Hawthorn/Trips and Collins/Hill third and fourth, Cabianca/ Bordoni fifth for Osca, and another Porsche sixth. That made the Championship score Ferrari twenty-four, Porsche fourteen, Lotus three, Osca two. Only Porsche could now prevent the 'Prancing Horse' from winning its fifth Championship.

A GLORIOUS FIRST OF JUNE

'Now, amid an orgy of back-slapping and hand-shaking, it is impossible to look anywhere without seeing scores of smiling Englanders, and who can wonder!' MOTORING NEWS, June 5th, 1958

The lessons of failure at Sebring and in the Targa Florio were not lost on Aston Martin, who strengthened and modified their 5-speed gearbox-cum-final-drive unit in preparation for Round Four of the Championship, the Nurburgring 1000-kilometre in Germany. This year Feltham sent a full three-car team of the sleek green DBRIs, and found themselves up against four Testa Rossas from Scuderia Ferrari, two ageing but still energetic Jaguars from Ecurie Ecosse, plus several formidable 1500s— Porsches, of course, and the interesting new fuel-injection Borgwards—which had no sense of respect and were prone to push amongst the bigger cars.

On June 1st, in glorious weather, fifty-four cars lined up for the 9am start of a race expected to last almost eight hours. Although Mike Hawthorn got his long legs moving well before anyone else at the Le Mans getaway, 'sprinter' Moss was into his Aston Martin and away like lightning while Mike was still starting his engine.

Ten minutes later, and the calico-tearing note of the Aston could be heard coming down the long switchback straight, then Moss hurtled past in splendid isolation. Another engine note, several, a concerted roar, and Hawthorn, Brooks (Aston), Trips (Ferrari) and Salvadori (Aston) crashed past in a tight group pursued by the rest of the field—scarlet Ferraris and Oscas, silver Porsches and Borgwards, blue Jaguars and green Lotuses, in a continuous, thrilling howl of sound.

Moss was completely out-pacing the Ferraris. 'If he keeps this up he'll bust it again', was the anxious feeling of many a watching Briton. By lap three he had a 21-second lead on Hawthorn, and had broken his own 1957 lap record of 9 minutes 49.9 seconds by 6.9 seconds. But where were his team-mates? Tony Brooks had an adventurous second lap, skidding round at the Karussel and stalling. When he pressed the starter, over-rich mixture caught fire under the bonnet and blistered a large area of the Aston's beautiful green cellulose before the speed of forward motion blew the fire out. That set him right back to fourteenth place, but Roy Salvadori was even less lucky, the gear-selector mechanism breaking on his third lap, compelling retirement.

So Moss had to 'go it alone'—which he did very capably, building up a 60-second lead before handing over to co-driver Jack Brabham. The Australian was a newcomer to the Aston team, and also to the Nurburgring, being able to turn only four practice rounds in the DBRI—an unenviable position for the man who was to become Champion of the World the following season.

There was no time for words at the changeover. Moss leapt out and Brabham leapt in and was away, the stop lasting just seven seconds! 'Just keep it going, Jack—for Pete's sake don't drop it!'— Moss had said when working out their race campaign beforehand. And Jack didn't 'drop it', even though Hawthorn chose to pass him right in front of the pits, before 100,000 Germans! By the thirteenth lap the Ferrari had a two-and-a-half-minute lead, but Moss was waiting to take over again the following round when the real drama came.

Hawthorn crawled in late with a burst rear tyre, and while the Ferrari pit struggled to jack the car up, Brabham came in and off streaked Moss, the Aston leading again! Twenty seconds later and the Ferrari tore away in pursuit, Peter Collins now at the wheel.

Again Stirling built up a commanding lead, this time almost two and half minutes, before handing back to Brabham for a spell after twenty-four laps. Jack now knew Nurburg and his car a little better, and when Moss took over five rounds later, the British car still led by over one minute, despite all Collins's efforts. Clearly nobody was going to catch the flying DBRI that day.

By lap thirty-three, with eleven to go, Moss had over four minutes' lead on Hawthorn/Collins, who were followed by Trips/Gendebien and Brooks/Lewis-Evans. But now misfortune smote the Ecurie Ecosse Jaguars. Masten Gregory, co-driver with Ron Flockhart, had turned a lap in 9 minutes 58 seconds, the fastest ever achieved in a Jaguar of any capacity at the *Ring*, and was lying fifth when a brake locked on the North Turn. The D-type spun off generously, and *en passant* struck a metal fence post which pierced the perspex screen, missed Gregory's head by inches, then emerged from the tail fairing of the car! Next Ivor Bueb's car had to retire with steering trouble, leaving the Jack Fairman/John Lawrence Jaguar the only survivor.

During his final laps Moss eased slightly, but his remarkable consistency was seen on his thirty-eighth to forty-second laps, each completed in exactly ten minutes. One lap from the end his team-mate Brooks had wretched luck, his car being forced off the road by a slower car, a Peugeot 403 saloon, and being too damaged to continue. The usually even-tempered Brooks vowed, in a towering rage, that he would never race under mixed conditions again; like Fangio, Ascari and others, he preferred the experts-only fields of Grand Prix racing.

Moss and Brabham won the race at 84.36mph, a new sports car record at the *Ring*. Four minutes later came the first of four Ferraris, driven by Hawthorn/Collins, followed home by Trips/Gendebien, Musso/Hill and Seidel/Munaron. Two works Porsches were next in, although the fastest, the Behra/Barth RSK, had to retire when holding third position.

Although Ferrari did not win, they were now sitting pretty for the Championship, with thirty points to the fifteen of the runners-up, Porsche. With two more rounds to go, the chances of the C.S.I. Cup going anywhere but to Maranello for another twelve-month sojourn seemed pretty remote.

SATURATION ON THE SARTHE

'*Well, we cannot truthfully describe that as the most inspiring of Le Mans races.*' Rodney Walkerley, THE MOTOR, July 2nd, 1958

Four weeks later the Championship circus gathered in full strength for round five, the Le Mans 24-hour race. Nine Ferraris (three works ones), four Aston Martins (three works ones), four Jaguars (two Ecosse, two private), two Lister-Jaguars and a Maserati were there in the 3-litre category, while amongst the thirty-eight smaller-capacity entries were the inevitable Porsches and Lotuses to hustle and ruffle the dignity of some of their larger rivals.

With such incredible swiftness did Stirling Moss get going at the 4pm release that those in pursuit forgot to stage their usual opening 'Grand Prix', and apart from a spasmodic flare-up between Hawthorn and von Trips in Ferraris and Brooks's Aston Martin, the race quickly settled down.

The skies were blue and sunny, but this was mere meteorological treachery, covering the marshalling of stormy battalions. The first two hours brought some drastic eliminations, beginning, most astonishingly, with those Le Mans paragons, the Ecurie Ecosse Jaguars. One, the Sanderson/Lawrence car, went out after just two laps, while the Fairman/Gregory car followed suit on lap four, both with damaged pistons! On lap fourteen the Allison/Graham Hill 2-litre Lotus retired with cooling trouble, and after two hours came the biggest blow for Britain, when the leading Aston Martin broke a connecting rod, leaving Moss to walk home.

He reached his pit just in time, for heavy clouds rolled up, a sinister twilight fell, and suddenly there came a torrential downpour of rain, flooding the course within seconds, and sending spectators scrambling frantically for shelter, while drenched drivers floundered round unhappily at reduced speed, fruitlessly wiping their goggles with their hands, or pulling in for vizors. When that first rainstorm eased off, there were three cars less in the race—Charles's Jaguar, a French-owned Lotus and a Panhard, all involved in a mêlée at Arnage.

So now it was Ferrari first and second, Gendebien/Hill

ahead and both showing a superb surefootedness under the trickiest of conditions. Another who motored magnificently was the exuberant Duncan Hamilton in his own Jaguar, who put on speed regardless of the conditions, passing first the Hawthorn/ Collins Ferrari into fourth place, then displacing the Brooks/ Trintignant Aston Martin from third.

But others were not so surefooted. As night fell, track conditions became trickier. Out went the Bianchi/Mairesse Ferrari— upside down at Mulsanne. Out went the Lewis-Evans/Salvadori Aston Martin after a dizzy series of spins on the Dunlop Bridge curve past the pits; out went a Stanguellini, a Lotus and an Alfa Romeo, all after accidents. Then 'Jean Marie's' D-type Jaguar and Bruce Kessler's Ferrari contacted near the Dunlop Bridge, both crashing; Kessler's car caught fire and was burnt out, while poor 'Jean Marie' was fatally injured. Out went another Lotus and a 2-litre Ferrari after colliding under the same bridge. Out, for mechanical reasons, went the Rouselle/Dubois Lister-Jaguar and the Gomez Mena/Drogo Ferrari.

Meanwhile, Ivor Bueb in Hamilton's Jaguar was carrying on the good work of harassing the Ferraris, passing Trips/Seidel, then closing spectacularly on Gendebien, to pass into the lead on lap ninety-three. Ferrari and Jaguar bickered awhile until Bueb pitted, then Gendebien moved ahead once again. Next, Seidel ditched his Ferrari at Arnage, much to the annoyance of co-driver von Trips, letting the Brooks/Trintignant Aston Martin up into third place.

By midnight only twenty-nine of the fifty-seven starters remained. An hour later there were twenty-eight, the Hawthorn/ Collins Ferrari departing with clutch trouble. Then the rain stopped and Phil Hill took over the leading car, speeding up through the night and steadily drawing away from the Jaguar. By the time a grey, watery dawn broke, he was three minutes ahead, and one of the Italian cars' most dangerous opponents, the Brooks/Trintignant Aston Martin, had retired with transmission failure. That was the last works DBRI, and now all Feltham's hopes were vested in the privately-owned, four-year-old DB3S of Peter and Graham Whitehead, lying fourth behind the Behra/Herrmann 1600 Porsche.

Now the rain teemed down again, to depress the morning influx of spectators and the weather-weary drivers, but the Whiteheads, urged on by the Aston pits, were motoring hard and brought the DB3S on to the same lap as the Porsche by 8 o'clock. Soon brake trouble struck the German car and the Aston moved into third place. Scorching back into the race, Behra indignantly caught it again, but the Porsche then lost a further four and three-quarter minutes at the pits, and the Whiteheads were unassailably third.

At 11am came more rain, lashing down with an accompaniment of thunder, and with it came Fate's last blow at the British cars. Coming up to pass a slower car in blinding spray, Duncan Hamilton left the road at Arnage at about 120mph, damaging himself and his Jaguar, which skated round and round for about 150 yards before hitting a bank. That meant Aston Martin were now second—a place they had occupied for the third year running!—while the Gendebien/Hill Ferrari soft-pedalled the last hours to victory, thirteen laps ahead, at 102.88mph.

A tremendous effort by Behra took his Porsche back from fifth to third place at the finish, while Porsches were also fourth and fifth, and a Belgian-entered Ferrari sixth. Heroic was the effort of Bruce Halford and Brian Naylor in their Lister-Jaguar, which developed serious gearbox trouble when lying sixth; they drove the last four hours in third gear, to finish fifteenth. In all there were twenty finishers in one of the dreariest and most uncomfortable Le Mans races for years.

Now Automobili Ferrari had their fifth World Sports Car Championship in the bag. Taking their four best performances, they already had four outright wins at eight points each, i.e. thirty-two points, whereas their closest competitor, Porsche, had eighteen. With but one qualifying round to go, the C.S.I. Cup was already won—which, as it happened, was bad luck for the final event. This was the twenty-third Tourist Trophy race, held, not at Dundrod of fond and feared memory, but at Goodwood.

THE T.T. RETURNS

'This was never an exciting race but for Aston Martin it was a magnificent achievement.' AUTOCOURSE, November 1958

When it became obvious that the Dundrod circuit in Northern Ireland would not be used again for motor racing, owing to the heavy cost of the required modifications, the British Automobile Racing Club and the Duke of Richmond and Gordon, a lifelong motor-racing enthusiast, took steps to revive Britain's Championship-race, the Tourist Trophy, at Goodwood in Sussex.

The idea of this classic British race being moved from a 7.4-mile road course in its old home, Ulster, to a 2.4-mile airfield circuit, no matter how refined, seemed appalling at first, but the Club rightly considered it was better than letting a great race lapse into obscurity and lose its international status. Goodwood had excellent facilities, and had already staged three nine-hour sports car races successfully, the venue was readily accessible from all parts of the country, while valuable sponsorship from a newspaper had been secured.

So the British Automobile R.C. went ahead, and with the cancellation of the Venezuelan G.P., the 1958 T.T. at Goodwood on September 13th became the final round of the World Sports Car Championship. It was to be of four hour's duration only, which meant, under C.S.I. rules, that fewer points would be earned than in full distance (i.e. 1000-kilometre or 6-hour) races the T.T.-winning marque getting four points; second, three; third, two; and fourth, one. This was purely academic so far as the Championship winner was concerned, since Ferrari was now untouchable, but it could well alter the second and third placings.

Ferrari had entered one works car only, for Mike Hawthorn to drive, while Ecurie Nationale Belge nominated another Ferrari for Rouselle/Bianchi. The other 3-litre class contenders comprised three DBRI Aston Martins, two Ecurie Ecosse entries (one a Tojeiro, the other a Lister, both Jaguar-powered), three other Lister-Jaguars, one from Belgium, and two private Jaguars.

Then disillusion began. Ferrari said they couldn't come owing to lack of a co-driver for Hawthorn. Certainly the tragic death of Luigi Musso at Rheims and Peter Collins at Nurburgring had hit the Scuderia hard, while von Trips had hurt himself at Monza, Phil Hill was back in California, and Gendebien was busy winning the Tour de France. One feels that, had the Championship been at all in doubt, Ferrari would have found drivers quickly enough, but as it was, they withdrew, to everyone's regret.

Then the Belgians were unable to bring their Ferrari and Lister over, and the Ecurie Ecosse withdrew their Tojeiro and Lister entries, substituting just one veteran D-type Jaguar. A works Osca and a 2-litre Ferrari were also scratched so that, apart from Behra/Barth and de Beaufort/Heins in the two Porsches, every driver and every car in the race was British.

As the only make to have vanquished Ferrari during 1958, the Aston Martins were not surprisingly the fastest cars in the race. They led from start to finish, giving the British crowd an impressive demonstration of their performance. Stirling Moss and Tony Brooks drove a model race together, winning at 88.33mph from team-mates Salvadori/Brabham and Shelby/Lewis-Evans.

Such opposition as there was to the Feltham fliers petered out all too quickly. Ivor Bueb's Lister-Jaguar was involved in an incident wherein Salvadori's DBRI just contacted a Lotus while oversliding out of Madgwick corner. The Lotus spun and was hit by the Lister, both retiring while the Aston emerged unscathed. Bueb walked back to the pits and took over the Ross Jensen/John Bekaert Lister, working it up to fourth position. Then he handed over to Bruce Halford, but the latter's run was very brief, a kingpin breaking near the Chicane.

After meeting keen opposition from the young New Zealander Bruce McLaren, in a 2-litre Lotus, until gearchange trouble forced him out, the Behra/Barth Porsche took a firm hold on fourth place, but never worried the Astons. Behind, there raged a spirited inter-Jaguar struggle for fifth place, Innes Ireland and Masten Gregory coming out best on behalf of Ecurie Ecosse, heading that great Goodwood specialist Duncan Hamilton and his co-driver Peter Blond.

Aston Martin's victory in this short, rather dull T.T. brought their total Championship points up to eighteen—exactly the same as Porsche's score. However, on their overall performances, the German make took the honour, such as it was, of being runners-up in the 1958 C.S.I. Championship, a contest far too easily won for it to be exciting in the later stages.

CHAMPIONSHIP SCORE-SHEET 1958

Make of Car	Buenos Aires 1000-km., Argentina	Sebring 12-hour, U.S.A.	Targa Florio, Sicily	Nurburgring 1000-km., Germany	Le Mans 24-hour, France	Tourist Trophy, Gt. Britain	Total Score	Best Four Performances
Ferrari	8 (1st)	8 (1st)	8 (1st)	6 (2nd)	8 (1st)	—	38	32
Porsche	4 (3rd)	4 (3rd)	6 (2nd)	1 (6th)	4 (3rd)	*1 (4th)	20	18
Aston Martin	—	—	—	8 (1st)	6 (2nd)	*4 (1st)	18	18
Lotus	—	3 (4th)	—	—	—	—	3	3
Osca	—	—	2 (5th)	—	—	—	2	2

SCORING: First 8 points; second 6pts.; third 4pts.; fourth 3pts.; fifth 2pts.; sixth 1pt.

*NOTE.—T.T. Race of only 4 hours' duration, therefore fewer points awarded by F.I.A. regulation.
SCORING: First 4 points; second 3pts.; third 2pts.; fourth 1pt.

CHAPTER 7

FERRARIS MEET THEIR MATCH

No ARGENTINIAN *Temporada*—that was the first news concerning the Sports Car Championship of 1959. Already in the previous autumn the City of Buenos Aires had intimated that there would be no money available for the annual three-race programme in the New Year. Thus both the Grand Prix and sports car seasons reverted to the pre-war habit of starting in the spring, which in many ways was no bad thing at all. Instead of the Buenos Aires 1000-kilometre race, then, round one of the contest for the Coupe de la Commission Sportive became the Sebring 12-hour race on March 21st.

UNSEASONABLE SEBRING

'Rain! In Florida! What do they think they're up to!' (The late Ivor Bueb)

The Championship 'circus', when it gathered at Sebring, was seen to be lamentably sparse and colourless, with many of the old faces absent. Considerable changes had been made in the Ferrari team, for besides the loss of Collins and Musso, poor Mike Hawthorn had met his death on the Guildford By-pass, three weeks after announcing his retirement from motor racing. Now there were new names on the Scuderia strength—Jean Behra, Cliff Allison, Dan Gurney the promising American driver, also Chuck Daigh of Scarab fame, who had been 'borrowed' for Sebring only.

Opposition to Ferrari was weak, although Stirling Moss and Ivor Bueb formed an interesting new combination in the latest disc-braked Lister-Jaguar with revised bodywork designed by aerodynamics expert Frank Costin. Two other Listers also ran, driven by Americans, all three entered by Briggs Cunningham, and using 2·4-litre Jaguar engines enlarged to 3 litres.

Aston Martin were there, but less than half-heartedly, since David Brown had decided the team should concentrate on Le Mans and ignore other Championship races, Feltham now being preoccupied with their new Grand Prix car. Thus only one DBRI ran at Sebring, in the hands of Roy Salvadori and Carroll Shelby, while Porsche put in Trips/Bonnier and Fitch/Barth to spur their 3-litre rivals along. Amongst numerous independent Ferrari entrants was Lance Reventlow, whose own highly success-ful Chevrolet-engined Scarab sports-racing cars were oversize for a c.s.i. Championship event.

The race was somewhat depressing, because of the weather and lack of excitement. Rain poured down, most unseasonably, through most of practice and much of the race, catching out many Americans who don't expect that sort of thing in Florida. Not many laps were run before it became obvious that Ferrari had found a lot more steam for their latest, much better looking Testa Rossa VI2s, fitted at last with disc brakes. Roy Salvadori executed a magnificent Moss-like Le Mans start and roared away into the lead with the green DBRI, but soon his clutch began to give trouble, and he was quickly overwhelmed by Italian red.

First Gurney, then Behra overtook him, followed by the Listers of Walt Hansgen and Ivor Bueb, and soon the Aston dropped right back. Shelby took over from Salvadori for a spell, but he was forced to retire when the gear lever, suffering under clutchless gearchanging, broke right off.

Sebring's harsh demands on transmissions also took its toll on the Phil Hill/Gendebien Ferrari, which chewed up its final drive, and now Lister moved in to stir up the Italians awhile, Stirling Moss, taking over from Ivor Bueb, began gaining fast, soon taking the position he likes best—the lead—from Jean Behra's Ferrari. His pleasure was regrettably brief, however, for the squat blue-and-white car ran out of fuel on the far side of the 5.2-mile circuit. It was a long walk back, so Moss borrowed a ride on a motor-cycle, thereby incurring disqualification for receiving outside assistance.

So Ferrari had things their way again, and apart from routine stops, the Italian cars just went on and on and on, through pelting rain and watery shine, through a magnificent evening rainbow, and on into the night and the relief of the 10pm finish. *Regenmeisters* Hill and Gendebien took over the Gurney/Daigh car after their own retired, so that even without the Argentine 1000-km. 1959 still had its four-driver/one car victory. Behra/ Allison had trouble with their disc brakes, and had to pull out all the stops to shift the inevitable Porsche which had nosed into second place, Cliff Allison making the fastest lap.

Between them, Porsche and Ferrari occupied the first eleven places at the finish, von Trips and Bonnier taking third with their 1600RSK, Sesslar/Holbert and Fitch/Barth placing fourth and fifth, and the Reventlow/Martin Ferrari sixth. The two remaining Lister-Jaguars, dogged by diverse troubles, got home twelfth and fifteenth, Stirling Moss taking over the latter car awhile from Briggs Cunningham and Russ Boss, rather than remain inactive in the pits.

The Championship opening score, then, was Ferrari first as usual, with eight points, Porsche second with four, and nobody else in the running—so far.

THE OLD ORDER CHANGETH

'. . . *how could one enthuse when the winner was known in advance ?*' THE AUTOCAR, May 29th, 1959

Two months after Sebring, on May 24th, Championship round two, the wildly contrasting Targa Florio, took place. There was no Cavaliere Vicenzo Florio to greet the competitors this year, the founder of this unique Sicilian race having died early in the year. But one of Florio's last requests was that his race should be continued, and his twenty-six-year-old grandson Vicenzo Paladino, Signora Florio, and a local committee, had taken up the torch and organized the race in its traditional pattern as the last of the real road races.

No Aston Martin turned up this time; the only British car was a plucky little Austin Healey Sprite driven by Tommy Wisdom and the French photographer Bernard Cahier. But in the Championship class Ferrari, of course, were present in force, with Gendebien/Hill, Allison/Gurney and Behra, co-driving with Tony Brooks, who had also joined Scuderia Ferrari that season.

For this particular race, Behra was probably wishing he had his mount of the previous year, the RSK Porsche, in which he had finished second to Ferrari. He, better than any other of Porsche's rivals, knew of the splendid compromise between power, handling and road holding in the little silver 'bombs' from Germany; now that they had even more power and improved rear suspension, there was little peace in prospect for him or any other Ferrari drivers.

There was no Le Mans-style start in the Targa; the roads weren't wide enough for such indulgences. Instead the fifty cars drew up in single file, to be dispatched class by class, one car each half-minute from 5am—an uncharitable hour, but unavoidable with fourteen laps to be covered this year, requiring twelve hours and more for all categories to complete the distance.

Giving an insight into his ability and that of the prototype Le Mans Ferrari, with six Weber carburetters and a reputed 330bhp under its bonnet, Dan Gurney led the opening lap on time by 8 seconds from the more experienced Behra. But the Porsches were massing behind them, and already disaster had struck at Ferrari when Gendebien's 3-litre broke its differential housing, due to Madonie's heavy calls on bottom and second gear, and Cabianca's new 2-litre v6 'Dino' Ferrari also dropped out with transmission failure.

The second long lap and, to Tavano's consternation, Joakim Bonnier the bearded Swede, in his Porsche, was picking up rapidly on Behra and Gurney; by the third round he was leading by fourteen seconds! Soon the taciturn Edgar Barth also took his growling Porsche past the two Ferraris, which for all their 140 extra b.h.p. over the German cars, had nowhere to use the power to advantage on this tortuous circuit.

Still worse was to befall Ferrari. Lap five saw Dan Gurney go out with rear-drive failure as on Gendebien's car, leaving Behra alone to uphold the proud Ferrari colours. Alas, Jean overdid it near Campofelice and the Ferrari skated helplessly off the road and overturned, the driver squeezing himself deep into the cockpit and out of danger, just as the car landed on the full-width screen and pounded it to pieces. Out crawled Behra, to enlist the aid of some peasants to right the car, whereupon he drove back to the pits and handed over one decidedly second-hand Ferrari to a singularly ungrateful Brooks!

With the steering now very sub-standard, Tony Brooks further battered the car against some stone markers, but completed a round before retiring with the same axle trouble which had dogged his team-mates. Every Ferrari was out, and Porsche had the race in their pocket!

Trouble still stalked, however. The Maglioli/Herrmann RSK broke its gearbox far from the pits, leaving Herrmann stranded for the rest of the race. Not even Bonnier and co-driver von Trips were to enjoy the hard-earned fruits of victory, for their 1600 RSK broke its experimental rear suspension when they had a twenty minutes lead in the race, just fourteen miles from the finish—a cruel blow indeed. Their win was inherited by their team-mates Edgar Barth and Wolfgang Seidel, who averaged a steady 56.7mph in a 1500 Porsche, taking 11 hours, 2 minutes 21.4 seconds to complete the distance.

Four Porsches finished the race, and took the first four places and the fastest lap, which went to Bonnier at 62.2mph, slightly slower than Moss's absolute record with the 3-litre Aston Martin. Could victory be more complete? Or Ferrari's defeat more absolute?

An old 2-litre Maserati was a valiant fifth, and Colin Davis, son of the illustrious Sammy of Bentley and *Autocar* fame, was sixth in an Zagato-bodied Alfa Romeo. And the Wisdom/Cahier Sprite? Despite four stops to refill their tiny fuel tank, and a broken throttle on the final lap, they brought it home eighteenth, and third in its class.

Four hours after Porsche had won the forty-third Targa Florio, they finally collected Hans Herrmann in his stranded RSK. He had elected to stay by it, rather than entrust it to the locals, and subsisted on food tossed to him *en passant* by his more fortunate team-mates!

That embarrassing debacle for Scuderia Ferrari cost them the lead in the Championship; Porsche now moved into first place with twelve points, while Ferrari had eight, Maserati two and Alfa Romeo one. The Italians could but hope to retrieve the situation at Nurburg in the 1000-km. race.

HAT-TRICK IN THE EIFEL

'The Nurburgring is one of my favourite circuits' Stirling Moss, THE SUNDAY TIMES, March 27th, 1960

It is a curious fact that the German motor racing public will only throng to a motor race when there are good prospects of seeing German cars in action. Thus when Mercedes-Benz were star performers, the Nurburgring saw crowds of a volume which would practically inundate Silverstone, totalling 250,000 and more. When only British and Italian cars have raced there, however, attendance figures are far lower, and in 1959 prospects of a paying gate for the Formula I German G.P. at Nurburg were so poor, that the race was taken instead to the Avus track in Berlin.

Yet when the Nurburgring 1000-kilometre race was held on June 7th, 1959, a colossal crowd totalling 230,000 gathered around the *Ring* to watch a race lasting practically eight hours. The big draw, said an A.D.A.C. official, was not Moss or Aston Martin, not Ferrari and their team of star drivers, but Porsche, the German marque which beat Ferrari in the Targo Florio, and currently led the World Sports Car Championship.

Despite this patriotic fervour, at the end of the race the German crowd were wildly applauding, not the feats of Porsche that day, but the truly magnificent performance of an Englishman in an English car.

Aston Martin had not originally intended to compete at Nurburg, being too engrossed in preparing for Le Mans a fortnight later. It was Stirling Moss who persuaded David Brown to enter a spare car for the German race, at a time when 'the Patron' could not see beyond the Le Mans victory he so ardently desired for Aston Martin. The car Moss was given was the original DBRI prototype, four years old, and the very one he had driven to victory at Nurburg the previous year.

It seemed a slender challenge to three 1959 Testa Rossa Ferraris, with the newest 340bhp V12-engines in two of them, but the strongest weapon in the Aston armoury was their No. 1 driver, Stirling Moss.

His Le Mans start was 'real Moss'; the crouch, the lightning sprint across the road, the agile leap into the cockpit, and the purposeful roar as he gave the Aston its head, leaving two long black lines as he rocketed away. He was first off by a good second, and he increased that second fifteen-fold by the end of the first 14.2-mile lap. His pursuers, needless to say, were the Ferraris, led by Dan Gurney and Phil Hill, themselves pursued by the upstart Porsches.

After ten laps, Moss's lead was over 90 seconds, and by lap seventeen, when he handed over to Jack Fairman for six laps, his lead exceeded six minutes, and he had already broken his own sports car lap record of 9 minutes 43 seconds (87.5mph) five times. Unfortunately, just as Fairman, one of Britain's most experienced and dependable drivers, took off with a full tank, rain fell heavily, making the circuit treacherously slippery. Like Brabham the previous year, one could sympathize with Fairman in such a situation. By ill luck he had run straight into bad conditions and had to 'play' himself in, yet upon him depended the entire Aston Martin effort. Inevitably his lead began to diminish, while Tavoni of Ferrari, well aware of the situation, speeded up Gurney and Behra to gain every second they could while Moss was not driving.

Yet Jack Fairman still had four minutes in hand on his sixth and last lap, before handing back to Moss, when *it* happened; he came rapidly upon a slow car right in his line round one of Nurburg's blind bends, took evasive action, and slid helplessly into a shallow ditch near Brunnchen. Desperately he hunted round for a lever, 'found' a suitable piece of fence-post; desperately he heaved and tugged and sweated at the tail, levering that Aston out inch by inch.

Back at the pits they waited anxiously. Gurney's Ferrari came screaming past, now leading, followed by Behra; other cars followed, drivers giving the 'spin' sign as they passed the Aston pit. Still no Fairman. Stirling Moss resignedly packed his helmet and goggles into a bag, and made ready to leave and catch a plane, when there came a shout, 'Here he is!' and a grimy, anxious Fairman brought the car in, shouting explanations. Moss frantically unpacked his gear again, donned it, took a flying leap into the car, and shot away to retrieve the situation.

He re-entered the race fourth, 90 seconds down on two Ferraris and Maglioli's Porsche. Five rounds later he was second, six rounds and he was back in the lead! By the thirty-second lap the Aston Martin had 2 minutes 43 seconds over second place-men Hill/Gendebien, and Jack Fairman took over for two more laps. When he returned, with the Ferraris now only ten seconds or so behind, Stirling's legs were in the cockpit before Jack's were scarcely out, so fast was the changeover. Five seconds was the actual time the car stood stationary, yet in that time, plus the slowing and acceleration time, the two Ferraris had flashed past, Hill now leading by twenty-two seconds.

Three laps later, the Aston came past the pits one second behind Phil Hill, and the crowd rushed to the rails to watch the battle. Green car closed on red as they rounded the South Curve; they ran two lengths apart behind the pits, and beyond the North Curve, to roars of excitement, Moss passed the American to lead once again. He went on to score a great British victory by forty-one seconds from Hill/Gendebien, breaking the lap record, in all, sixteen times, and leaving it at 89.2mph!

Third came the Behra/Brooks Ferrari, fourth the Maglioli/Herrmann 1.6-litre Porsche, fifth the Gurney/Allison Ferrari, plagued with a slipping clutch, and sixth another Porsche. Ecurie Ecosse had fielded two of their vintage D-type Jaguars for Flock-hart/Gregory and Ireland/Lawrence, but both cars retired with rear axle trouble. Brian Naylor in Graham Whitehead's new private Aston Martin DBR1 had the gear-lever break away, while Michael Taylor's Lister-Jaguar crashed.

After this great exhibition of the Moss genius, and Aston Martin's splendid 'hat trick', it was suggested that Moss and the Feltham marque should jointly be given the Nurburgring for 'keeps'! Their success against three to one odds now gave Aston Martin a fighting chance in the World Championship, if they cared to take it up. They now had eight points, placing them third to Porsche the leaders, with fifteen, and Ferrari, with fourteen. So to Le Mans. . . .

IF AT FIRST . . .

'We're not far from flat out all the way down the straight' Cliff Allison, SPORTS CAR ILLUSTRATED, September 1959

The principal actors in the Nurburg drama next took the stage for the twenty-seventh G.P. d'Endurance at Le Mans. Aston Martin had three meticulously prepared DBRI 300s, but Ferrari opposition was massive, with three works' Testa Rossas, and eight private entries. Ecurie Ecosse were there again, with one of their faithful D-type Jaguars and a more modern Tojeiro-Jaguar, while Brian Lister had entered two Lister-Jaguars, supplemented by one from the Ecurie Nationale Belge. Graham Whitehead's private DBRI Aston Martin and a Swiss-entered DB4 Grand Touring coupé completed the 3-litre contenders— the class from which the outright winner must come, on the excessively fast 8.36-mile Sarthe circuit. Not even Porsche wizardry could be expected to vie with the bigger cars there, not on 1600cc only, and practice, in fact, closed the issue further, indicating a straight Ferrari–Aston Martin fight.

And so it proved, right from the start, when Stirling Moss gave his usual matchless run-and-jump performance and bellowed off into the lead with his Aston Martin. As the opening laps were reeled off, it became clear that his chief adversary was Jean Behra, whose determination to displace the British car before his countrymen tended to overcome respect for his Ferrari's rev. counter. He made up for a bad start within eighteen laps, and slammed past the green Aston Martin to lead the race. This was exactly what Moss and the Aston pit management, knowing Behra's temperament, wanted.

Barring routine pit-stops, the Frenchman and his partner Dan Gurney held the lead for over six hours, during which time the Ferrari works strength was weakened by loss of the Cliff Allison/ da Silva Ramos Testa Rossa with gearbox and valve trouble. It found several companions already in the dead car park, including two blood relations in the private Testa Rossas of Bianchi/de

Changy and Ginther/Carveth, also the works Lister of Hansgen/Blond.

They were joined at about 9pm by a distinguished newcomer, the Moss/Fairman Aston Martin, out, alas, with dire engine maladies. Its second place was taken by an old Le Mans campaigner, the Ecurie Ecosse Jaguar of Masten Gregory and Innes Ireland, but the veteran's splendid effort ended just after quarter-distance with a ruined piston, letting the carefully restrained Salvadori/Shelby Aston Martin up a place.

Some cars never got as far as the dead park. A Frazer-Nash was left perched on the sandbank at Arnage; Brian Naylor crashed the Whitehead DBR1 at White House and had to abandon it there; two hours later at the same spot a Stanguellini suddenly slowed and was rammed into the wrecked Aston Martin by Jim Russell's Cooper Monaco. All three cars caught fire, and Russell suffered burns, a broken leg and ribs, which combined to end his racing career for two seasons.

The penalty of Behra's early 'Grand Prix' pace was now exacted, the Ferrari developing diverse troubles, including a broken gear-lever and headlight trouble, which frittered away many valuable minutes in several chaotic pit-stops, and let the Salvadori/Shelby Aston Martin take over command of the race. Behra and Gurney struggled on, dropping to third behind Gendebien/Hill, and finally ended in the dead car park with lack of oil pressure after 1am.

Now one works Ferrari remained. But that one was driven by those two heady strategists, Gendebien and Hill, who contrived somehow to motor fast without overstressing their car, which is the particular genius of the Le Mans expert. The pair closed implacably on the Aston Martin, soon to rob it of first place when the British car stopped for a complete change of disc brake pads, the entire operation being effected in five minutes and twenty seconds.

'Let it go, let it go,' said Reg Parnell, as the Ferrari screamed past; he knew his Le Mans too, and with twelve hours yet to go, bade his drivers 'hold their horses'.

Meanwhile the cruel hours whittled the field down. The Herrmann/Maglioli Porsche broke a valve, the Bueb/Halford Lister broke a con. rod when holding fourth place; the Flockhart/ Lawrence Tojeiro warped its head and blew a gasket, and the Graham Hill/Jolly 2.5-litre Lotus-Climax kept jumping out of fourth gear, over-revved and threw a rod.

Then Sunday morning brought an unexpected but wholesale massacre of the usually reliable Porsches. Bonnier/Trips, lying fourth, broke their crankshaft; Barth/Seidel had a broken gearbox; de Beaufort/Heins had clutch failure. Two private Porsches also died, leaving not a single Stuttgart representative in the race.

Now Salvadori, holding second place two laps behind the Gendebien/Hill Ferrari, reported misfiring and serious vibrations, apparently in the transmission. Team manager Reg Parnell had the rear wheels jacked up, climbed into the car and revved the engine in gear. 'Tyre,' he said, and investigation revealed a damaged tread on one rear wheel which was lifting under centrifugal force. A new wheel was fitted, a plug lead replaced (the vibration had dislodged it) and away went Shelby, now several extra minutes down on the Ferrari. But behind, giving moral support, came the other Aston of Trintignant/Frère, a notably dependable Franco-Belge combination.

With less than five hours to go, just when the Aston Martin pit were considering speeding up their cars to reduce the three-lap advantage held by Ferrari, the Ferrari saved them the trouble. Shortly after Phil Hill had handed over to Gendebien, the latter saw his temperature gauge rising, the engine began to run raggedly, and the car to slow. Excitement gripped the Le Mans thousands at this new development in an otherwise boring race, while in the rival pits tension reigned.

Round came the leader, now definitely slowing, his engine stammering, the temperature soaring. Next lap Gendebien pulled in, to climb out with an air of finality while mechanics raised the bonnet, releasing a gush of steam and watching the last few drops of water leak away from a joint in the cylinder block. 'Ca, c'est Le Mans,' muttered Gendebien, glumly throwing down his helmet as they pushed the car away to join its fellows.

The last Ferrari was out, and Aston Martin led. More, they were second as well, richly rewarded for their dogged patience and reliability, in the race where these attributes count most.

Both cars eased off to cruise the final hours—Roy Salvadori and Carroll Shelby, the Londoner and the Texan, eventually achieving David Brown's ten-year-old ambition by winning Le Mans. They averaged 112.57mph, a speed bettered only in 1957 by Flockhart/Bueb's 113.85mph.

Second, six miles behind, came the other Aston Martin of Trintignant, who was suffering a badly burnt foot—and Paul Frère, heading a string of private Grand Touring Ferraris which saved Maranello's face by occupying the next four places, ahead of a British 2-litre A.C.-Bristol and a Lotus Elite. Only thirteen cars finished out of sixty-one starters.

Said Mr David Brown, 'I am a very happy man'. A magnate in the gearcutting, tractor and industrial worlds, he had taken over the Aston Martin concern in 1947. In 1949 he entered his first cars for Le Mans, and Aston Martins have raced there every year since, yet always victory eluded them. In 1955, 1956 and 1958 the marque had finished second; now at last they had won, thanks to well-planned race strategy, reliability, magnificently ordered pitwork and thorough organization—and thanks, also to Ferrari's contrastingly bad pitwork and general disorganization that year.

DRAMA AT GOODWOOD

'Biggest casualty of all was Reg Parnell's briefcase, which went up in smoke with a rather sizeable chunk of the firm's money inside.'
Jesse Alexander, SPORTS CARS ILLUSTRATED, December 1959.

After Le Mans, Aston Martin's Championship score rose to sixteen points, compared with Ferrari's eighteen and Porsche's fifteen—a challenge which the British, Italian and German makes could scarcely ignore. The fifth and crucial round, unless the Venezuelan G.P. unexpectedly came to life again, was the British Tourist Trophy race at Goodwood, and the organizers could be certain of full Aston Martin, Ferrari and Porsche entries, with no fear of Ferrari backing out this time.

No charge of dullness could be levelled at the second Goodwood T.T., as it had been at the first. With the Championship at stake the race proved highly exciting from the Le Mans start to the finish, six hours later. The duration had been increased from four hours to six so that full Championship points could be earned, rather than half as in 1958.

As in the Nurburgring 1000-km., the hero of the race was Stirling Moss. Right from the start, in which his were easily the first legs to move, his pace was terrific, so much so that within half an hour he had over twenty-three seconds lead on the second car, Carroll Shelby's Aston Martin. Phil Hill's Ferrari broke a valve on the opening lap, a harsh blow for the Italians, though Dan Gurney did his best for them by moving up fast into third place, nagging hard at Shelby's tail.

Jack Brabham's Cooper-Monaco cancelled out its formidable speed potential on a tight circuit like Goodwood by several pit stops, eventually retiring, while Graham Whitehead's private DBRI staged a private fire in its electrics on the Lavant straight, but continued after repairs.

Then came the first routine pit-stops, notable for a crafty innovation on the Aston Martins, conceived by Reg Parnell to dish the rival Ferraris of several valuable seconds during tyre changing. Consumption of rubber on Goodwood's somewhat abrasive surface is heavy on the bigger cars, so Astons employed built-in pneumatic jacks, operated by compressed nitrogen from a cylinder in the pits by the mere insertion of a hose into an intake nozzle near the driver's door. Similar jacks were used at Indianapolis that year, while the actual principle was first employed by Mercedes, way back in the 1908 Grand Prix! The total weight of four jacks on the Aston Martins was only 17lbs., and they raised the car off all wheels within two seconds, considerably bettering the time required by racing jacks.

Carroll Shelby's stop for four tyres, fuel, and a change-over to Jack Fairman, took 32.2secs., whereas Gurney's stop, also for four tyres and fuel, and changeover to Tony Brooks, occupied 39.2secs. Brooks lost further time in spinning near Lavant owing to a pad on one front disc brake becoming detached, which sent him back to the pits for repairs, much time—and Ferrari's Championship chances—trickling away while the mechanics worked.

Meanwhile Phil Hill took over Gendebien's Ferrari, Moss

handed over to Salvadori, and Trintignant to Frère, this Aston Martin's pit-stop for all wheels and fuel taking only twenty-seven seconds—a race record. Although Ferrari morale seemed shaken at that stage the Porsches remained an ever-attendant menace, even if the advantage of their amazing lap speeds was largely dissipated in their pit-stops, their five-stud wheel fixings costing minutes at each tyre change. On the other hand, their tyre consumption was less than on the 3-litre cars.

The race was two and a half hours old when Salvadori brought in the leading Aston Martin to refuel and hand back to Moss. Fuel was gravity-fed from fifty-gallon tanks set up on twenty-foot towers behind the pits, the business end of the hose being controlled by a simple gate valve. Bent on saving split seconds, the mechanic rushing with the nozzle to the tank filler had the valve open and fuel gushing out while the engine was still running. As Salvadori switched off, there came a stab of flame from the exhaust, an almighty 'whoooffff' and the car was ablaze.

The mechanic dropped the hose, still gushing fuel through the part-closed valve, and within seconds the pits, too, were blazing. Roy Salvadori leapt out, rolling on the grass strip to extinguish his burning overalls, while a frantic effort to turn off the main tap beneath the fifty-gallon fuel tank resulted in the whole tower, tank and contents crashing down into the flames and spreading them further.

Aston Martin's three pits, their lap charts, tools, tyres, other equipment, drivers' gear and the team manager's briefcase were all burnt, while the DBRI which had proudly led the race now stood, a smoky, blistered mess, covered in fire extinguisher foam. While the Goodwood fire brigade dealt expeditiously with the blazing pits, Aston Martin personnel pushed the burnt car out of the way, then got down to the business of racing again.

The pit problem was solved by Graham Whitehead, who nobly withdrew his own DBRI in order that Reg Parnell and his currently not-so-merry men could take over the pit space and the refuelling system. Then Jack Fairman brought his car in, lying second to the new race leader, the Bonnier/von Trips Porsche, and after a refuel and wheel-change, it was Moss, not Shelby, who hopped in and set off in his well-known role of saving the team's bacon. 'Just tell me how far I am behind,' he shouted as he accelerated.

Over half a minute ahead, the Porsche was travelling at remarkable pace for a 1600, leading the Ferraris as it had in the Targa Florio. But Moss remorselessly closed the gap, and just one hour after Aston Martin had lost first place through that terrifying pit fire, they were leading again.

Now the Ferrari pit woke up, and while Tony Brooks was busy breaking the absolute Goodwood sports car lap record at 94.12-mph, trying to better fifth place after those early brake troubles, Gendebien in the other car (also driven by Phil Hill and Allison) was closing on the second-place Porsche, moving past when Bonnier stopped for fuel. But Gendebien himself had soon to stop, whereupon Brooks, who had handed his own car over to Dan Gurney, took over, some twenty seconds behind the Porsche, now handled by von Trips.

Yet Brooks failed to close the gap appreciably, and as the last hour of the race ran out, Tavoni in the Ferrari pit awoke to the fact that their signals could well have misled him; they were giving him 'plus fourteen', 'plus thirteen', 'plus ten and a half', 'plus nine and a half', as the gap varied on each lap, suggesting to Brooks that he was ahead instead of behind the Porsche. It was only when Brooks himself saw Trips's Porsche scuttling ahead that he realized the situation and put on full speed.

The Ferrari pit crew almost went mad, urging Brooks along faster, but between him and his prey were numerous smaller cars and the two Aston Martins of Frère, two laps behind with one magneto inoperative, and Moss, a lap in front. Passing all these cost Brooks many seconds, and with ten minutes to the finish he was still eight seconds behind the Porsche.

Von Trips fled round at magnificent speed, until with four laps to go, the gap between Porsche and Ferrari was 6.6 seconds. Two laps and it was down to 2.9 seconds, and on Brooks's final desperate round the Porsche tore over the line, just two seconds in front, and second in the race.

Further drama attended that dramatic finish, Edgar Barth pulling up just short of the line, his Porsche's engine very sick to await Moss the winner, while Gurney's Ferrari burst a tyre with two laps to go, and came 'lolloping' round to queue for the flag behind Barth—thereby presenting the Trintignant/Frère Aston Martin with fourth place.

Incidents other than the great fire had punctuated this race, notably when the highly promising young Londoner Chris Bristow, driving a works Porsche with Herrmann, collided with Stacey's 2-litre Lotus near St. Mary's. Both cars were put out of the race, evoking pungent comment from Stacey's co-driver Graham Hill, and from the Porsche pit. Then Masten Gregory saved his own life by quick thinking when the steering on his Ecurie Ecosse Tojeiro-Jaguar failed at high speed down the Lavant Straight. The car charged straight on at Woodcote, but Gregory climbed out of the seat, being catapulted out beyond the car when it hit the bank head-on at about 80mph. The Tojeiro, which caught fire, was a virtual write-off, its frame a heap of mangled tubing, while Gregory broke a leg, ribs, and hurt his shoulder—but was alive.

Final race order was Moss/Fairman/Shelby, winners for Aston Martin at 89.41mph, von Trips/Bonnier (Porsche), one lap behind, Gendebien/Hill/Allison/Brooks (Ferrari), Trintignant/ Frère (Aston Martin), Brooks/Gurney (Ferrari) and Ashdown/ Ross in the fantastically fast 1100cc Lola-Climax.

Thus, with the guarded use of that irritating phrase 'subject to confirmation', Aston Martin, in winning the T.T., had won the World Sports Car Championship for Britain. Like Mercedes-Benz in 1955, they achieved it with three straight victories, easily bettering Ferrari's best three 1959 performances of a win, a second and a third.

There was just one slight fly in the ointment—the F.I.A. of Paris—who soured the Aston Martin victory by their failure to confirm cancellation of the Venezuelan G.P., originally listed as the final 1959 round of the Championship, until three weeks after the T.T. But there was little real doubt as to which was the true Champion marque, and Aston Martin's honour was well earned. Few teams were ever run more efficiently, and few cars were so superbly prepared; the stringent standards of Feltham's competition department, sometimes likened to that of Mercedes-Benz, had borne the richest fruit.

CHAMPIONSHIP SCORE-SHEET 1959

Make of Car			Sebring 12-hour, U.S.A.	Targa Florio, Sicily	Nurburgring 1000-km, Germany	Le Mans 24-hour, France	Tourist Trophy, Gt. Britain	Total Score	Best Three Performances
Aston Martin..	..	..	—	—	8 (1st)	8 (1st)	8 (1st)	24	24
Ferrari..	..	..	8 (1st)	—	6 (2nd)	4 (3rd)	4 (3rd)	22	18
Porsche	..	..	4 (3rd)	8 (1st)	3 (4th)	—	6 (2nd)	21	18
Maserati	..	..	—	2 (5th)	—	—	—	2	2
Alfa Romeo	..	..	—	1 (6th)	—	—	—	1	1

SCORING: First 8 points; second 6pts.; third 4pts.; fourth 3pts.; fifth 2pts.; sixth 1pt.

CHAPTER 8

TOWARDS GRAN TURISMO

THE YEAR 1959, in which Aston Martin won the Coupe des
Constructeurs for the World Sports Car Championship, was also
the year in which that eminent British marque withdrew from
sports car racing. At a gathering of Aston Martin drivers, top
team personnel, and other artificers of the victory who were
celebrating at Helene Cordet's in Hamilton Place, London, 'the
Patron', Mr David Brown, announced that Aston Martin would
be seen no more as a works team in sports car racing, giving as
his principle reason the unrealistic regulations permitted under
Appendix C, which produced cars much closer akin to racing
machines than high performance road vehicles.

In asking the big question, 'What is the purpose of sports car
racing', David Brown said: '. . . it seems to me that it has departed
very much from the original intention, when this class of racing
first started. I would like to see sports car racing where the cars
are very closely allied to what the public can buy.'

Mr Brown was not alone in his condemnation of the class.
Enzo Ferrari also weighed in with some caustic comments at his
traditional end-of-season party at Modena. Although he did not
go so far as to withdraw from sports car racing, he declared that:
'World Championship sports-racing cars are things of the past,
and I hope that this class will disappear altogether. . . . All the
competition has been removed from the Championship, and I
repeat my suggestion, made eighteen months ago, that the contest should be confined to Gran Turismo cars. This is a type
which sportsmen buy for ordinary use during the week and for
racing on Sundays; it is the car that represents the production
standards of its manufacturer, and it is a car that costs less than
a sports-racing car—and has a definite purpose'.

Another manufacturer, Brian Lister of Cambridge, whose

competition cars were definitely of the 'sports-racing' class, and
had scored countless successes in home events, had withdrawn
from sports car racing by the late summer of 1959, his main
reason being 'the incessant changes made to sports car regulations by the c.s.i.', as well as the uncertain future of sports car
racing, and the heavy expense of competing with larger concerns.

THE 'DEEP SCREEN' RULE

The primary cause of these critical outbursts was the 1960
edition of Appendix C, first drawn up by the c.s.i. at a meeting
at Geneva in April 1959, and finalized in October. Again
broadly following the regulations issued for Le Mans, 1960, the
Appendix was aimed at bringing the competition sports car closer
in character to the Grand Touring type. In this laudable aim,
however, it did not go far enough, and one wonders why the
f.i.a. lacked the courage to 'kill' the anachronistic 'sports-racer'
there and then instead of attempting to control the breed by
enforcing complex new regulations.

Apart from various dimensional revisions of the kind which
obviously irritated Brian Lister and Aston Martins—such as the
provision of 65cm. × 40cm. × 20cm. of 'luggage space', forming
an integral part of the body, a minimum ground clearance of
13cm., and a turning circle radius of not more than 6.5 metres—
it was also laid down that the windscreen must be not less than
25cm. (9.85 ins.) in vertical height (former minimum height,
15cm.) with a chord width of 100cm. for cars of over 1000cc,
and measuring not less than 80cm. between the top of the screen
and the lowest part of the seat cushion. In addition, at least one
automatic wiper had to be fitted.

These new rules also applied, with slight variations, to Grand
Touring cars, save that one hundred examples of the latter were
to have been built within twelve consecutive months. But no
restriction was imposed on the type of engine used in the Appendix C sports car, other than its top capacity limit of 3 litres. In
short, the f.i.a. had left the door open to the 'two seater special'
for another twelve months.

With the new screen and luggage boot rules, it was thought at first that the future Championship contender would be a saloon, but this did not prove so in 1960; instead some remarkably grotesque 'motorized windscreens' or 'F.I.A. specials' as they were dubbed, appeared. Obviously the F.I.A. desired that drivers should look *through* their screens while racing, rather than *over* them, as hitherto, which on the face of it seemed a logical desire. But it posed new problems for manufacturers, the great disadvantage being that, in circuit racing, a heavy scum of oil, dust, mud and flies quickly collected on the screen, obscuring the view—and at speeds of up to 170mph, clear visibility was absolutely vital to safety.

One formidable newcomer to Championship fields, grotesque enough in appearance even without the F.I.A. screen, and quite hideous with it, was the Tipo 61 Maserati—the car which greatly rekindled interest in the contest, lost through the withdrawal of Aston Martin and Lister. By careful nursing of Officine Maserati through a stormy financial period, Count Omer Orsi had contrived a limited but very welcome racing 'come-back' for the famous Trident.

The first post-crisis competition Maserati was the Tipo 60, a tilted 4-cylinder twin o.h.c. 2-litre sports car, designed by Ing. Alfieri. It had a 5-speed gearbox, disc brakes, and a remarkable multi-tubular space frame of countless small-diameter steel tubes, which earned this amazingly ugly car the nicknames of 'Spaghetti Special' and 'The Birdcage'. Being very small, low and light, the new Maserati had a formidable power-to-weight ratio and a striking performance, as Stirling Moss demonstrated by winning the first time out, in the up to 2-litre Rouen G.P. of 1959.

Now Alfieri had produced the basically similar, 260bhp 2888cc 4-cylinder Tipo 61 for Championship-class racing, but, being unable to operate a team themselves, Maserati supplied a number of these cars to American customers, including a new racing organization known as Camoradi-U.S.A., which planned to operate a team of Maseratis with the collaboration of Modena, on an International scale.

The name Camoradi derives from 'Casner Motor Racing Division', sponsored by Lloyd 'Lucky' Casner, a strong-minded, keen and wealthy Miami motor dealer, anxious to see America do well in 'big time' motor racing. He signed Carroll Shelby and Stirling Moss, both ex-Aston Martin, also Masten Gregory, ex-Cooper, and Dan Gurney, ex-Ferrari, to drive for his team in various races, and although he had not received all three Maseratis on order by the time the first Championship race took place, Camoradi-U.S.A. was 'all set to go'.

THE BATTLE OF THE SCREENS

'I do not know of a single wiper that can cope with an oil-dust-rain mixture even at 40mph, let alone 170' Stirling Moss

The revival, after a season's break, of the Buenos Aires 1000-km. race over the 5.88-mile autodrome-cum-motorway circuit indicated that the promoters had solved their 1959 financial problems. There was £3500 prize money in the kitty, to be shared between three classes—up to 1600cc, 1601–3000cc, and—significant, this —Grand Touring up to 3 litres, the F.I.A. now permitting the inclusion of this class, concurrent with all the major sports car events.

Ferrari sent two of his latest V12 Testa Rossas for Hill/Allison and Trips/Ginther, supplemented by a 2.5-litre sports car with V6 engine evolved from the 'Dino' racing unit. This was driven by Scarfiotti and our old friend Froilan Gonzalez, who found the call to a works Ferrari irresistible on his home ground.

Porsche sent out a tough trio of under 1600s, for Gendebien/Barth, Bonnier/Hill—(not Phil but Graham Hill, new British member of the German team) and Herrmann/Trintignant—the latter also a 'new boy'. Camoradi fielded just one 2.9-litre 'Birdcage' Maserati, which quickly became the talk of the Autodrome, initially because of its apparently wilful ugliness (nobody, least of all the Italians with their keen aesthetic sense, *had* to make a tail like that, or put round wheels in square wheel arches)—but later because of its remarkable speed. Masten Gregory drove it, setting up some sizzling lap times in practice which goaded the Ferrari team into tremendous counter-action, Phil Hill pulling out every stop and eventually bettering the Maserati's lap time by 1.3 seconds.

But even the advent of Camoradi faded before the big screen row which boiled up before race day. The works Porsches turned out wearing low 'look-over' screens instead of 1960 F.I.A. pattern, of the regulation 9.85in. vertical height—team manager von Hanstein justifying this indifference to the latest Appendix C by saying that Porsche had sent an appeal to the F.I.A. to revoke the big screen ruling, and had so far not received a reply.

But Tavoni of Ferrari, whose cars all complied with the new regulations, insisted that the Porsches should do likewise, while the Argentine A.C., whose delegates had assured von Hanstein that the new screens would not be insisted upon in their race, intimated their willingness to run it without Championship status. Ferrari naturally jibbed at this, and so did Porsche, though still refusing to fit proper screens!

Following practice, many drivers reinforced Porsche's stand, and eighteen of them cabled the F.I.A. in Paris, urging that the windscreen clause be withdrawn in the interests of safety. But the F.I.A. would not budge, replying that 'regulation screens must be used', so Porsche and the others had to give in. It was noticed that Porsche seemed to have regulation screens ready 'just in case' anyway, these unsightly things spoiling the appearance and aerodynamics of the beautiful little silver 'bombs'. They also dropped their lap times by four to five seconds per lap, which could help to account for Ferrari's insistence on the rules being enforced!

So to race day, January 31st, when the starter was that distinguished Argentinian Juan Manuel Fangio, looking very dapper and somewhat thicker about the waist since his retirement from racing. He raised the flag, swept it down, and lanky Dan Gurney did a 'real Moss', scorching off in the Camoradi Maserati to lead the Ferrari 'hounds' of Phil Hill and Richie Ginther—three Americans fighting for the lead, a striking sign of the times. Alas, another American, popular Harry Blanchard, crashed his Porsche after striking a kerb on the first lap, and was killed.

Gurney pulled purposefully away, the 'Birdcage' showing its remarkable speed despite mildly unsuitable gear ratios. Setting up the fastest lap of the day at 103.66mph, he left the Ferraris puffing hard, and when, after one and three-quarter hours, he

F

pulled in and handed over to Gregory, his lead was 2 minutes 45 seconds. The halt enabled Phil Hill to forge past, but Gregory, not yet back in form after his Goodwood crash in the 1959 T.T., spun and damaged the Maserati's tail, possibly owing to shock absorber defects now manifesting themselves.

So Hill and Cliff Allison now romped away, and at fifty-seven laps, just after half-distance, the Maserati retired with a broken gearbox, to general disappointment. The Camoradi team's standard of pit-work and general organization were impressively high, and would obviously merit watching in future.

The race now degenerated into a dullish Ferrari procession, with Hill/Allison leading Trips/Ginther home, while Froilan Gonzalez suddenly stopped on the course with apparent ignition trouble on the 2.5-'Dino'. Had 'Pepe' but looked beneath the bonnet, he would have found a condenser lead adrift; as it was, he retired. The Gendebien/Barth Porsche broke a connecting rod, but Graham Hill, going strongly in partnership with Bonnier, worked up into third place at the finish.

An older 3-litre six-cylinder Maserati, well handled by two Brazilians, Barberis and Bino Heins, finished fourth after a spirited battle with a similar car driven by Bonomi/Milán, whose run ended abruptly with a broken crankshaft. A quartet of Porsches filled the next four places, followed by a Ferrari 250 coupé, which won the poorly contested Grand Touring class.

Ferrari's winning average was 99.24mph, and could obviously have been higher, though once again the 'Prancing Horse' kicked off with an eight-point Championship lead, followed by Porsche with four and Maserati with three.

A LETTER TO THE F.I.A.

After their first experience of racing with the regulation deep screen, the exasperated drivers in Buenos Aires got together again, this time forwarding to the F.I.A. a strong complaint, written by Joakim Bonnier and signed by Gurney, Hill, von Trips, Allison, Gregory, Trintignant, Herrmann, Barth, Gendebien, Gonzalez, Munaron, Seidel, Scarlatti, Moss, Brabham, Schell and Shelby, with Fangio adding his name for good measure.

Stressing the dangers of driving with the screens when they became covered with oil, rubber, flies, etc., particularly at night and in the rain, Bonnier's letter concluded:

'In the name of safety we therefore once more request the F.I.A. to abolish this new regulation and return to 1959 windscreen height.

As the windscreen regulation was decided by the F.I.A. without asking any of the professional drivers, we now strongly feel that if there is an accident resulting in injury to the public and/or competitors, the entire responsibility rests with the President of the F.I.A. Sports Commission, M. A. Perouse, alone.

This was real 'fighting talk', but the F.I.A. still would not budge. Their reply was to sanction the cutting of a rectangular slot, not more than 5.9ins. long, and 1.38ins. deep, in the 9.85in. screen, to afford the driver added vision when the rest of his screen was obscured! This was reducing the dispute to a farce, and after a few experiments with slots, nobody bothered with them any more. The concession actually made nonsense of the F.I.A.'s Rule 208 of Appendix C, which stipulated that: 'If the windshield is broken or loses its transparency on more than three-quarters of its width in the course of a race on a closed circuit, it must be urgently replaced at the pit under pain of exclusion from the race.' Here was a stick to beat the F.I.A. which nobody apparently took up.

Engaged in fighting an even sterner battle with the F.I.A. over the new Formula 1, manufacturers and drivers finally gave up the windscreen issue for the time being, and turned to round two of the Championship at Sebring, only to run into further trouble.

A NEARLY 'NATIONAL' SEBRING

'*Again, Sebring picks the* Unleaded *Premium Gas !—For the seventh successive year, Amoco-Gas—and only* Amoco-Gas—*will power the cars at the 12-hour Florida International Grand Prix of Endurance. . . .* Advertisement issued by the American Oil Co., SPORTS CARS ILLUSTRATED, April 1960

Ferrari, Porsche, and their new rivals, Camoradi–U.S.A., were confidently expected to meet in combat again at Sebring on March 26th, and certainly appeared in early entry lists. But a big snag arose. The American Oil Company, manufacturers of Amoco fuel, were sponsoring the race, as they had, in fact, since 1954, and their 1960 terms of sponsorship required that all competitors should run on Amoco petrol.

But Scuderia Ferrari had a fuel contract with Shell, and Porsche with B.P., both teams declining to use Amoco. The organizers, who in order to secure adequate backing for the race, had tied their own hands, felt bound to insist—'Amoco or nothing'. At this, Enzo Ferrari, with eight Championship points already in the bag, and with several useful Ferraris running at Sebring in private hands, withdrew his team cars in a huff, declaring that he would not contest any further Sports Car Championship events, apart from Le Mans, owing to general dissatisfaction with the contest.

Porsche, on the other hand, had fewer Championship points than Ferrari, so took advantage of a loophole in the regulations and arranged that their new 1600 competition models became 'private' entries for Joakim Bonnier and Olivier Gendebien who were thus able to use any fuel they liked, though with a full complement of works mechanics in attendance!

Camoradi–U.S.A. had no such problems, and entered three 2.9-litre 'Birdcages' this time, for Moss/Gurney, Gregory/Shelby and Rathmann/Koehne, as well as a Testa Rossa Ferrari, two Corvettes, a Porsche and an Osca! Two other Maserati 'Birdcages' were also to run, one for private owners Causey and Stear, the other entered by Briggs Cunningham for Hansgen/Crawford. Cunningham also fielded two Corvettes, and also made a provisional entry of a new Jaguar, rumoured to be the long-awaited 'E'-type. It didn't materialize at Sebring, but everyone was saying 'Wait until Le Mans'.

Two other 3-litre Testa Rossa Ferraris were to run, one for Nethercutt/Lovely, and one for N.A.R.T., these initials denoting yet another new organization, the North American Racing Team, who nominated Richie Ginther/Chuck Daigh for the TR, and those two remarkable Rodriguez brothers from Mexico, twenty-year-old Pedro and eighteen-year-old Ricardo, with a 2-litre 'Dino' Ferrari.

Apart from the semi-official Porsches, however, the organizers had an all-American field for their Championship-qualifying race, with a large proportion of GT cars in the entry. One result was a smaller than the usually small crowd, while there were reports of local motels actually having rooms to spare—the first time ever at Sebring! Somebody felt moved to remark that, 'Sebring 1960 was the biggest S.C.C.A. National ever held in Florida!'

Camoradi suffered a serious blow in practice when Stirling Moss had a con. rod pop out through the crankcase on one of the newer, better looking Maseratis, and he and Gurney took over the Rathmann car instead. The Moss Le Mans start was for once a dismal failure, the Maserati refusing to co-operate and leaving him well hemmed in mid-field, way behind Corvettes, Ferraris and Porsches. Peter Lovely and Richie Ginther led on lap one with their howling Testa Rossas, but Moss was soon scything his way through the field and took the lead on the third round.

Behind him came another Maserati, Hansgen's red Cunningham entry, but Gregory in Camoradi's other 'Birdcage' had poor luck, a piston breaking early in the race. As in the Argentine, the Moss/Gurney car fairly whistled away from the opposition, and by half-distance was two full laps ahead of Daigh's Ferrari and Crawford's Maserati, with the Gendebien/Herrmann Porsche a dangerous fourth.

Soon a thick trail of blue smoke heralded the end of Daigh's racing for the day, while further smoke betokened the blowing up of Bonnier's Porsche in which Graham Hill was pacing Gendebien. Then Crawford spun the Maserati into a sandbank and dug like fury for half an hour to get it out; repairs at the pits ensued, but in the end its differential broke.

In the hot, dry, dusty weather, drivers were finding the F.I.A. deep screens trying but not wholly impossible to race with, many resorting to the use of cushions and other packing to enable them to see over the top! By 6pm, when the Camoradi Maserati had almost six laps lead over the Gendebien/Herrmann Porsche, Moss brought it in, the brake pads were changed, and Gurney took over. A few laps later, and he returned, looking gloomy. 'Diff's going' he said, whereupon Moss tried the car for a round or so, only to crawl back, looking even gloomier. Engineer Bertocchi jacked the car up, turned a wheel, grimaced, and made 'take it away' gestures to the mechanics.

Meanwhile Hans Herrmann, seeing the Maserati halted, put on all speed and was rapidly making up the six laps deficit when he saw the blue-and-white car being sadly pushed away. He promptly eased off again, thereafter 'pussy-footing' to victory. The Stuttgart cars now ran 1-2-3, with the only 'Birdcage' left, the Causey/Stear entry, holding fourth place. It moved up to third when the von Dory/Mieres Porsche retired, but not even one Tipo 61 Maserati was destined to finish, Causey/Stear's transmission chewing up with only half an hour to go.

That let the well-driven Nethercutt/Lovely Ferrari up behind the Porsches of Gendebien/Herrmann and Holbert/Schechte/Fowler, while behind sped four Ferrari 'Berlinetta' coupés and a 'California', giving an impressive display on behalf of the 'Prancing Horse.'

Once again, then, the incredibly fast 'Birdcages' had broken up, their sole honour being a new lap record for Moss at 94.99-mph. Reliability had gained the day for Porsche, who won at 84.9mph, placing them on a Championship par with Ferrari, each having twelve points. 'It was an easy promenade,' said Gendebien, and with the next round the Targa Florio, Stuttgart had every chance of augmenting their score—especially if Enzo Ferrari meant what he said about withdrawing from all Championship races apart from Le Mans.

THIRD TIME UNLUCKY

'Perhaps there was a certain sadness in the Maranello camp. . . .'
THE AUTOCAR, May 13th, 1960

But of course Ferrari didn't mean it; he could hardly ignore the Targa Florio—Italy's round in the C.S.I. Championship. Nor could 'Lucky' Casner, so depressed by Camoradi's failure at Buenos Aires and Sebring that he had declared the cars would not race again until Le Mans, giving the Targa Florio and the Nurburg 1000-km. a miss as the 'Birdcage' transmission was not up to these courses.

But in the end he yielded to the Targa's magic call—and to the persuasion of Officine Maserati, who had worked hard 'getting the bugs out of the Birdcage', and entered one car, besides entering himself with a Porsche Carrera. He secured the services of one of Italy's few remaining top sports car racing drivers, Umberto Maglioli, to drive the Type 61 Maserati. Chosen as co-driver in the ten-lap, 720-km. race was a talented 'local boy', twenty-seven-year-old Nino Vaccarella of Palermo, and between them the Maserati pilots certainly augmented the Porsche-versus-Ferrari dramatics.

Ferrari defence had originally comprised four cars, two 3-litre TRs and two V6 'Dino' models, but unfortunately one V12, fitted with new all-independent rear suspension, deflated a tyre while Cliff Allison was practising, ending up badly damaged in a ditch. Allison, unhurt, therefore took the older 3-litre for the race, sharing with Ginther. Phil Hill/von Trips had an all-independent 'Dino', and Willy Mairesse, new Belgian member of the Scuderia, shared the other with Scarfiotti. Another 2.5 'Dino' was also entered by N.A.R.T. for the Rodriguez brothers.

The Porsche challenge was strong with three RS60s, two enlarged to 1678cc, one driven by poker-faced Swede Bonnier and cheerful German Herrmann, the other by Gendebien, while Barth/Graham Hill had the under 1600cc car. Interesting was the rear-engined 2.5-litre Cooper Monaco-Maserati, only slightly better looking than the Camoradi Birdcage, and driven by Colin Davis, while there were several other Porsches, private Ferraris and numerous Gran Turismo entries making up the sixty-nine-car entry list.

Much rain had fallen during practice, and unseasonable grey skies greeted all on race day, May 8th, the locals being happy to blame this on the French atomic bomb, exploded a few days earlier in the Sahara! But in spite of muddy roads and the F.I.A. deep screen, bearded Jo Bonnier was in brilliant form, turning a first lap in 45 minutes 49 seconds, and leading Maglioli by twenty-three seconds. The Birdcage seemed more of a handful than the sleek silver Porsches, so superbly suited to the Sicilian terrain, while the Ferraris were well out of things initially. Allison lay fourth behind Gendebien's Porsche, while von Trips had contacted a mountain on lap one to the detriment of his car's front end and his lap time.

The order remained Porsche, Maserati, Porsche, Ferrari until the fourth round, when a determined Trips had forced his 'Dino' up into third place, then handed over to Phil Hill, while Ginther took over from Allison. Then Bonnier, too, shot into his pit, and Teutonic efficiency went into action; the car was swiftly refuelled, and Herrmann took over. But Bonnier's hard-won two-and-three-quarter-minute lead soon became a deficit, for Herrmann could not match his partner's pace that day, and soon Maglioli had taken the blue-and-white Camoradi Maserati past into the lead.

But Maglioli's own turn to stop came on lap six, when he had about three minutes in hand over Herrmann. Bertocchi refuelled the Maserati swiftly but when Vaccarella climbed in, the car wouldn't start. Many willing Sicilian hands promptly came forward to push their local hero off (no irksome 'outside assistance' rules mar the Targa Florio!), and Vaccarella responded by pulling out an opening lap in 46 minutes 24 seconds, maintaining the Maserati's lead.

Meantime the merciless course had caught out 'first year man' Richie Ginther, who crashed Allison's Ferrari and walked in. The Mexican Rodriguez boys, too, had battered their 'Dino' considerably by now, but pressed on. Colin Davis in the Cooper lost time early on at the pits, then retired with a broken header tank.

Now the sun had broken through, the roads were drying, and the pace increasing. Phil Hill lapped in 44 minutes 52 seconds, to force Gendebien out of third place, then went round in 44 minutes 18 seconds, closing on Herrmann. By the end of the seventh lap Vaccarella was leading by 4 minutes 20 seconds, lapping in 44 minutes 35 seconds and confounding Porsche theories about his abilities as a co-driver to Maglioli. With Maserati pulling away and Ferrari now moving up, the worried Germans took action. Herrmann came in and Bonnier took over, a determined glint in his eye. As for the weary Herrmann, his rest lasted about two minutes, for he was promptly whisked into the third-place car as relief to Gendebien, who had driven from the start.

Then Birdcage luck prevailed. Maglioli waited at the pits, helmet and gloves on ready to drive the last two laps, but Vaccarella never came round. Up in the mountains the car suddenly ran out of fuel and coasted to an impotent halt before a group of villagers. Quickly they found more petrol for a fellow Sicilian, but as he set off again the fuel streamed from a rent in the tank, made by a flying stone, and again the engine died. It caught Vaccarella in neutral on a fastish bend, he lost control, hit a bank, and ended up in a gully.

Meanwhile Bonnier was travelling at tremendous pace, turning the fastest lap of the race in 42 minutes 26 seconds, only 8.5 seconds slower than Moss's absolute record with the 3-litre Aston Martin in 1958. With the Maserati out, victory was his for certain, although Phil Hill and von Trips behind were flogging the Dino Ferrari round in fine style, finding its compact size and weight far more suitable for the Madonie circuit than the bigger 3-litre. They finished 6 minutes after the brilliant Bonnier, who averaged 59.13 mph (best ever, Moss/Collins in a Mercedes, 59.6mph in 1955), while Herrmann brought another Porsche home third, but was unflagged, so carried on for another lap. So did Graham Hill in Barth's fifth-place car, both weary drivers waxing indignantly against flagmen in general when at last their driving was done!

The Scarfiotti/Mairesse Dino Ferrari was fourth, another Porsche ran sixth, while seventh, after a hectic race in which their F.I.A. screen was well and truly smashed, together with most of the rest of their Ferrari, came Ricardo and Pedro Rodriguez.

Third at Buenos Aires, first at Sebring, now first in the Targa —at this rate Porsche could win the 1960 Constructors' Cup! They now led the Championship with twenty points to Ferrari's eighteen, Maserati still trailing along with three. And Nurburg was next, with no works Aston Martins to better their 1957-8-9 hat-trick this year. Ferrari? Porsche? Maserati? Which would win?

'VOGELKAFIG' VINDICATED

'. . . it was all one long drama. Especially for the wretched drivers, peering miserably through their tall screens and uttering such very naughty words about the F.I.A. as they swirled through the fog at a spanking 140*mph plus. . . . O Safety, thy name is FIAsco!'* Philip Turner, THE MOTOR, June 1st, 1960

The Germans came out in force again, to the record strength of 250,000 on May 22nd, to watch their valiant Porsches grapple with Ferraris and Maseratis of almost twice the capacity on the famous Nurburgring. In all, there were eighteen Porsches of various types running, with three works' RS60s—two 1.7 litres, one 1.6—forming the spearhead of their defence.

But attack is perhaps the better word, for that was Porsche policy from the word go. The Championship contest had now been reduced to probably five events, for the B.A.R.C. had taken a bold and far-sighted step in deciding to run the 1960 Goodwood T.T. for Grand Touring cars only, even though it meant the loss of C.S.I. Championship status. With the strong likelihood of the final round, the G.P. of Venezuela, being cancelled owing to a political flare-up, this left Nurburg and Le Mans only for Porsche to extend their narrow lead over Ferrari.

Nurburg's twists and turns offered the better chance for the nimble little German cars, and their belligerent mood became evident right away, when the brilliant Bonnier was fastest of all on both practice days with his 1.7-litre RS60.

But the opposition was very strong. Ferrari had two 3-litre Testa Rossas for Hill/Trips and Allison/Mairesse, and two 2.4-Dino V6s for Scarlatti/Seidel and Ginther/Scarfiotti; Camoradi-U.S.A. had two factory-prepared 2.8-litre Birdcage Maseratis (the Germans called them the '*Vogelkafig*') for Moss/Gurney and Gregory/Munaron, and there was welcome British representation in three DBRI-300 Aston Martins. Two of these were ex-works, one entered by the Border Reivers team for Roy Salvadori and up-and-coming Jimmy Clark, the other belonging to Ian Baillie, who drove it with the Hon. E. G. Greenall; the third DBRI was Graham Whitehead's, co-driven by Henry Taylor.

The mounting interest in the GT class was accentuated by the appearance of the first 3-litre rival to the numerous Ferraris—the Aston Martin DB4-GT entered by Taylor and Crawley, driven by Innes Ireland and Jonathan Sieff. The latest short-wheelbase, disc-braked Ferrari coupés were obliged to run in the sports car class, because they did not as yet comply with G.T. regulations, while the Aston Martin failed to start for the same reason.

Race day saw the normally glamorous *Ring* at its most depressing, with drizzly rain falling, and cold, clammy mist hanging in the trees and cloaking the Schloss Nurburg and other lofty parts of the scenery. One thousand kilometres—621 miles, 44 laps, of this, driving behind buzzing wipers and F.I.A. deep screens—was a dreary prospect for Championshp contenders in open cars.

Again the Birdcage Maserati nearly spoiled a 'Moss getaway' through a momentary engine falter as he accelerated, to be challenged by Jimmy Clark's blue Aston Martin, which led round the South Turn and along the back of the pits, then fell back. Masten Gregory in the second Camoradi car moved up behind Clark, and on lap two passed into second place, presenting a warming spectacle to 'Lucky' Casner and his pit crew. The Camoradi team at Nurburg was under the sage management of 'silver fox' Piero Taruffi, who had retired from active motor racing after his 1957 Mille Miglia victory.

But the 1-2 Maserati ascendancy was rudely disturbed on the third lap, first by bearded Jo Bonnier, who thrust his Porsche past Gregory, soon to be followed by von Trips on behalf of Ferrari. But no one could approach the flying Moss, master of Nurburg, even though by the fifth lap the mist had thickened considerably, and the famous illuminated lap scoreboard became invisible to the packed stands and enclosures. Now drivers found a hair-raising increase in the number of Nurburg's already numerous blind bends, each likely to conceal a GT car or an '850'!

On lap six Britain's Aston Martin effort was suddenly reduced by two-thirds when both Jimmy Clark and Graham Whitehead retired with mechanical troubles. The Ginther/Scarfiotti v6-Ferrari also dropped out, but now 'Taffy' Trips in the v12 was pressing Bonnier hard, managing to put the Porsche comfortably behind him before his first refuelling stop on lap eleven.

Phil Hill took over, now third again, until Bonnier came in to hand over to Gendebien, when the race order reverted to Maserati-Ferrari-Porsche.

Then Moss brought the Maserati *Vogelkafig* in for fuel after fourteen laps, his lead of 2 minutes 23 seconds being reduced to just under one minute while the ingenious adjustable seat, contrived to give the driver a view above the F.I.A. screen, was lowered to accommodate the lanky Dan Gurney, who then shot away into the gloomy mist. The multitude, now facing the empty pits and fog all round, settled down to be bored when, on lap sixteen, came a repeat, on a more frightening scale, of the Aston Martin T.T. pit fire of 1959, the victim this time being Scarlatti's 2.4 Dino-Ferrari.

As a mechanic swung the pressurized fuel line across to insert it in the tank filler, petrol splashed over the driver and car, an exhaust flash-back doing the rest. There came an orange flash, Scarlatti leapt out, his overalls blazing like a torch, while a great column of flame and smoke enveloped the Ferrari. A concerted rush upon Scarlatti by quick-thinking people (Stirling Moss amongst them), with coats to wrap around him, saved the Italian from serious burns, only his hands suffering. But the car was doomed.

The pressure hose steadily fed more fuel to the flames until the hose itself caught fire, and the gravity tank above the pits emptied its contents with a great gush and a 'whooofff', which sent blazing petrol in all directions. A burning river of fuel ran over pit counters, presenting to the appalled public the apparent spectacle of concrete burning! More bangs followed as the Ferrari's tyres exploded, and then Nurburg's firefighters brought out an immense fire extinguisher which, by a miraculous smother of foam, reduced an impending holocaust to a wintry-white scene of desolation and sullen smoke, all within seconds.

More drama came after half an hour, when the leading Maserati came to its pit, Gurney shouting urgently at Bertocchi and Taruffi, then clambering out. Was this the end of another Birdcage effort? The answer meant much to Porsche and Ferrari, denied victory as long as the Camoradi car ran well, But the Maserati mechanics were slaving away at the engine.

renewing a broken oil pipe, while another wiped the pedals, cockpit floor and the inside of the screen clean of much surplus lubricant.

Then came the rising whine of a V12, and Phil Hill burst out of the mist, slammed past, and disappeared into the murky distance; next came the deep beat of a Porsche and Gendebien went through. Then another Ferrari, that of Allison/Mairesse, tore by, and when at last Dan Gurney climbed in and shot back into the race, 5 minutes 16 seconds had ticked by, and the Maserati was a mere fourth.

It looked like a 'Moss job' to recover all that lost distance, and pundits shook their heads on noting that Gurney was still at the wheel. But the Californian's subsequent drive established his truly remarkable prowess in motor racing. Forcing on through that maddening mist, he overtook his rivals one by one, never putting a wheel wrong as was so fatally easy in such greasy, murky conditions under duress of making up lost time. On lap twenty Gurney was 3 minutes 35 seconds behind the leading Ferrari; by lap twenty-eight, aided by Ferrari and Porsche pit-stops to change drivers, he was back in the lead! Two laps later, when 9 seconds ahead of his compatriot Phil Hill, he swept back into the pits and handed over to Moss.

The stop lasted just over one minute, the Maserati rejoining the race third, the leader now being Bonnier, who, thanks to smart pit-work by Porsche and his own ability, had got the better of von Trips in the Phil Hill Ferrari. And Trips, moreover, was in trouble, suddenly dropping back and stopping with mechanical malaise while the tempestuous Moss snarled past.

By the time Ferrari realized that their best car was out, the Porsche was well ahead. With Championship points at stake, Tavoni moved swiftly. Lying fourth behind Bonnier, Moss and the Herrmann/Trintignant Porsche was the Allison/Mairesse Ferrari. Mairesse promptly got the 'come in' signal, Phil Hill leapt in, and went off like a scalded cat.

Seven laps from the end, with the fog thinning slightly, Stirling Moss set up the fastest round of the day in 9 minutes 37 seconds, and caught Bonnier's game Porsche, to lead again for Camoradi until the finish of a dramatic, exhausting race, while Phil Hill stormed past Trintignant into third place, snatching a vital extra Championship point for Ferrari. Gregory/Munaron in the second Camoradi Maserati also finished, taking fifth place when Barth's Porsche went off the road near the end. Maserati's '1960 luck' had certainly changed for the better!

Porsches were also sixth and seventh, the latter an Abarth-modified model with Porsche-designed disc brakes. The sole surviving Aston Martin placed twenty-second—a slight change from 1957, 1958 and 1959!

The 1960 Nurburg 1000-km. was not only a striking victory for the new Maserati, for Dan Gurney and for Moss (it was his fourth joint win in this race!); it also stands out as a great victory for an American team, under the most taxing conditions. As one of 'Lucky' Casner's pit helpers later remarked, 'Jeez, what a motor race that was—if only we coulda seen it!'

Second place for Porsche was gratifying for the crowd, placing the German marque four points ahead of Ferrari for the C.S.I. Cup with twenty-six to twenty-two, while Maserati now had eleven. But with one race to go, unless the Venezuelan G.P. suddenly materialized, it rested between Porsche and Ferrari alone. So to Le Mans.

A FINE DAY—FOR SOME

'So when it started to rain during practice, my first thought was that I would like to take everyone in the C.S.I. who had voted for the present high screen for a quick lap around the circuit, so that he would be aware of the responsibility he had undertaken.' Paul Frère, THE AUTOCAR, July 29th, 1960

Le Mans, 1960, lasted over three times as long as the Nurburgring 1000-km. race, yet was scarcely a third as interesting. Technically, its main significance was the appearance of the new Jaguar originally entered for Sebring; this was not a works entry, but developed by Coventry for that great American enthusiast, Briggs S. Cunningham. A logical evolution of the D-type, and popularly but erroneously termed the 'E'-type, it had all-independent suspension—first ever by Jaguar—and a 3-litre six-cylinder fuel-injection engine with new light alloy block and crankcase. Externally, its lines were beautifully clean, the F.I.A. regulation screen and luggage space being embodied in the design, and not appearing to have been reluctantly stuck on, as with so many other sports-racing cars.

Alas, there was but the one Jaguar, to be driven by Walt Hansgen and Dan Gurney, the former unofficially approaching 180mph during early tests at Le Mans and lapping little slower than the Ferraris. Another Jaguar, a veteran D-type which must practically have known its own way round the course, was entered by Ecurie Ecosse, while the only other British cars in the Championship class were two Aston Martin DBRIs, that of the Border Reivers to be driven by Salvadori and Clark, and Ian Baillie's by himself and Jack Fairman.

Porsche had four official entries, two just over 1600cc, one just under, and one a 1500, with their usual cosmopolitan team of drivers. Ferrari also had four team cars, all 3-litre TR VI2s, with two others entered privately by N.A.R.T. There were also half a dozen handsome closed Ferraris running in the Grand Touring class which contributed so many to the fifty-five-car starting list.

As for Camoradi, feared newcomer to Le Mans, Lloyd Casner had entered three Tipo 61 2.9-litre Maseratis for Gregory/ Daigh, Scarlatti/Munaron and Casner himself, co-driving with Jim Jeffords. The stumpy tail of the Birdcage had been improved considerably, as had the aerodynamics, by use of a longer, shaplier tail on the Gregory/Daigh car, which also bore a fantastic mockery of the F.I.A. 9.8in. screen, extended forward almost to the radiator, and merging into the streamlining of the nose. It was ludicrous, but within the letter of the law.

Camoradi-U.S.A. also fielded a single Chevrolet Corvette in the Grand Touring class, while Briggs Cunningham had three Corvettes in, so that the United States blue-and-white was greatly in evidence at Le Mans that year.

Heavy rain during practice accentuated the handicap imposed by the F.I.A. screen, most wipers proving inadequate to cope with the ever-blurring screen at racing speeds. Thus drivers had the option of crawling miserably round or stopping altogether until the rain ceased—hardly the way to go motor racing—or they resorted again to piles of cushions and layers of Dunlopillo, in order to peer over the top of the screen. This reduced their 'feel' and control of the car, and often brought legs into contact with steering wheels, scarcely contributing to the 'safety' which, the F.I.A. avowed, was their primary concern.

Whatever drivers may justly think of the hazards of Le Mans, there is no denying its immense attraction to the public. In spite of grey skies and an occasional spatter of rain on the afternoon of Saturday, June 25th, the crowd was simply colossal, estimates running as high as 310,000. Every stand and enclosure was packed tight, with the greatest human mass around the start area. Lined up by engine capacity, the four big Corvettes stood at the head of the long line of cars, with the two Jaguars, the Aston Martins and no less than twelve Ferraris next in order.

There was no Stirling Moss to perform his famous sprint start this time (he was not entered, and in any case lay in hospital after a crash at Spa), and it was Jim Clark who effected the best getaway, his Border Reivers Aston roaring off to lead under the Dunlop Bridge, with a Corvette and Flockhart's Jaguar leading the pack astern. Gradually the field spread out, while up from nineteenth place, spurting past car after car at sensational speed, flew Masten Gregory in the Camoradi Maserati.

By the end of the opening round he was well in the lead, slamming past the packed stands to a hubbub of excitement. Gendebien's Testa Rossa Ferrari was next and, a great thrill for the British, Hansgen in the sleek new Jaguar third. Though not fully extended, Gregory's Maserati was travelling at a prodigious pace, and he held a seventy-second-lead after one hour from a solid phalanx of Ferraris. Trouble quickly struck at the new Jaguar, first with a broken fuel pipe, then with the injection system, which set it far back in the field, to widespread disappointment. Bonnier's Porsche suffered shock absorber trouble and then, sensation, both the von Trips/Phil Hill and Rodriguez/ Scarfiotti Ferraris ran out of fuel, owing to a miscalculation in fuel consumption or tank capacity!

Nothing could hold the Birdcage—and nobody tried to, the remaining Ferraris maintaining the 'hasten slowly' policy which pays so well at Le Mans. Gregory clocked a comfortable 169.6-mph through the flying kilometre and then, with the race one and three-quarter hours old, he swept into the pits for fuel, and handed over to Chuck Daigh. Daigh pressed the starter button— and nothing happened.

Every electrical ruse was tried to get the car into action, but it remained obstinately dead. They tore the starter out, dismantled it, found an internal wire broken, repaired it and frantically reassembled the unit. And as they worked, the heavens opened with tropical violence, rain pounding down, reducing the fastest cars to a comparative crawl.

The Maserati mechanics worked on through the downpour, but the new race leader, the Gendebien/Frère Ferrari, had gained twelve laps before the Camoradi car was ready again— a heartbreaking blow after so promising a start. Thereafter the Ferrari was never headed throughout the twenty-four hours, and as the long hours passed and their rivals dropped out one by one, interest in the race diminished. Lucky the GT class, with roofs at least over their heads when more rain fell furiously during the evening, bringing further misery for those in open cars.

But Gregory and Daigh, in a magnificent do-or-die effort, fairly slashed through the rain trying to make up their twelve-lap deficit, until a broken connecting rod finally put them out during the sixth hour. The Munaron/Scarlatti Maserati had suffered electrical trouble, retiring in the second hour, while the last Birdcage, the Casner/Jeffords car, likewise afflicted with starter motor disease, finally dug itself into the Mulsanne sandbank, sand getting into the gearbox and putting it out of action.

Piston trouble eliminated both the sleek new Jaguar and the Trintignant/Herrmann Porsche, and it was a sad blow when the gallant Ecurie Ecosse D-type Jaguar of Flockhart/Halford broke its crankshaft early in the morning when lying fourth. Malign Fate really had it in for Porsche, too, who lost their second 1600, the Bonnier/Hill car, on Sunday morning, while the Barth/Seidel 1500 developed transmission trouble which forced it down to a lowly twelfth position at the finish.

An interminable race ended as a fine victory for Olivier Gendebien and Paul Frère, and a magnificent demonstration of high-speed reliability by Ferrari, whose cars occupied first, second, fourth, fifth, sixth and seventh places! The second-place Testa Rossa was driven by Mexican teenager Ricardo Rodriguez and the Belgian André Pilette, while the Tavano/Loustell 3-litre coupé in fourth place won the GT class, leading three more GT Ferraris and a GT-class Chevrolet Corvette home.

Greatly to the gratification of the large British contingent present, the intruder in third place was the Border Reivers' dark-blue Aston Martin of Salvadori and Clark, while the other DBR1 of Baillie/Fairman also finished the course in ninth spot, having dropped two places when a weary Jack Fairman took to the Mulsanne sandbank, and lost an hour getting free again.

To the majority, this was not a great Le Mans, although Ferrari doubtless thought well enough of it after their remarkable 'grand slam', which seemed to clinch the 1960 Championship for Maranello once again. But like Aston Martin in 1959, Ferrari were unable to announce their Championship victory immediately, owing to uncertainty concerning the Venezuelan G.P. This was due to be held five months later, in November, whereas the C.S.I. Championship rules stipulated three-months' notice of cancellation of a qualifying event, which left the issue in doubt until August.

When at last the Venezuelan A.C. made up their minds that the race could not be held, and the F.I.A. confirmed it, the final score could be calculated. It proved quite complicated, as the chart will indicate.

Ferrari's total score was thirty points, gained in all five events, whereas Porsche's score of twenty-six was gained in four events. But by C.S.I. ruling (to quote: 'For each make shall be added up all the points awarded in a certain number of events where its placing was the best. This number shall be $\frac{1}{2}$ plus one—or, in the case of an uneven number, $\frac{1}{2}$ plus $\frac{1}{2}$—of the total number of events actually promoted') only the three best performances of five qualifying events could count, which reduced Ferrari's score to twenty-two, tying with Porsche!

However, Article Seven of the Regulations says that: 'In the case of a tie, the make having obtained the highest number of first places, or second places, etc., as the case may be, will be declared Champion.' And that settled the impasse in favour of Ferrari who had two thirds to Porsche's one.

Undoubtedly Ferrari were in every way a Champion sports car marque, yet there were many who regretted Porsche's narrow defeat from the sporting aspect; the performances of the German cars on under 2-litre engines, compared with their opponents' 3 litres was truly remarkable, and a victory for the Stuttgart 'David' in a contest already won five times by the Maranello 'Goliath' would have been warmly welcomed.

CHAMPIONSHIP SCORE-SHEET 1960

Make of Car	Buenos Aires 1000-km., Argentina	Sebring 12-hour, U.S.A.	Targa Florio, Sicily	Nurburgring 1000-km., Germany	Le Mans 24-hour, France	Total Score	Best Three Performances
Ferrari..	8 (1st)	4 (3rd)	6 (2nd)	4 (3rd)	8 (1st)	30	22
Porsche	4 (3rd)	8 (1st)	8 (1st)	6 (2nd)	—	26	22
Maserati	3 (4th)	—	—	8 (1st)	—	11	11
Aston Martin.. ..	—	—	—	—	4 (3rd)	4	4

SCORING: First 8 points; second 6pts.; third 4pts.; fourth 3pts.; fifth 2pts.; sixth 1pt.

CHAPTER 9

1961—THE LAST CHAMPIONSHIP

A SWITCHOVER to the Grand Touring class for C.S.I. Cup events was generally anticipated in the motor racing world for 1961, and it thus came as something of a surprise when the F.I.A. decided to postpone the 'demotion' of the sports-racing car from Championship status for another year.

Italian influence was undoubtedly in part responsible for this, since her Ferraris and Maseratis were the only serious contenders apart from the smaller engined Porsches. Nor did the Italians allow design to stagnate in this final year; instead they departed still further from conventional sports car practice by following the trend already revolutionizing Grand Prix car design, and moved their engines to the rear.

Ferrari put their 2½-litre v6 engine of G.P. origin behind the driver in a new 'sports car', the Type 246, a machine of striking ugliness, having a 'nostril' nose and cut-off tail in Cooper 'snow plough' style. Maserati's effort, the Type 63, was little improvement in appearance on their front-engined Type 61 'Birdcage'; it appeared during the season both with four-cylinder and new v12 power units, the latter derived from an experimental racing unit.

Ferrari also fielded an improved Testa Rossa front-engined model, the 3-litre v12 TRI/61, with similar high, cut-off tail, and both types appeared in Round One of the 1961 contest at Sebring in March, opposed by Maserati and Porsche in the Appendix C bracket, and by GT cars in ever-increasing numbers.

THE ELEVENTH SEBRING

'There is no doubt that the lessons taught by Cooper and Lotus in

185

Formula I racing—and the long-term example set by Porsche—are being applied by the Italian factories . . .' THE AUTOCAR, April 7th, 1961

In a race depressingly lacking in British contenders of Championship class, Ferraris were to be seen in force. There were three works cars, one the rear-engined v6 for Wolfgang von Trips and Richie Ginther, who was responsible for much of its testing and development work; the others front-engined TRI/61S for Phil Hill/Olivier Gendebien and Willy Mairesse/Giancarlo Baghetti, the latter a newcomer from Formula Junior destined to hit the headlines that season in Formula I racing. And there were three older, privately owned front-engined 3-litre Testa Rossa cars, and one or two hybrid variations in American hands.

Opposing them were three Type 61 Maseratis—two of them Camoradi entries—and two of the new rear-engined cars, plus several smaller Porsches including two 1.7-litre works cars. Stirling Moss and Graham Hill shared a Camoradi Maserati Type 61, which refused to start at flag-fall and required a new battery before it burst into life. After the usual bickering in the opening stages, the order settled down with von Trips/Ginther ahead in the rear-engined Ferrari from Phil Hill/Gendebien and the Rodriguez brothers, twenty-two-year-old Pedro and twenty-year-old Ricardo, in the N.A.R.T.-entered front-engined Ferrari— the very car with which Gendebien and Frère won at Le Mans in 1960.

By the end of the third hour, Moss and Graham Hill in the Camoradi 'Birdcage' had worked up to second place, when Hill came in and had to retire the car with a broken exhaust manifold. Moss promptly took over the Masten Gregory/Lloyd Casner Type 63, only to be forced out an hour or so later with broken suspension.

But others had their troubles too, and the leading Ferrari of von Trips/Ginther suddenly retired with broken steering, the pair then taking over the Mairesse/Baghetti front-engined car. Thus the race issue now fell between the fiery young Rodriguez brothers and those old foxes of sports car racing, Phil Hill and Gendebien. The last Maserati, Briggs Cunningham's Type 63 driven by Walt

Hansgen and New Zealander Bruce McLaren, had departed with transmission failure, and now the Ferrari team men, suffering the indignity of being led by two youngsters in an older Ferrari, set out to retrieve the situation.

Yet it was brake trouble on the Rodriguez car three hours before the finish which finally took a works car to the front, and Phil Hill and Gendebien stayed there to the finish. In all, the enterprising young Mexicans lost 17 minutes while all brake pads were changed, and thereafter they put up a vain but valiant effort to make up ground, finishing third behind Hill/Gendebien and the Mairesse/Baghetti/Ginther/von Trips car. The only non-Ferrari in the first eight places was the Holbert/Penske 1.5 RS61 Porsche which came fifth, so the score before Round Two stood at eight points to Ferrari, two to Porsche, and none to Maserati.

RECORDS TOPPLE IN THE TARGA

'. . . . *the Targa Florio has been one of the few remaining venues where baroque-minded aficianados of old-style open road racing can get their jollies. . . .*' Henry Manney, ROAD AND TRACK, August 1961

It was to Sicily and the Targa Florio next, for one of the most exciting in all that lengthy series of races. Ferrari, Porsche and Maserati were all there, and over the tortuous 710-cornered, 44.7-mile mountain circuit the odds between them were far closer than on the Sebring runways. This time Scuderia Ferrari fielded two rear-engined type 246 V6 cars, plus the Sebring-winning V12. Porsche had Bonnier/Gurney in a new, longer-wheelbased car with 1966cc engine giving better torque, and Moss/Graham Hill had the Camoradi RS60, also with 2-litre engine. Maserati had two rear-engine Type 63 'fours', both entered by the Scuderia Serenissima, one for Trintignant and local star Vaccarella, who did so well in 1960, and the other for Maglioli/Scarlatti.

On the first of the ten laps, Stirling Moss took the lead from

Bonnier and von Trips, while Phil Hill, somewhat put out by Gendebien's last-minute decision to change over to von Trips car, came up with the latter after 25 miles. Rear vision on the high-tailed, rear-engined Ferrari is very poor, and von Trips, unaware of Hill's presence, was using all the road. After a few fruitless efforts to pass, Hill gave von Trips' tail a bump or two, where-upon von Trips, thinking his car was ailing, eased off, Hill's car hit him harder, and finally both spun off!

They got going again, but meanwhile Moss had turned the heat on further, and broke his 1958 lap record with a second round in 41 minutes 9 seconds—the course, incidentally had been improved and some corners eased off since 1960. On lap three Moss brought the record down to 40 minutes 58.5 seconds, by which time Phil Hill had left the road in a big way, snapping off two concrete posts with his Ferrari. Ricardo Rodriguez also crashed, holing the fuel tank on his forward-engined v12, which limped in to retire with Phil Hill a rueful passenger.

On lap four Moss did 40 minutes 58.2 seconds despite stopping to hand over to Graham Hill, but an overlong pit stop made the order von Trips/Gendebien, Moss/Hill, Bonnier/Gurney. Hill did two rounds, then handed back to Moss, who lowered the lap record yet again to 40 minutes 41 seconds and caught Gendebien on the eighth lap when the Belgian drew in and handed over to von Trips. On round nine there were 65.7 seconds between Porsche and Ferrari, and in a final desperate lap von Trips turned a fantastic lap in 40 minutes 3.2 seconds—67.0mph—and crossed the line the winner, to the surprise but immense delight of the Sicilian crowds.

And Moss? With the race secure despite von Trips amazing last lap, the differential on his Porsche had run dry, owing to oil escaping through stretched casing bolts, and his magnificent drive ended near Campofelice, about four miles from the finish.

But Porsche were second and third with Bonnier/Gurney and Herrmann/Barth while—surprise!—both Serenissima Type 63 Maseratis survived the 447-mile, 7-hour race in fourth and fifth places, heading yet another Porsche. So now Ferrari led the Championship by sixteen points to Porsche's eight and Maserati's modest three.

SNOW AND RAIN AT THE RING

'What a beautiful sight the chequered flag must have been for Masten Gregory, after beating not only the newest type of car of the same make, but the entire Ferrari team and the official Porsche factory team as well. . . .' Jan Norbye, CAR AND DRIVER, September 1961

From the sunny mountain slopes of Sicily, the scene next shifted to Nurburgring, in Western Germany—and a very damp, cold and cheerless *Ring* it was on May 28th, 1961, when the teams gathered again to do battle. This time Ferrari's team comprised two rear-engined sports cars only, plus a very fast GT car for Mairesse/Baghetti, Porsche had the long wheelbase RS61 for Bonnier/Gurney, a shorter one for Barth/Herrmann, a 1.7-litre disc-braked Carrera, and a 1.7 RS61 for Moss and Graham Hill, ostensibly a Camoradi entry but with factory backing. Maseratis had two Serenissima Type 63s and the older Camoradi front-engined Type 61 of the type which won the race in 1960.

The irrepressible Rodriguez boys were also running their hard-worked V12 Ferrari, while Jimmy Clark drove John Ogier's DBRI Aston Martin. It was Jimmy, in fact, who repeated his 1960 act by being the first on the move at the 9am Le Mans start, but Stirling Moss accelerated savagely in the Porsche and took the lead. On the second lap Phil Hill forced past, to be followed on lap three by Ginther, but Hill was motoring at tremendous pace, lowering the sports car record on laps 3, 4, 5, 6, 7 and 8, and leaving it at a staggering 9 minutes 15.8 seconds (91.72mph in a sports car!).

First pit-stops then confused the order, but not so much as did the suddening darkening of already sullen skies, a fall of snow and then drenching rain. Moss and Graham Hill, with Dunlop SP rain tyres on their Porsche, came into their own, whereas the more powerful Ferraris were now at a disadvantage; Gendebien spun, and then both cars began misfiring intermittently, owing to the ducts to the rear disc brakes imbibing unhealthy quantities of water, which upset the carburation.

Just when Moss was up to second place and gaining, his engine stopped very firmly and he skated out of the race, and next the von Trips/Hill Ferrari, leading despite its misfiring, was missing. Hill had run off the road, a small fire which had started was quickly put out, and the Californian became a pedestrian. That let, not the sister car of Gendebien/Ginther, but the Gregory/Casner Type 61 'Birdcage' Maserati, up into the lead, with 'Lucky' Casner driving with praiseworthy skill and restraint under harrassing conditions, holding off the Rodriguez Ferrari and the works 2.5 v6.

The Aston Martin had retired after lying fourth, the Serenissima Maserati when third, and then, as the fog lifted, the rain stopped and the skies brightened, Pedro Rodriguez had a front wheel collapse at the Swallowtail corner, and drove the Ferrari in with the wheel a mess of twisted spokes and rubber. Von Trips and Hill, who had taken over the Ginther/Gendebien car, put on a spurt in an attempt to catch the Mexican, but Rodriguez held them off to the end, scoring a highly popular second behind the Camoradi Maserati. Fourth and fifth came two GT Ferraris and sixth a GT Porsch, indicative of the diminishing field in the sports-racing class.

BACK TO THE STATUS QUO

'Out of the revolt of two Mexicans is born a new record' AUTO-ITALIANA, July 1st, 1961

The Fourth Round of the Championship took place at Le Mans, where already, in April, Ferrari had put their new cars through their paces. Ginther had proved fastest with the 2.5-litre v6, lapping the ultra-fast, 8.36-mile circuit in 3 minutes 54.6 seconds—128.33mph, bettering Phil Hill's best in the front-engined 3-litre v12 by .6 of a second. On race day, June 10th, however, only one v6 was there for von Trips/Ginther, the Ferrari strength being made up by two v12s for Hill/Gendebien and Mairesse and the British driver Michael Parkes, who had been offered the drive after his performance in the April tests. Alongside the works machines, and destined to prove a sharp thorn in their sides, was the N.A.R.T. 3-litre Ferrari of Pedro and Ricardo Rodriguez, with 'Papa' Rodriguez and Luigi Chinetti in control in the pits.

Maserati produced three wonderfully impressive V12 rear-engined Type 63s, two entered by Briggs Cunningham, one by Scuderia Serenissima, while two ageing Aston Martin DBR1s turned out for England, one the Ogier car for Roy Salvadori and the promising South African Tony Maggs, the other the Border Reivers car for Jim Clark/Ron Flockhart.

Were it not for the Rodriguez brothers, the 1961 Le Mans story would have been duller, for these lads pitted their Ferrari against the newer works cars, defied the accepted Le Mans tenet, 'hasten slowly', and drove as hard as they could go, in spite of the beseechings of the official Ferrari pit to ease off.

It was cold and windy on race day, and after the usual impressive hush, the start signal, the patter of drivers' feet and the whirr of starters, it was good to see the Aston Martins snatch the lead from the Ferraris, Clark leading Salvadori, with Kerguen's DB4 GT also well up. But inevitably a Ferrari led after lap one, Ginther's V6 heading Hill's V12 and Hansgen's screaming V12 Maserati. Then the Rodriguez car moved up, battling for the lead in spite of drizzling rain after two hours' running, until it was time for the first refuel stops.

The rain increased, but Ferrari tenure of the lead remained unbroken. Hansgen in the 12-cylinder Maserati crashed, as did Bruce Halford in the Ecurie Ecosse Cooper Monaco, while Vaccarella's retirement meant two Maseratis gone. By one-third distance (8 hours) the rain had eased off, and the Rodriguez boys in the leading car put on speed. Stirling Moss and Graham Hill, driving a GT Ferrari, had worked their way into an astonishing fourth place, but their efforts were ill-rewarded when a radiator hose broke and they had to retire during the small hours.

Jim Clark's Aston Martin was another casualty during the night, and dawn showed a dry track and Ferraris solidly in the lead, still with the flying Mexicans heading Hill/Gendebien. Mairesse/Parkes and Ginther/von Trips. By 6 o'clock there was only 10 seconds between them, but an hour later a faulty condenser cost the N.A.R.T. car 27 minutes and five whole laps—a cruel blow after which anyone might give up the fight and settle for a comfortable place. Not so the Rodriguez pair, however! Undaunted, they tore back into the race, and began turning in laps at around 4 minutes dead, which compelled Tavoni of Ferrari reluctantly to speed up his cars in defence.

Then the works team had a shock when von Trips ran out of fuel on the course owing to a miscalculation over the consumption of the 2.5-litre v6. But the Salvadori/Maggs Aston Martin having by this time retired with a leaking fuel tank, only the Maserati of Pabst/Thomson remained to disturb the Ferraris.

Four hours to go, and the Mexicans were back in third place and out to catch the Mairesse/Parkes car, but two hours later their sorely tried power unit at last gave up, and their valiant run ended in a cloud of smoke, to widespread regret and several 'I told you so's' from the Ferrari pit. 'We'll be back next year' said the Rodriguez boys, who at least had the the fastest race lap in 3 minutes 59.9 seconds to their credit.

So Hill and Gendebien boomed on to another Le Mans win, rain falling dismally as they crossed the line to average 115.90 mph for the 24 hours, followed by Mairesse/Parkes, Noblet/Guichet in a GT Ferrari, the Pabst/Thomson 'Birdcage' Maserati, and two more GT cars.

THE LAST ROUND

'*It is fitting that the house of Ferrari should score their final Sports Car Championship victory on that great Pescarese circuit where Commendatore Enzo Ferrari himself won the first Pescara G.P. with an Alfa Romeo back in 1924. . . .*' TUTTOSPORT, August 17th, 1961

After Le Mans, Ferrari had a total of thirty points to the thirteen of Maserati and eleven of Porsche, and with but one race to run, the Maranello marque just couldn't lose the Championship. Because of this there was talk of the final round, the Pescara G.P., not being held, but as the C.S.I. stipulated a minimum

of five events, the Championship would have been nullified for
1961 without Pescara. However, it was decided that the race
duration should be reduced from the original six hours to four,
which reduced the number of points to 4 for a win, 3 for second,
2 for third, 1½ for fourth, 1 for fifth and ½ for sixth.

Race date, August 15th, being an Italian public holiday, the
Italians being lovers of motor racing, and Pescara being a magnificent 15.9-mile road circuit on the warm Adriatic coast, the
race had every chance of succeeding in spite of its hollow value as
a Championship qualifier. But Enzo Ferrari came under fire from
the Italian press for entering just one 2.5-litre v6 Type 246 for
Baghetti and Richie Ginther and no more. No Phil Hill, no von
Trips, no Gendebien! The worried organizers finally persuaded
the Commendatore to make available another Ferrari, a 3-litre
front-engined v12, for the Scuderia Centro-Sud, who nominated
Lorenzo Bandini and Giorgio Scarlatti to drive it.

Things still looked a bit thin, but there were several GT
Ferraris, and smaller Oscas, and then Joakim Bonnier arranged
to drive the highly exciting v12 Type 63 Maserati for Scuderia
Serenissima, while the Sicilian Vaccarella took the 4-cylinder
car. A third Maserati was Lloyd Casner's well-used Type 61,
already winner in 1961 of the Nurburgring 1000-km and the
Rouen G.P. Being right out of the Championship, Porsche kept
away from this race, but were lending support to private owners
Tommy Spychiger and Orthuber, the latter having works man
Edgar Barth to co-drive his 1.7 RS61.

As befits the Adriatic coast in August, the weather was hot and
cloudless when, at 9.18am, the Pescara G.P. began with the
traditional Le Mans start. Casner was quickest off, but Ginther
soon caught him and led the race. Bonnier had a bad time in the
ear-splitting v12 Maserati, which wouldn't start, and then broke
a half-shaft during lap two, perhaps to his relief as the cockpit was
like an oven. Lorenzo Bandini's v12 Ferrari was losing oil from
the tank filler, costing him vital time at the pits, while Mairesse
crashed his very fast GT Ferrari.

On lap three Richie Ginther stopped to check on the handling of
the Type 246, letting the Maseratis of Casner and Vaccarella by,
but he caught them up again in the next round or two, while

Bandini was slicing his way back through the field. Vaccarella passed Casner, but had to retire with transmission failure after nine laps, and two laps later Baghetti, who had taken over from Ginther just after the latter had set the fastest race lap in 9 minutes 55.5 seconds, pulled in with a broken steering link and was out.

'Lucky' Casner's Maserati now had a five-minute lead over Bandini/Scarlatti, but four laps later the American crashed when trying to pass a slower car, the Maserati landing on top of him. Indifferent officials and a very leisurely ambulance service meant he suffered serious burns from hot oil and water before he was removed to hospital by helicopter. Meanwhile Bandini moved into the lead and won the 22-lap race, while Carlo Abate, holding second place in a GT Ferrari, ran out of fuel a few kilometres from the finish.

The Orthuber/Barth Porsche therefore inherited its place, third was Boffa's 2-litre Maserati, fourth and sixth were GT Ferraris, and fifth the British driver Colin Davis in a 1600 Osca.

Thus did Ferrari consolidate the 1961 C.S.I. Cup victory which was theirs already, giving the final emphasis to their undoubted pre-eminence in the World Sports Car Championship series, which they had now won seven times out of nine contests!

It was at their May congress at Monte Carlo that the C.S.I. confirmed that the Championship in 1962 would be for Grand Touring cars conforming to Appendix J, with no limit on engine capacity, but this did not mark the death of that anachronistic but fascinating beast, the 'sports-racing car', for the C.S.I. also announced that there would be a series of events run solely for Appendix C sports cars, with the present 3-litre capacity limit in force. Screen height would be reduced to 15cm again, and those farcical items of equipment, 'hoods', need no longer be carried.

Demoted though it is from Championship status, the sports-racing car is thus given a further lease of life. Whether it will succeed, or whether the GT car will oust it from its former position, remains to be seen. If racing should be a lesson, not a spectacle, as the late Charles Faroux once declared, then the GT car has it all the way, but for sheer spectacle only a Grand Prix car can outmatch the sight—and sound—of a big sports-racing Ferrari or Maserati in full flight. Perhaps there will be a place for both.

CHAMPIONSHIP SCORE-SHEET 1961

Make of Car	Sebring 12-hour, U.S.A.	Targa Florio, Sicily	Nurburgring 1000-km Germany	Le Mans 24-hour, France	Pescara 4-hour, Italy	Best three Performances
Ferrari	8 (1st)	8 (1st)	6 (2nd)	8 (1st)	4 (1st)*	24
Maserati..	—	3 (4th)	8 (1st)	3 (4th)	2 (3rd)	14
Porsche	2 (5th)	6 (2nd)	1 (6th)	2 (5th)	3 (2nd)	11
Osca	—	—	—	—	1 (5th)	1

SCORING: First 8pts.; second 6pts.; third 4pts.; fourth 3pts.; fifth 2pts.; sixth 1pt.
*Race of under 1000-km, or 6 hours duration, therefore reduced points:
  First 4pts.; second 3pts.; third 2pts.; fourth 1½pts.; fifth 1pt.; sixth ½pt.

39/6 + 1/6 p & p.

Lockwood Eng. Products.
Margaretting Tye
Ingatestone
Ex.